A Tug
on the
Thread

A Tug
on the
Thread

From the British Raj
to the British Stage
A Family Memoir

DIANA QUICK

virago

VIRAGO

First published in Great Britain in 2009 by Virago Press

Copyright © 2009 Diana Quick

A CIP catalogue record for this book
is available from the British Library.

ISBN 978-1-86049-844-2

Typeset in Goudy by M Rules
Printed and bound in Great Britain by
Clays Ltd, St Ives plc

Papers used by Virago are natural, renewable and
recyclable products sourced from well-managed forests and certified in
accordance with the rules of the Forest Stewardship Council.

Mixed Sources
Product group from well-managed
forests and other controlled sources
www.fsc.org Cert no. SGS-COC-004081
© 1996 Forest Stewardship Council

FSC

Virago Press
An imprint of
Little, Brown Book Group
100 Victoria Embankment
London EC4Y 0DY

An Hachette UK Company
www.hachette.co.uk

www.virago.co.uk

For Mary and Bill

and for my brothers Clive and Richy, and my sister Julie

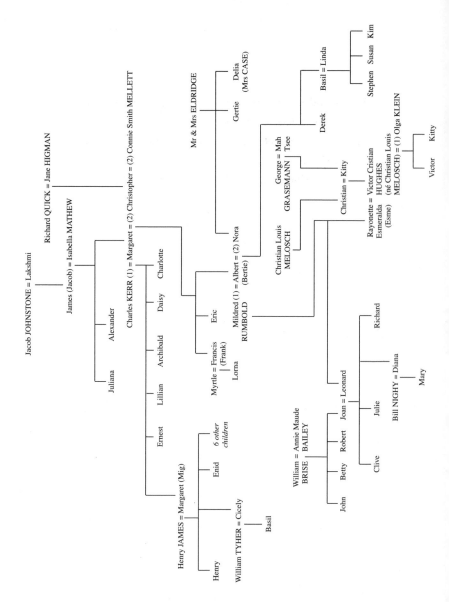

In the end, we all become interested in our personal history. Some of us become interested in our tribal history, even when it stretches back 2000 years. In the end, history is all we have.

Hunter Davies, The Independent, 31 May 1999

India and Pakistan

Contents

Preface

If you dig deep enough, all our secrets are the same . . . deep
down below there is the hard rock of the common
denominator, the sameness of our secrets.

Amos Oz on BBC's *Start the Week*, 25 February 2001

It all started when I was playing a fugitive from the Third Reich in
Kindertransport by Diane Samuels. Eva had left her family behind
in Nazi Germany to make her way by train – the Kindertransport –
to a new life in Britain. When, against all the odds, her mother survives the extermination camps and turns up in England to reclaim
her daughter, Eva cannot respond with love. I am not your daughter any more, she says, you sent me away. Don't you understand I
would rather have taken my chance with you in the camps than survived alone without you?

We see a woman who, up to now, has seemed very controlled,
even dispassionate, crack up to reveal the hurt child inside. Eva has
had to grow up far away from her parents, she has made a life for
herself and is to all intents a middle-class, middle-aged English
woman. The crisis of the play unfolds as we discover that this is far
from a successful transformation, for it was made by denying her
true identity. She rejects her mother because the cost of re-opening

those old wounds is too high, but in refusing this opportunity she ruins any chance that she has of healing herself.

As far as I know I am not Jewish, but when I was asked how I went about playing Eva it set me thinking. As an actor you fish into any memories, stories, observations you may have collected on your way through life and, if they chime with the situation you are required to act out, you use them. Of course imagination plays a large part, too, but it always starts with something you feel you know about. For *Kindertransport* I had thought about my own father a great deal. He had been raised in India, and was sent away to a school in the Himalayas aged five. He came to England at seventeen to go to dental school and never went back, barely had any connection to his family again. As I worked on Eva I thought about the emotional cost of leaving your family behind; of how my father was very controlled but loving, and yet – like Eva – he could also be curiously unapproachable and unknowable.

The play was very successful. We were in the West End for a six-month run and there wasn't a night when people were not waiting at the stage door to talk about it and, above all, about their own experiences. The play had acted as a trigger, and for many – many! – it was the first time they had been able to look at compli-cated, painful, ambiguous feelings. There were so many who wanted to thank us for opening these particular doors. I have always thought that the theatre is a place to open people up. It's a place to entertain, of course, a place to divert ourselves, but it has another function, as a forum for ideas and as a mirror to nature, in which we can sometimes see ourselves and our fellows reflected, amplified and made clearer.

I think this happened because of our timing with *Kindertransport*, playing it as we did some fifty years after the end of the war, as the generation who had survived were reaching an age at which they realised that if they did not pass on their experiences to their children now it would soon be too late to tell them. It was also a time at which the widespread wish to belong to English society, to fit in, was starting to give way to a desire to celebrate where people had come from, to uncover ancestors, to trace roots. We caught hold of the Zeitgeist with this play, and it gave me one of my most exciting and humbling experiences of my career.

In thinking about how, as an actor, one uses one's emotional life to furnish a character, I started to want to explore further, first my father's life and then how I had developed the emotional dimensions of characters I had played. Was there a common theme to them? And if I had been influenced by things in the family cupboard, did that determine how I was myself, when not acting?

In order to address these questions, I was going to have to look at my history in a new way. Growing up in the sixties I had always taken pride in being able to go with the flow, but now I wanted to look at some of the roles I have acted, to see how they have informed who I am, and how I have drawn on my own character to create others further on in my career. I knew I would have to start by looking at what had happened in my father's family, for there had always been a degree of silence about his life before he arrived in England, and I had a hunch that if I could unlock that, then I might be able to understand better.

I knew very little about my father's childhood, since he had died when I was a teenager. But I had always intended to find out more and I now embarked on an enquiry that has taken nine years, thousands of miles and a hard look not only at Eva but at why in my career as an actor I have played so many outsiders, exotics and people in denial of their true selves.

It started at school; Rosa the gypsy girl was created especially for me by – me! Aged thirteen, my class wrote and performed an operetta in which Rosa is carried off by the wicked Sir Jasper to live happily ever after. I found a fantastic Hungarian peasant costume at my grandfather's house (I still don't know to this day how he had acquired it), with a bodice embroidered in scarlet, bright blue and cerise, and a panelled velvet skirt. That was it: I was lost to show business. I knew I was nothing like a real gypsy, of course: I had met one when off at a Girl Guide camp. It had been my job that day to collect wood for the campfire. I'd never had to do that before, and so gingerly set off into the undergrowth. Suddenly there was a slim, brown, crop-haired girl. It was as if she'd appeared from nowhere. Joan was a traveller; her family's van was camped a short distance away on the edge of the wood. She and I got talking and she offered to help me collect the wood. In no time at all she had got a massive stack together and I started to see with her eyes, to spot where the wood was and to make my own pathetic pile into a decent-sized bundle. We took it all back to the camp and, my chore accomplished, I happily followed her to another part of the wood where she showed me a rope tied high in a tree growing by the water's edge, which you could run with and jump on to swing far out over the water before splashing down. It was heaven. I knew I'd never be her or have her familiarity with the woods, but I wanted to be like her, and there was a sort of osmosis by which I could mimic her and her ease in the countryside, her smooth passage amongst the trees, her delight in moving through the water. I daresay wanting to play Rosa the gypsy was in some way a tribute to that brief encounter.

When I started to get professional work some seven years later, it was mainly to play peasants. I was cast as the token peasant in Sam Spiegel's last epic film, *Nicholas and Alexandra*, getting trampled to death at the Bloody Sunday demonstration, and as a Greek peasant girl in love with the Christ figure in Kazantzakis's *Christ Recrucified*. When I made it to the National Theatre it was to play an Indian princess in a version of Racine's *Phèdre* set in the British

Raj. In fact, I played so many exotic parts that I thought I would never be cast as anything else, and threatened to fire my agent and set up my own agency.

I did knock the exotics on the head for a while by refusing the relatively easy pickings that were coming my way, and sitting it out until I began to be cast in other parts. Over my career, however, I have played many such parts and feel very comfortable doing so. The question I found myself asking is, do I feel so comfortable as an outsider because of some unconscious aspect of my family history? To all intents and purposes I am an English woman. I am probably still best known as Lady Julia Flyte in *Brideshead Revisited*, yet if you look closely at Julia you soon see that she is an outsider too: some of her relatives are dark and foreign, her family is Roman Catholic and her father, brother and herself all flout the conventions of the social class to which they belong. So why, I wonder, have I been always drawn to play those who live outside the pale? Can it just be chance? Or is it that somewhere in my family is a history of denial that, unknowingly, I have drawn upon, and which, if uncovered, could perhaps explain my choices?

I

Two Unreal Things

There were two unreal things. The first bit was going over the handlebars of my bike and knocking myself out. I was cycling back to college from a lecture – unusual for me, since I had long been in the habit of skiving off lectures to make more time for rehearsals. I seem to recall that this lecture had been by Isaiah Berlin, and though not part of my English Literature course it was absolutely unmissable. I'd gone on my Pink Witch bike – also unusual, since more often than not I couldn't find it. I was a scatty girl, continually mislaying the bike around Oxford, but because it was so distinctive – neon pink with bits of bright metallic blue – it usually turned up again somewhere.

I was wearing a minidress so short that when I'd finished sewing it I realised I'd have to make knickers to match. Today, though, decency was preserved by a long scholar's gown that covered my legs. I was on the home stretch when the gown's dangling pointed sleeve somehow got entangled in the front wheel and I went clean over the handlebars. I was out cold for a moment or two, and when I came to it took a while for me to realise what had happened. I wasn't badly hurt, just a bit scraped and bruised, and more embarrassed than anything else.

I took off my mangled gown and started to make my way back to
the red brick façade of Lady Margaret Hall. As I wheeled my bike
along I consoled myself with the thought that I'd had more luck
than my older brother, Clive: he spent a lot of his adolescence sal-
vaging old bicycles from dumps and rebuilding them, and once,
when he was testing a re-assembled beauty on the heathland in
front of our house, the gears had jammed and he too had knocked
himself out going over the handlebars. He'd lost his memory for several days, and couldn't even hang on to the name of his beloved cat,
let alone those of his siblings. I was a lot younger than him and
found the whole episode spooky. Five years on and I'd done the
same thing. I now knew what seeing stars meant too, but at least I
also knew who I was and what I was doing.

I was a month off my nineteenth birthday and in my second year as
an undergraduate. It was 1965, and it felt as if the world really was
my oyster. I took for granted that the young were the centre of the
universe. My leaving home had coincided with the great flowering
of youth culture of the sixties, and it was people my age or not
much older who were making the music and the films and the plays
and the art and the magazines that dominated the headlines.

I had no sense of history, of how radical a change this was from
the cultural style of the previous decade. In fact I was a baby
boomer, born as a result of my father's first leave after the war. My
early childhood had been defined by talk of the war and what the
family had had to do – digging for victory, going off to be land girls
while the men were at war, avoiding doodlebugs, hiding in the air-
raid shelter, evacuation. Some of the family didn't make it back
from the war. My aunt's fiancé had been wiped out by a bomb just
after he'd enlisted, before he saw any active service, while sitting
outside his barracks at his basic training camp. At home there had
been an attitude of 'make do and mend': clothes were handed down

or sometimes the seams unpicked and the fabric re-cut and re-sewn, jumpers unravelled and the wool knitted again, and paper and string and everything really saved for re-use. Old rubber gloves were cut up for rubber bands, and you always had to eat everything on your plate, with an exhortation to think of the poor little children starving in Africa.

I'd left home as soon as I could, and by seventeen was delighted to skip off to college. Looking back, it feels as if I was far too young to manage my life but I adored being in charge of myself and making my own choices, even if they turned out to be duds. I don't think I ever got into a proper routine of study, because the theatre had seduced me as soon as I got to Oxford. The lecture that day had been a sop to my academic conscience before I went off to spend the rest of the day in a rehearsal room as my alter ego, Victoria Groves. The false name was necessary because I had already used up my annual allowance of acting parts: my college rather grudgingly conceded that we might appear in one play a year in any year without exams, and since that meant only the summer of the first year, after prelims (the preliminary exams in Anglo-Saxon, Latin and Milton if, like me, you were reading English) and one some time in the next, I had adopted my middle names for the cast list in order to escape the notice of the college. This was my fifth play and it was only my fourth term.

I'd come to Oxford to study literature, and my college clearly had faith in me, but the theatre was my real passion. I had no thought for the future; all I wanted was to get to my rehearsal for *The Horse*, a Hungarian satire on life under a communist regime that the university's Experimental Theatre Club was staging in its English premiere. In 1965 Hungary was still regarded as an heroic victim of communist Russia after the suppression of the Uprising nine years earlier, but the playwright, Julius Hay, had obtained permission to come out of Hungary to attend our rehearsals; his son Peter was a

fellow undergraduate and had translated the work himself. The
play was an allegory of life under a totalitarian government:
Caligula appoints his horse consul, and even nightingales are forbidden to sing. I was to be Ameana, the horse's hapless bride. The
national press was interested; I had a wonderful part; it all felt terribly important.

When I walked into college there were messages for me everywhere – in my pigeonhole, with the porter, pinned to my door:
Contact your tutor IMMEDIATELY. This was Kathleen Lea who, as
well as teaching me Elizabethan literature, was my moral tutor
and my champion; it was she who had recommended me for the
senior scholarship when I was only sixteen and appallingly ill-
read, she was the one who fretted over whether I was eating
enough and insisted that I attend meals in hall at least once a
day (at the time I was a robust size 14 with a 38-inch bust).
Lately she had been concerned that I was spending rather too
much time with the muses Polyhymnia, Melpomene and Thalia
(mimic art, tragedy and comedy), as she put it, to the detriment
of Calliope and Erato (epic and lyric poetry). That was how she
often spoke, and I had had to learn a whole new language and
style in order to communicate with her. I liked and admired and
respected her, hence the pseudonym: I wasn't going to stop being
in plays but I didn't want to upset her. She had impeccable manners, a tiny frame, a face like a rosy wizened apple and a large
decanter of sherry for occasions such as this. She made me sit
down and told me that my father had died that morning of a
heart attack.

When I got home the house was, as usual, full of family, but now
doing their bustling in silence. Sisters and aunts filled me in with
the details; where were the two boys, my brothers? I've very little
memory of them in all this. I understood, vaguely, that the service

would be a full Catholic requiem. I wasn't sure if I'd ever been in a Catholic church – perhaps once or twice, for a wedding. I glanced at my mother's face and decided that it wasn't the moment to ask why we were having a mass. From the moment I'd gone over the handlebars the day had had an unreal spin to it: seeing stars; learning that my father was dead at the age of fifty when he had seemed to us all to be fit, athletic and full of energy; and now this absolutely unknown ritual we were going to go through, a full Requiem Mass for a man who had never once mentioned that he was a Roman Catholic.

At the morgue, he was behind glass. Now when I think of him, which I do often, I think of him being in a glass box like Snow White. His body looked calm, as if he were only sleeping. But the second unreal thing was the colour of my father's ears. I thought I might hear the inevitable snore in a minute, and would jiggle his foot to stop it as we'd always done, but no, the purplish-blackish-blue accumulation of blood in his ears gave the lie to that. No more jigging his foot, no more cuddling up in an armchair or on the beach. This was it. It was over. He had gone away. I stood for a long time and stared. When I left I kept walking for twenty paces or so then found myself clinging to my sister and howling at the sky.

I don't remember much about the service. It was in the little local church. Later I was to learn that my parents had been married there, and during the mass I dimly recognised it as the place my sister had also been married, age twenty, to a Roman Catholic. Of the four children three of us were to choose partners who had been raised as Catholics, but of course that was not clear then. I didn't know the extent to which our father's upbringing would impinge on our choices in adult life.

At twelve I must have had an inkling that the family had started out differently. There was some talk about the older children going to confession when I was too tiny even to be entrusted with collection money in the cool, light-filled, perfumed church near the house in which I first lived, but I didn't know if they had ever gone.

'Please Miss Abraham, I think I'm supposed to be a Catholic but I don't know where the church is . . .'

The monumental head of the junior school, with her iron-grey hair shorn up the back of her neck, her tremendous bosom straining against the buttons of her cardigan and against the hearty tweed of her skirt, dismissed my half-baked request peremptorily. 'Ask your parents,' she said, but I would not be asking questions. Not in our house, because they'd be brushed aside – not harshly or angrily, but carelessly like crumbs swept off the table.

I'd never got to the bottom of the facts of life, for instance. At school the others would ask in the playground, do you know the facts of life yet? Bet you don't know what a rubber johnny is. But at home when I'd asked about a pack of sanitary towels my brother Richard and I had found in a cupboard, I was dismissed with 'I'll tell you about it when the time comes.' What time, we wondered and wandered off to mine the treasures in other cupboards with pads dangling under our chins and looped over our ears. Nobody seemed to notice.

When the time did come, blood pouring between my legs and soaking my pants with a brownish-red metallic goo as I played hookey from Sunday school, I believed it was a sign that I was being punished for my waywardness, for stealing tins of condensed milk and spoonfuls of dried egg powder left over from the war from the larder, which were washed down with our special drink. You took all the Refreshers of one colour from two tubes of the little round sherbet sweets – blue or pink or yellow or green – and chewed them up, spat them into a beaker, mixed in some water and served as if it was a proper milkshake. All this was done while perched in the branches of the treetop highway, a circle of tall elms where you could climb from one tree to the next without ever having to come down to the ground. It was much more fun than the mile walk across the heath (children could roam freely in the fifties) to the white-boarded St Barnabas's, the Anglican church where my sister rang the bells every Sunday.

At the weekend our parents were mostly out having fun; golf or tennis or motor-racing, or dancing with friends. So when I ran out of tissues to staunch the flow of blood I reluctantly hobbled home and was dealt with firmly but silently by my grandmother, who kitted me out with a sanitary belt of Germolene-pink elastic and one of the bulky pads that had previously dangled from my ears, and tucked me up in bed with a hot-water bottle and a bowl of bread and milk (a panacea in our house), saying by way of explanation only 'This will happen every month, now you are a woman.' I was eleven. When my parents came home they too treated me like an invalid. Was this what all the fuss was about, then, three years earlier when my sister had danced around chanting 'I know something you don't know.' 'What?' 'You'll know when you're eleven.' So now I knew. And I stopped going to Sunday school.

I don't remember much about the funeral or its aftermath. I spent a few days at home with my mother, who was silent and stunned by grief. A week later I was back at university. No time for lectures now; the play was to open in less than a week. There was a lot to catch up on. Our playwright Julius Hay gave an interview in which he said, 'A nation who can laugh at their tyrant is on the way to freedom. Laugh, dear people, laugh with us.'

No time to mourn – I was a week behind. I still had to catch up with the academic work and for the play there were still lines to learn and costumes to make, as well as technical and dress rehearsals. Many years later, after my mother had died, I found

some of my letters home among her papers. I wrote this in the week
I got back to college after the funeral:

8–11–65

Darling Mummy,
I wrote to say hello and how are you? We've been rehearsing
like MAD since Friday afternoon and now don't know whether
I'm coming or going.

They've built our set – it is sort of ruined Roman, but giving
a tremendous impression of light. There are some lovely
columns and a huge staircase – they need it with such a large
cast – about fifty, I think.

Everybody has been so nice – my tutors, and everyone in
college, and everyone connected with the play.

I suppose it is a good thing I've got so much to keep me
occupied. I have lovely costumes too – yellow and white, and
russet and gold, and my hair in a very elaborate style.

Can you let me know exactly how many tickets are wanted
when? I can't remember anything.

We think about you and dear Daddy a lot. Please give my
love to everyone, but most of all to you.

So I spent the two weeks up to my nineteenth birthday trying to
make people laugh. The reviews were kind to me, less so for the
play. But to be in the play and be praised for it distracted me from
my grief. It was a definite consolation. I was already a veteran of
student drama as, since my debut in the primary school's Nativity
aged six, playing a shepherdess, I had performed in about twelve
plays. I was the Princess in *The Princess and the Swineherd* and Rosa
the gypsy. I'd been Captain Bluntschli in Shaw's *Arms and the Man*
and Benedick in *Much Ado About Nothing*. (I was tall for my age and
always ended up as the boy.) At the local amateur theatre, where

my father was stage manager and my mother helped out with the costumes and the coffee, I'd been Juliet, and Beauty in *Beauty and the Beast*, Katharine in *Henry V* and Fay in *The Boy Friend*. Between school and going up to university I'd been Hermia for the National Youth Theatre at the Queen's Theatre, Shaftesbury Avenue, and because that made them trust that I might be able to act I was cast as Abigail Williams in *The Crucible* in my first term at Oxford when someone more senior had fallen ill. I'd played one of the leads in a musical called *You Can't Do Much Without a Screwdriver* and been the girl in the Oxford revue at the Edinburgh Festival with Michael Palin, turning down Cressida at the National Youth Theatre to do it. I wasn't really much cop as a singer, but then I'd been approached by two young men called Lloyd-Webber and Rice to sing Mary Magdalene in a musical they were writing about Jesus. I'd refused, not trusting my singing to be good enough.

I'd written, directed, designed costumes, done publicity and been both stage manager and production manager. Yet if anyone asked me what my plans for after my degree were, I was cagey. Not out of prudence, particularly, nor lack of confidence, I was simply living in the moment. I couldn't think about the future because the present was so interesting, and time stretched ahead infinitely.

Now, with my nineteenth birthday, I had to catch up. The play was finished and all the academic work that had been on hold for three weeks had to be done. I'd be sitting quietly reading or writing, and would find that a sob would rise up from the well of my belly and burst out of me. More would follow in a great uncontrollable wave. It was almost as if it was happening to somebody else, and even as my body shuddered and howled the actress in me was observing from one side – so this is what a person does in deep grief. And then, as suddenly as it had started, it would be over.

My father's death was the first thing that had ever gone wrong for me. Throughout my teens I was clear, undistracted, fully engaged in whatever I was doing and confident that if I wanted to do something I could get it with concentration and hard work. Nothing had ever happened to prove me wrong. And I was very blinkered: I had no critical perspective whatsoever.

I was amazed, for instance, when Polly Toynbee, whom I'd known and admired at the National Youth Theatre and as a regular player in our Sunday morning football team (girls only allowed to be strikers) left Oxford in the middle of her course, hugely dissatisfied. I couldn't imagine that anyone could be having less fun than I was. Or that they wanted anything other than fun. There were some brilliant and beautiful people among my contemporaries: Emma Rothschild had come up on a scholarship in PPE* at fifteen and Marina Warner, who later became a novelist and cultural historian, was in my year at Lady Margaret Hall, exquisite and cultured, and the belle of every social event. Tariq Ali and William Waldegrave were making political waves on opposing sides at the Union and Sarah Boyd-Carpenter (now Baroness Hogg) dwelt in the sophisticated realms of journalism and Westminster. Somewhere in the University Christopher Hampton was writing a play that would be snapped up by the Royal Court Theatre while he was still a student, and would launch him into his professional career as a playwright. Long before he was to become notorious as a marijuana dealer, Howard Marks held sway in the druggy court from which several of my friends were exiled and then sent down when Joshua Macmillan, grandson of the former prime minister, was found dead in his bed. I'd never got into the habit of watching television, and I was more or less blind to film – even when the tyro film director John Birt, later to be chair of the BBC, held auditions for a film he was making and asked if I'd be willing to strip off . . .

* Philosophy, Politics and Economics

The world beyond the university barely impinged at all. I loved rock'n'roll but really only heard bands if they had been hired to play at some ball where I happened to be doing cabaret. I did manage to see some great ones that way, and I remember the Rolling Stones being really pissed off at having to turn up to play a commemoration ball in the middle of their first American tour. I'd known some of the band before they were famous, because they came from the same town as me, and I had to laugh when they were dragged back from America because I'd last seen Mick in the Carousel Coffee Bar on West Hill, Dartford, one Saturday morning two years earlier. He'd been agonising over whether to go on the road with the band, who'd just got their first serious gig, or stay on at the London School of Economics and complete his degree. They were going to replace him as lead singer if he didn't go.

I never read a paper, didn't own a radio. I remember hearing with some amazement that Winston Churchill had died, some two years after it had happened. I didn't actually live in an ivory tower – my college was solid red brick and, some claimed, the inspiration for Toad Hall in *The Wind in the Willows* – but I was as cut off from the outside world as if I did. But now, with my father's death, I was forced to take notice of that world.

When term ended I went home for a few days, and then returned to Oxford: the American Rhodes scholar who had played Caligula was getting married. I enjoyed the distraction of it, and I drank a lot of champagne and got sleepier and sleepier. In the car on the way back I could hardly keep my eyes open and by the time we'd gone the sixty-odd miles home it was difficult to rouse me. The doctor came round, a family friend, and I can remember snatches of conversation in which he speculated about meningitis or polio. It was hard for my mother; it was only a few weeks since she had buried her husband and now here was another crisis. In fact, all of us children were to react to our father's death in quite extreme ways. My sister miscarried her first, much longed-for, child; my little brother, the only one still at home, was to muck up his A levels and take a year or two to sort himself out; and my other brother's private life reached a crisis. It was as if our family life had prepared none of us for any sort of crisis. Looking back, it feels as if we had enjoyed a sort of idyll through our childhood, untouched by the usual privations and losses that come to families. No deaths of close relations, no serious illness, enough creature comforts to be comfortable but not enough to make for a sense of being set apart by privilege.

I was sent off to an isolation ward in what had formerly been a plague hospital out on the Thames marshes and by the time I was admitted I was in a coma. No one had noticed at home, but in the hospital they thought me very dark – later my nurse said they had thought I was Indian. It was jaundice: I turned bright yellow. When I woke up ten days later my eyeballs were like orange conkers, I could barely see and my arms and legs were paralysed. It was quite bad as the bile had set up secondary irritations in the glands of my armpits and groin, and at the back of my eyes. I felt hopelessly weak and disoriented and could do nothing but try to stay on the bed – I kept finding myself in a heap on the floor – and think.

My father's requiem kept coming back to me. Why had he had a full-blown Catholic service? I'd thought I was very close to him, but I'd had no idea about his faith. When I really thought about his background I realised that all I knew for sure was that he had been born and raised in India, and had come to England to be a student at Guy's Hospital a few years before the Second World War. What world had he come from, then?

It was the world of Mowgli and Kim, as far as I was concerned. I'd read *The Jungle Book* and the *Just So Stories* when I was small, and any thoughts I had of India were mixed up with that early reading. I remembered my father speaking with a deep passion of the

Himalayas, which he would sometimes pronounce 'Himaaaliyas' with a big grin on his face. I didn't really know where he'd been born or anything much about his circumstances. His father had been a doctor and dentist in Rawalpindi, and he had gone to school somewhere in the foothills of those same Himalayas. There was an icy lake fed by the surrounding snowy peaks in which the school swam before breakfast; there was a school dog that had once terrified him as a boy. He and a friend were hurrying back to school to meet the curfew after taking too long on a walk when they heard something padding through the jungle behind them. When they eventually plucked up courage to look they saw not a bear or some other great beast but the school dog, its guts and eyes falling out where it had been savaged by a black panther. I'd particularly loved this story, dwelling as it did on the precise nature of the dog's injuries. And didn't a black panther seem altogether slinkier and more exotic than a common-or-garden spotted one? I used to terrify myself at bedtime with the idea that the sand pits next door to our garden were inhabited by wolves and alligators, and every night they would start an inexorable climb up the steep sides of the pits towards the big curved white balcony that surrounded my bedroom. They were going to climb the fig tree and break through the balcony door to get me. There was a delicious frisson of terror every night as I lay in bed imagining their progress up and across the vegetable garden, past the pigsties and chicken runs and fruit trees, circling the billiard room, through the low white curving walls that separated the grass from the gravelled drive, eyeing the trellis next to the fig tree. Luckily the climb was difficult and slow, and dawn would always arrive before they could make their final assault, or, more likely, my eyes would close in sleep. My father's story of the black panther, however, could always knock my night-time creatures into a cocked hat.

Some mornings he couldn't go to breakfast because a bear would

be snoozing on the verandah of his dorm. I'd always longed for a
dorm, any dorm – an Enid Blyton Malory Towers brick turret would
have done, let alone a veranda'd bungalow surrounded by jungle.
The North-West Frontier. That meant boys' stuff, I'd thought. I
only really liked the Kim part of it, a small boy adrift in a multitude
of exotic peoples. There were Hindus and Muslims, Sikhs and
Pathans. Sometimes my father would be persuaded into a few words
of Punjabi or Urdu or Pushtu. '"*Sterai ma shay*," say the Pathans,'
he'd say. 'May you never be defeated. May you never die.'

His death was an altogether sobering experience. And now,
acutely ill myself for the first time, I had momentarily surfaced from
my coma to hear a doctor's voice saying 'You must prepare yourself,
Mrs Quick: she may not survive the night.'

'Dear God, no – oh no,' my poor mother, not two months widowed, groaned. I had no feelings other than surprise at the
unexpectedness of it. To stop at nineteen. *Sterai ma shay*. I sank
back into the black hole of the coma for another few days.

When I returned to college a term later, it was to a long, slow con-
valescence. I could no longer count on a limitless reserve of energy
to get me through. No more partying and acting in several plays
at once, no more writing through the night to get an essay done
in time for a tutorial. That life had become a physical impossibility,
and I felt distanced from almost every aspect of it. I didn't even
recognise my reflection. I was also three stone lighter and that
was the best thing to come out of the whole experience. I remember going into a department store and trying on hats. As I checked
myself out in the mirror I suddenly realised that my cheeks were
hollow below what looked like . . . cheekbones! Always before I
would suck in my cheeks to get rid of my face's schoolgirl plump-
ness. This time when I sucked in my cheeks in a reflex action to
look at myself in the white leather pill-box there was no change

in the shape of my face. (What I really wanted was a leopard-skin pill-box hat like the Dylan song, but Oxford stores and my limited budget wouldn't stretch to that. I settled for the white leather version.)

I was thin. Suddenly I had the trendiest figure imaginable: from being generously endowed I had become a waif. I looked good in the new tiny Biba dresses, which even I could afford because they were so unbelievably cheap. Until then I had made most of my own clothes because my mother had insisted that there wasn't enough money to buy me all the things I coveted. Through childhood I wore my three-years-senior sister's cast offs much of the time, and was beside myself with envy when she got a clothing allowance at fifteen, which she seemed to spend on little clutch bags and net petticoats. I never did get a clothing allowance myself, but my mother was a decent seamstress and she had taught me to make clothes, so I'd arrived in Oxford with an array of home-made frocks, most of which make me shudder to think of now. As the year progressed the outfits I made got bolder and shorter. There was one in particular, navy blue with very large white polka dots, that I wore with a bonnet made of white Michaelmas daisies tied under the chin with white satin ribbons. What can I say in my own defence? It was the sixties; I was not alone in my sartorial choices. At the time it made me feel fabulous.

I was back in Oxford having missed one term and two vacations – that equalled at least three missed opportunities to be in plays – and I celebrated by buying myself a little shift dress, the midriff section of which was made of netting. I lived in that dress. Oh, and my feet had grown a size or two bigger (bad) and for the first time in my life I had long, elegant fingernails (good). Both had grown while I was flat on my back.

The big theatre event of the summer was a production of Marlowe's *Doctor Faustus* with Richard Burton as Faustus and

Elizabeth Taylor as Helen of Troy. Nothing like it had ever happened before, two massive Hollywood stars coming to work on an OUDS* production with an otherwise student cast and crew. I had in fact been asked to understudy Miss Taylor – no one could quite believe that she would even make it to Oxford, since she was so frequently overwhelmed by illness, let alone survive five weeks' exposure to undergraduate drama – and though I baulked at the idea of playing second fiddle, even to a Hollywood diva, I was sorry to have missed it all. I listened, with a polite but wan smile, to the adventures of the student actors who had been working with them and were now off to Rome to make a film of it for Dino de Laurentiis. The university offered me an extra year, for there was no doubt I had had to slow down and catching up with the work I had missed was going to be a grind. Now I think I was mad to refuse it (a whole extra year to read!) but then I was impatient and accepted the challenge of completing my degree in the original time. But I did tend to rush through things, glancing neither to left nor right.

A recurring memory is of sitting in a crowd – in assembly at school; at a noisy summer party; a Union meeting; on a coach full of hockey players on the way to a match – and luxuriating in the feeling that my life stretched ahead of me full of possibility. I would play with the heady notion that I could be anything I wanted: an astronaut or a deep sea diver, an academic or a gardener, a doctor or the first female prime minister. I'd always felt immortal, but now, perhaps, was the beginning of the end of that. As Dr Johnson said, the prospect of imminent death does concentrate the mind wonderfully.

One way and another it was the end of childhood, and later my friends were to tell me that I had been hard to take 'before'. Some eighteen months after my return to Oxford Hermione Lee[1] played

---

* Oxford University Dramatic Society

Hippolyta to my Helena in a production of A *Midsummer Night's Dream* that we took to the United States, and as we wandered through a snowy New York, she said, 'You were insufferable, you know.'

'When?'

'Before.'

'Why?'

'So arrogant. Don't worry, it's all right now.'

It puts me in mind of what Max Beerbohm said: 'I was a modest, good-humoured boy. It is Oxford that has made me insufferable.'

So it seemed that fate was taking a hand. I'd been brought down a peg or two and, lurking in the back of my mind, was a vague recollection that my father had sometimes called his school in the foothills the Seminary. Had he been destined for the priesthood? Was he a closet Catholic all his life? Why had it been hidden? And if I had been so totally ignorant of this crucial fact about him, what other secrets might be there for the seeking?

2

Pure Blood

Searching around for scraps of memory that might give a clue to my father's background, I remembered visiting another hospital bed, ten years earlier. My Grandfather Quick had been taken ill at the age of sixty-six, and he thought he might be going to die in the cold, expensive, inhospitable place he called home, even though he'd only lived there for the past three years. He had spent his life in India: he was born there and schooled there, trained there, practised medicine and then dentistry there, and had only retired to England in the fifties. Now, as he perhaps lay dying, he'd asked to talk to the girls, me and my sister Julie. He didn't ask for our two brothers. It was only the second time we'd ever met him. Our father didn't seem to be on friendly terms with his own dad.

The first time we'd met had been in a dark flat in Carshalton or Esher or some other Surrey refuge for the returnees from the Raj, soon after their arrival from what was now Pakistan, but had, for most of Grandfather's life, been part of British India. They had not left at Partition in 1947. He had a thriving practice in Rawalpindi, and had in any case only known life in India. Even if he now called England home, his heart, his reference point, must always have been India. I did not understand any of this at the time – I was about six years old – but I did get a strange feeling of dislocation and tension. There was an atmosphere.

The flat seemed to be overrun with Pekinese dogs. I remember the dogs best, because we children had all stayed in the rather small kitchen while the dogs reclined on the sofas next door.

'Your name is Diane, not Diana, isn't it?' said the woman we'd been told to call Grandmother. 'So much nicer a name.'

'No,' I managed, baffled but aware that I must mind my Ps and Qs, 'I'm Diana.' She turned away with a sour expression and a pinched mouth. I don't remember her talking to me after that.

Now here was another conundrum. After a big gap, with no contact as far as I can remember, we were sent to see him on his sickbed. Grandfather lay tucked up to his neck under a starched white sheet, turning just his head to address us. I didn't recognise him, but he looked like the photograph of Kipling in my edition of *The Jungle Book*: bullet head, groomed moustache, a military bearing even when flat in a hospital bed. And that funny voice, which rose and fell in quite unexpected places. He fixed us with a gimlet eye and urged us, without preamble, 'Always do as your parents tell you, and be sure you marry a pure-blooded Englishman.'

Me aged nine, Julie twelve. The two commands – to obey our parents and to marry pure blood – were somehow connected. Would a Scotsman or a Welshman count as pure-blooded, I wondered. But we never mentioned this conversation to our parents, and they never questioned us about what had been said in our interview or why we'd been summoned but not the boys. As you do at nine, I slipped out of the room, was taken home and got on with the next thing – probably hanging upside down on the bar above the swing at my friend Jackie's and dreaming of the day Tommy

Trinder would announce my debut on the trapeze on *Sunday Night at the London Palladium*. I dreamed of being a trapeze artist and spent hours perfecting my act; I certainly wasn't thinking of love and marriage. In any case, I hardly knew anyone who wasn't English so what was the problem?

This is one of the most striking differences between the fifties and now. In a suburban town like Dartford, and even more living, as we did, in a big house on the edge of a heath with only two neighbours, I hardly knew anybody who wasn't white and middle or lower middle class. My parents had a golfing friend who had been a hero of the Polish resistance, and another friend who had married an Afrikaner called Frik and been whisked away to South Africa, while my father's sister Esme sent a long letter from Australia each Christmas, which was read out to us children. That was about it as far as foreigners went.

Oh, and then there was a Belgian who arrived from the airport – so exotic, he'd actually flown over the Channel in an aeroplane – with four tall plastic cylinders, one for each of us children, filled with the most dreamy chocolates I'd ever tasted; pralines, he said. I'll never forget their utter deliciousness, for treats like that were few and far between. I could still remember going once a week to collect my measly sweet ration, two ounces of sherbet lemons or liquorice comfits from Mr Knucklebones the grocer. Of course rationing was over by now and we did get a few pence each week to buy sweets. I'd walk over the heath to the hunting lodge turned sweet shop and buy twelve flying saucers (four for a penny), a sherbet fountain and a penny chocolate bar, or a tube of Love Hearts, or my beloved Refreshers, but nothing like these smooth, nutty jewels had ever crossed my horizon.

The only other foreign person I knew was my teacher, Miss Da Silva, whom I loved and who loved me back, with her golden skin and black eyes, and who used to sing out when her eye lighted on me, 'Quick by name and Quick by nature!' For a whole year I scurried everywhere, trying to live up to my new handle. In fact, her voice was very like Grandpa's, with its curious cadences, but it took me many years to realise that she, like him, was a child of the west coast of India.

And so for the time being it was pretty easy to do Grandfather's bidding: no impure blood on the horizon, and a mother and father who were easy to obey since they were nearly always out, leaving any discipline to the intermittent attentions of Nana or Great Aunt Kitty. Bedtime wasn't negotiable but almost anything else could be wangled. Mostly we were outside or, if it was wet, in the billiard room or one of the outhouses that were scattered around the garden, if not occupied by Nana's chickens or pigs, or down in the air raid shelter turned apple store called the Do Drop Inn, with its musty-apple smell and platoons of spiders. We only went inside to raid the larder. I don't remember many meals, but there was a large pantry with well-stocked shelves and the bread man delivered to the door each morning. If it was your turn you got to choose an extra loaf just for you, still warm. You'd cut the crust off one end on the big circular slicing machine then pull out all the heavenly white pap from the inside, crushing it into a gooey greyish ball (not too much hand washing went on) that would last you a good few hours. There was always milk in the fridge, and you might complement the bread with some lettuce leaves from the garden sprinkled with a spoonful of white sugar and rolled up into a little package. There was plenty in the garden, carrots and radishes and gooseberries and figs and apples and pears, and tomatoes in the greenhouse. If you got really desperate there were large tins in the larder that no one seemed to mind you raiding; dried egg powder, tins and tins of it left over from the war. I came to love the way it moulded itself to the roof of my mouth when I sucked it off the spoon because I hadn't a clue how to cook the stuff. For a treat I took to raiding the medicine cupboard for Ex-Lax chocolate – small squares that must have had a laxative effect, but it was worth it for the hit of sweetness. My brother Clive developed a taste for a cough medicine called Liquafruita, heavy with the tastes of fig and garlic; I could never quite see the point of it myself, but he loved it and spent much of his youth reeking of garlic, which was still a rarity in cooking in those days.

We certainly never went abroad, and it was a very big deal to eat at the one Greek restaurant when we went down to the coast for our summer holiday – a bit of taramasalata or hummus followed by steak and chips. Once in a while my father would decide to cook and then it would be a curry, the hotter the better. He would spend whole evenings grinding the spices and encouraging us to try ladies' fingers or halva. He'd go soft-eyed at the thought of papayas or mangoes but we never saw such exotica in our house. I imagined them hanging from the trees in the jungle where he had spent his childhood, with panthers and bears padding beneath. I never thought they would be something I would ever eat myself; it was inconceivable that, in a few years' time, they would be as familiar as apples or pears.

So, for me, Grandfather was very foreign, ineluctably so. The stiff bearing; the tune in his voice; the powerful sense that he was a rumbling volcano by temperament. Not someone to be ignored. And yet here was a funny thing: in my world he was more or less ignored. No one had ever talked to us children about him or his wife. We'd never even heard of them until the day we'd been taken over to their kitchen and met the Pekinese. They never came to our house, which was always so full of family: not just us and my mother's parents, but aunties and uncles and cousins and second cousins dropping in all the time. My mother had so many relatives it was hard to keep track of who they all were. It never bothered me, they were just our family and anyone over twenty-five was called Auntie or Uncle, whatever their actual relationship might be, and anyone younger was good to play with, especially my mother's brothers. One of them always called me Honeybunch, and the other was a racing driver. Before the war he had raced a Jaguar SS100 at Brands Hatch when it was a grass track, and when I first knew him raced 500cc cars. His favourite trick was to tie me up with a whole ball of string and leave me to untangle myself – sometimes it took hours.

But none of this rolled over to Grandfather and Grandmother. There was no feeling of warmth towards them whatsoever. Even their names were awkward, but it was unthinkable that they might be shortened to Granny and Grandpa. Everything to do with them was stiff, formal, cold and difficult. I was glad to escape from that spooky hospital room back to the familiar world of hugs and teeming family; pet cats and lambs and piglets; chickens to be fed and endless trees to be climbed and plays to be contrived with my little gang. I didn't give Grandfather a second thought.

It took another twelve years for these memories to surface, as I sat at another bedside with another man who was also dying, only this time it was acting. I was playing Julia Flyte in the television series of *Brideshead Revisited*. We were filming the death of Lord Marchmain – my father – who had returned to his family seat after many years abroad. As his older daughter I take upon myself the responsibility of bringing a priest to his bedside so that at the last he might be reconciled with the Roman Catholic Church that he had abandoned half a lifetime before, even though I myself do not follow the faith any more. This of course set up a strange echo for me, and as Laurence Olivier looked uncannily like a handsome version of the men in my family, with the same domed forehead and silver hair brushed back, a strong, somewhat broad nose and high cheekbones, art was clearly imitating life. Was it Errol Flynn who used to annotate his scripts with 'AR' (acting required) and 'NAR' (no acting required)? This was definitely a NAR situation.

3

A Tug on the Thread

It was a big deal to have Laurence Olivier in our series, a very big deal. We had been working away for months before he joined us as we had started filming, broadly, at the beginning of the story, and so far there were the two boys, Charles and Sebastian, their university pals and fleeting appearances by the other three children in the Flyte family. We hadn't got to the older generation yet, and thus far my character, Julia, had played what Waugh calls 'an intermittent and somewhat enigmatic part'. About halfway through what should have been a seven-month schedule there had been a major strike of all ITV technicians.

Even before the strike had halted our progress the director Michael Lindsay-Hogg had come to the conclusion that he would serve Evelyn Waugh best by working from the book itself, rather than the script commissioned from John Mortimer. John had originally been asked to prepare six fifty-two-minute episodes, stripping away or combining some of the minor characters and simplifying the structure to tell the story in a continuous present narrative rather than 'bookended' by Charles Ryder's later recollection of his pre-war involvement with the Flyte family, and this was precisely what he had provided. But, with Michael's decision to go back to the book, a new version was in preparation that, by the time the strike ended, consisted of a couple of milk crates containing a verbatim transcript of Evelyn Waugh's dialogue from the book. As yet, it could not be called a script: it had no scenes, episodes or linking framework.

The strike had also meant that we lost our original director: Michael could not keep himself free for the extra span of time the production would need as he was off to Hollywood to make a feature there and so Charles Sturridge – an outsider for this plum job since he was fairly junior at Granada – was appointed director. Charles had been saying for months in the privacy of dressing rooms and bars, 'Why aren't I directing this? I know more about the subject than anyone in England.' As it turned out, he possibly did: Oxford-educated himself, he had grown up in a large Catholic family with a father who first gave him the book to read before he was in his teens.

It was nonetheless a brave choice by the producer, Derek Granger, whose defining quality was and continues to be his capacity to enable others to do their best work, without a shred of rivalry, his openness to suggestions. Before work could resume on the series Derek, Charles and the associate producer spent three days holed up in a hotel near Castle Howard in Yorkshire with the crates of transcribed dialogue, thrashing out a new shape for the story and a detailed script for the last episode, which was the next to be filmed.

Meanwhile, it had been out of the question for any of the actors to go off and do another job during the strike, for it might have ended at a moment's notice, so we had all spent a great deal of time re-reading the book. When we reconvened our new familiarity with the book led to intense lobbying by all of us in the cast for the restoration of each of our favourite scenes, which had been cut away in the original script from what was already a slimmish book. Luckily for us, the wishes of producer, director and cast coincided and Derek lobbied hard to persuade Granada TV to increase the budget. The result was that in the end we included almost everything in the book; instead of the six short episodes originally proposed, it was to be shot as seven two-hour segments (though in the end it was re-cut and transmitted as a long first and last episode, with nine one-hour episodes in between). The schedule went from its initial seven months to twenty-one and the budget, spiralling upwards, took Granada a decade or so to recoup. It was an unprecedented situation in television production.

I had also spent time in the strike trying to learn about the Catholic faith in order to help me understand what was to happen to Julia later in the story. When she marries a divorced man she turns her back on Catholicism and spends her adult life denying it has any hold over her.

Then her father returns home after many years in exile from his family and the Catholic Church, and Julia is the one who must decide whether or not he should be allowed to die without absolution. The 'tug on the thread' of this chapter's title is borrowed from Waugh's 'twitch upon the thread', and he in turn is quoting one of G. K. Chesterton's 'Father Brown' stories. However far you roam, and however much you deny it, for a Catholic there will, sooner or later, be a twitch upon the thread that draws you back to the faith. I wondered if that was what had happened to my father on his deathbed.

This crisis of faith is at the heart of what happens to Julia, and indeed the point of the book is not just nostalgia for a lost golden age or gilded youth, though that was certainly the popular impression of the book and our film. Evelyn Waugh was an ardent convert to Catholicism and in writing *Brideshead Revisited* he was writing an apologia for his religion. I was going to carry a large part of the responsibility for communicating this solemn argument, but that all lay in the months of filming ahead. For the time being my priorities were to work out how I looked and how I spoke. I'd spent many happy afternoons listening to the cut-glass enunciation and high rapid delivery of the leading ladies in old British films, but it was clear that we couldn't use a full-on, between-the-wars toff's accent – even though we were the children of a Marquess between the wars – because it was felt that it would alienate the general viewer. Hardly anybody spoke like that any more, and certainly not in the world of the media. I regretted that decision in a way: I love accents and the detective trail of getting it spot on. Later, when I was playing a Burnley divorcee in the film *Vroom*, I spent three weeks on the streets of the town trying out what I had learnt phonetically in daily sessions with a voice coach, and eventually lived in the accent on and off set for the duration of the shoot.

As Julia, my role model was not Celia Johnson in Brief Encounter but Anthony Andrews, who played my brother Sebastian. He is what most people remember when they speak about Brideshead: the golden youth with his teddy bear, doomed to betray his early promise in an alcoholic haze in Tunis. He dominates the first half of the book, and when the narrator Charles first comes across Julia, he 'recognized her at once . . . her voice was Sebastian's and his her way of speaking'. We spent a lot of time doing mirror exercises, where you sit face to face – in our case mostly over a meal or a glass of something – and try to move in exact reflection of the person opposite. I got his way of flicking his hair back off his fore-head, the tilt of his chin, and copied his vocal inflections. He was blond and I was dark, but Waugh specifically says that 'her dark hair was scarcely longer than Sebastian's and it blew back from her fore-head as his did'.

The hair proved hellishly difficult to get right. We had attempted to film a crucial scene pre-strike, when Julia collects Charles from the station. In other scenes I wore the cloches of the period, well pulled down, but this was my first hatless scene and because Julia is precociously sophisticated we had opted for a Marcel-waved look with serpentine locks close to the head, no eye make-up and a dark red mouth, all strictly of the period. In the rushes I looked utterly wrong, a travesty, a hard-faced Wallis Simpson rather than a radiant eighteen-year-old hovering between childhood and adulthood. I was in fact thirty at the time, and well placed to play the older, sadder and wiser Julia, but all through the strike the ghastly inappropriateness of my young 'look' had haunted me and I have only learnt recently that it nearly cost me the part. Unbeknownst to me, my employers at Granada were equally worried and considering firing me and recasting Julia after the strike. Depressed at the prospect of resuming the work looking all wrong, it was lucky that I decided to do something about it and, without consulting anyone had cut my hair in a short, straight bob and made it a condition of extending my contract that I had a new make-up artist, who was able to soften the harsh lips, enhance the eyes with a discreet pencil and mascara and arrange my new short hair so that it blew back from the forehead as described by Waugh. Suddenly we were in business, although in fact it was to take another eighteen months before we got a satisfactory take of this, my first big scene. I recall that when we finally got that scene in the can I had been being thirty-seven for a scene in the morning, and then back to the eighteen-year-old after lunch, to complete a sequence we had started a year and a half earlier.

One of the new team's first tasks was to complete the casting of the parents. Charles secured the wonderful Mona Washbourne for our nanny, Claire Bloom for our Mama, Lady Marchmain, Sir John Gielgud for Charles's father, Stéphane Audran for our father's mistress, Cara, and Laurence Olivier for Lord Marchmain. To my lasting regret I had no opportunity to work with Sir John: his very brilliant scenes were all two-handers with Jeremy Irons. Later, when Sir Laurence had settled into the routine at Castle Howard, he would make very beady jokes about how, if he had read the whole of the novel before accepting, he would have insisted on playing Gielgud's part and not Lord Marchmain. He knew it was an absolute scene-stealer. I loved this glimpse of how the rivalry that had coloured their youth, when they had alternated as Romeo and Mercutio, continued throughout their careers to this point, when both were well into their seventies. Sir John, of course, said nowt. He didn't need to.

As it was, Sir Laurence arrived in our midst frail with illness. He had already survived two major ailments that would have finished a lesser mortal. He never referred to it, but he was suffering from a degenerative disorder that caused extreme pain in his palms and in the soles of his feet, which would periodically distract him to the point of oblivion. You would see his vitally present spirit retreat far back behind his eyes, and he would be taken from the set discreetly and we would take a break. He was on large doses of steroids and that alone must have made it hard to concentrate, yet he led the company in exemplary fashion; he knew the names of the crew from his first moments on the set – some forty or fifty people. That made people love him. He was, it goes without saying, punctual and prepared, but also unfailingly courteous, alert, solicitous of others, witty and voracious for gossip. He was as camp as anything, with a sort of high theatricality that you do not find much in non-gay actors of my generation. When he was filming with the boys on the streets of Venice they had all wandered off during a break to look at something and got lost: he was delighted and suggested they stay lost for the hell of it.

He had a very low boredom threshold; you sensed a gargantuan appetite for diversion and this was very useful for playing Lord Marchmain, a restless spirit drawn on the grand scale, a drinker in his youth and now a cosmopolitan habitué of Capri and Venice and

Rome for whom the years are closing in. When the time comes to die he hangs ferociously on to life.

In fact his own fear of boredom may have informed his characteristic habit of stressing an unlikely word or syllable in a sentence, which had no doubt been developed to force the audience to sit up and pay attention. Charles spotted this concern that the audience must never be allowed to be bored as a key to working with him: if he felt that Sir Laurence needed steering towards a different interpretation he found it was usually enough to say, 'Don't you think the audience might expect that? What if you tried this . . .'

Lately Lord Olivier had been cramming in several parts a year, often in indifferent projects, almost a travesty of his previous career as the world's pre-eminent actor, the only one to be created a life peer in those uncynical, pre-Blairite days. No doubt he was working so frenetically to secure the future for his still-young family, but I always had the sense of him as a man who loved to work, who was most fully alive when acting. And perhaps, too, the work kept him going; perhaps he was more like the character he was playing than we realised. Charles Ryder describes Lord Marchmain as a man who did not have so much 'a wonderful will to live' as 'a great fear of death' – which, as Marchmain's doctor goes on to explain, meant that 'he doesn't derive any great strength from his fear, you know. It's wearing him out.' Sometimes it's hard to know what is the play and what is reality. In any case, for much of the time an actor's work 'does not end with the imagination', as Burne Jones said of his life as an artist. We, like him, 'go on always in that strange land that is more true than real'.

What has stayed with me for more than twenty years is a sense of Olivier as being massively private, and it seemed to me that he was truly living out 'his own solitary struggle to keep alive' just like the character he was playing. He was at his most vivid in the long

soliloquy that he delivered during Lord Marchmain's final, inexorable decline towards death – twenty minutes at least – an eternity
in television terms. It was the scene that sold him the part and
it was to be filmed in one take, with no fancy angles or reverses.
There would be cut-aways to me and my sister Cordelia (so brilliantly played by Phoebe Nicholls), to Charles and to Cara, as
we sat around the bed but the scene was essentially his. Sitting
at that bedside, watching and listening, was where the collision of
memories really began.

Though Olivier was more handsome by far he had so much the
look of my grandfather and my father. His position in the bed,
reclining against pillows, eyes shut; his urgent wish to speak and
our difficulty as we strained to catch his meaning; my understanding at last that this man, as his life came to its end, was concerned
with not being an outsider, that he was perhaps frightened by the
idea of not conforming to the world; and, finally, the situation of
my character, who is there at his bedside with her sister beside her;
all these elements conjured up that last meeting with my own
grandfather. I remember an unusual air of solemnity on the set
while we filmed that affected everybody: it was partly the scene,
but mostly because it was Lord Olivier who was doing it, and
doing it brilliantly.

And then, for me, there were other images coming up, the nine-
year-old's memory and the nineteen-year-old's memory. The two
senior men of the Quick family, one sternly abjuring me about a
future that seemed so far ahead that it was unimaginable, the other
snatched away by death long before I had finished being close to
him. I sat with the others around that bed and listened – acting is
often about listening properly – and stirred up things that had been
lying undisturbed and undisturbing for decades.

I was in my early thirties when this collision of memory and
professional life happened. As an actor it is a commonplace to

ricochet between fragments of one's own past and the actions one is required to play for the part; it is the bread and butter of the work. It doesn't mean one has to have actually been the thing itself – you can play a felon without going to jail, a nymphomaniac without twenty-four-hour promiscuity – but this episode was taking place at a significant stage of my life. I had nearly always done things at a young age, but now, suddenly, my thirties had come upon me and it was no longer enough to be promising. I couldn't get away with that any longer: it was time to start being myself, not for ever a larva about to hatch. I'd been reading Simone de Beauvoir since my late teens, and something she had written about transcending the moment had always haunted me: 'There is no justification for present existence other than its expansion into an indefinitely open future . . . Every individual concerned to justify his existence feels that his existence involves an undefined need to transcend himself, to engage in freely chosen projects.'[1]

The trouble was, I wasn't free. These memories tugged me back into what the existentialists called immanence, and I didn't know who I was. Acting gave me as many clues as it hid me from. Until I was cast as Julia I had mostly played foreigners and mavericks; I'd made a pretty successful exotic over the years and now here I was inhabiting the life of an English aristocrat. But even Julia had something about her – the European relatives, her family's Catholicism – that, ignore it as she might, put her outside conventional Englishness. So where had *I* come from? As a girl I sometimes spent hours trying to see where my family fitted in to the English scheme of things: not quite posh, though two of my siblings went to public school; not quite working class, for though Nana and Pop spoke with ordinary Dartford accents he was called 'The Guv'nor' by everyone locally; not quite like our middle-class friends because there was something a bit bohemian about the family too. There was a very dark, almost Semitic look to many of my mother's family, but if you asked where that had come from – were we perhaps Jewish? – you were met with blank looks and a hushed 'Oh no, I don't think so'. And then there was the fact of my father's life in India and why did it matter so much to me that my father had been buried with a requiem after twenty-eight years of ignoring his Church? And why was the injunction to marry a pure-bred Englishman the one thing that had stuck in my memory about Grandfather?

I am not suggesting that an actor must know his family history to act well. On the contrary, I think the tension created by the gap between oneself and the character can often make a performance crackle into life – the strange land that is more true than real. But I wanted more clarity, more information. I wanted to understand how my father had come to turn his back on the world he'd grown up in, to the point where he could only tell his children romantic yarns: the morning dip in the icy lake, the constitutionals through the jungle and the rush to get back before the curfew released wolves and tigers and panthers back onto the trail that seemed so harmless, almost like suburban Surrey, in the daylight. Perhaps that's why so many old India hands chose Surrey when they made it home; it reminded them of the wooded hills rising all along the southern side of the Himalayas. Like Grandfather, cut off in his gloomy flat with a critical wife and a pack of pampered Pekinese. How did he become this angry misfit from the Punjab? How had he come even to be there?

To understand that, I needed to find out about his parents. That took a lot of digging as I didn't even know their names. I started asking a lot of questions of my Uncle Basil, the only member of the Quicks now in England who had been part of their life in India. He was my father's younger brother – no, half-brother, the child of both Grandfather and Grandmother. So here was already something interesting: Grandmother wasn't my father's mother, but his

stepmother. All the fairy stories I'd ever read – where the stepmother was always wicked – set up a little alert in my brain, but her
story would have to wait. I wanted to go back a generation and find
out about Grandfather's origins first. My uncle gave me the basic
facts: the Quicks were originally from Devon or Cornwall, maybe
from Tavistock, and someone called Christopher had gone out to
India in the army, probably in the 1870s. That was the information
from which I started. A little vague, but enough to get cracking. It
wasn't too difficult to track down a likely Christopher Quick in the
registry of births as, luckily, the name is relatively uncommon. But
when I tried to find this particular soldier in the army records, he
proved to be far more elusive.

4

Alias Tom Jones

In the birth records I soon found that a Christopher George Quick had been born in 1853 to Richard Quick, a miner, at Calstock on the River Tamar, which marks the boundary of Devon with Cornwall. Calstock was a mining town on the southern boundary of Dartmoor: mines were often sited around the edge of moorland as the tilting of the upland brought seams closer to the surface, making the business of digging out the copper, tin, arsenic and tungsten found here in abundance much easier. During the 1860s, there was a boom in copper production in the area. I could see from the 1861 census returns for Devon that other Quicks in the town were doing well from the mines – John and Nanny Quick lived at 19 Collycliff with their six little daughters and a couple of servants – but there is no sign of the Richard Quicks. There was no protection for miners and they had to nominate which seam they planned to work on a yearly basis. It was a gamble: if they struck lucky they could do brilliantly well; if not, they and their family would starve. The owner of the mine took no responsibility for the men who worked his seams. Perhaps Richard's luck had run out and he'd moved away.

Trawling through the records in Cornwall and Devon was frustrating: there were plenty of Quicks, especially around St Ives, including ten Richards aged from two months to fifty-seven years, but no sign of my Richard or of little Christopher. I enjoyed the landscape, which still has remnants of the once-thriving mines: between Tavistock and the Tamar it is marked with the tall chimneys and ruined walls of mine shafts. But however atmospheric the countryside of my great-grandfather's childhood, I wasn't getting very far with the hard facts of his life.

Frustrated, I went to the India Office at the British Library. My Uncle Basil said that my great-grandfather had gone out to India as a soldier. I worked backwards, starting with the baptismal record for my father then tracking his parents from the information I found in that, and then back to my great-grandparents. I learned that Christopher George had been a gunner in the 3rd Battery of the Premier Brigade, Scottish Division of the Royal Artillery. Now that I knew where my great-grandfather had been born and which regiment he had served with in India, I thought it would be a piece of cake to track his career back to its beginning, even if the fate of the Richard Quicks was still eluding me.

In fact, I met a brick wall – the first of many in the search for my family. I went to Woolwich, the headquarters of the Royal Artillery, and looked through their records. I searched in vain through the military records of British India in the India Office library. Weeks passed. There was a mass of information about officers, but Christopher was a humble gunner. It was the first indication of what was to be a recurring frustration: the great divide between the officer class and the other ranks. Any officer can be tracked in great detail, from first commission to final pension payment, but unless I found some more specific details about Christopher he would be lost in the swirling ranks of those who served in India without individual distinction. I tracked the baptisms, marriages and deaths of anyone called Quick in India since records had first been kept there in the early eighteenth century. The name was not

nearly so rare as I had once imagined – there were hundreds to add
to the many I'd found in the West Country census lists – and as I
continued to thrash about it started to feel as if Christopher was a
needle in a rapidly expanding haystack.

I had masses of information by now, a thick A4 notebook filled
with lists of names and dates that might somehow fit into the family
tree once I had found the key. I needed to narrow my search somehow, and worked out that the earliest Christopher could have sailed
for India was in 1869, when he would have been sixteen, and the
latest was in 1887, as his first son was born in Meean Meer later that
year. If nowhere else, his name would surely be on the embarkation
rolls for troops going out to India. There even the humblest and
most junior soldier would be named.

At last I found a 'C. Quick' – no other details on the bare roll –
who had tried to sail from Portsmouth on the HMS *Malabar* in 1871.
He was on a waiting list and there was a line through his name, suggesting that he didn't actually make it on to the boat. All this was
taking ages: I was thrashing about and didn't seem to be getting anywhere. However, I did uncover some incidental facts, even if I couldn't
nail my man down. I learnt that 3333 regular soldiers went out to
India in the year from 1872 to 1873, the majority of them infantry.
There were just 272 cavalry and 22 engineers, and 972 artillery and
horse artillery. Somewhere in that number was my great-grandfather,
but why on earth was he proving so elusive? I also learnt that most
artillery would have embarked at Woolwich, near their headquarters,
or at Sheerness in Kent, not Portsmouth, and the mystery deepened.
Perhaps this C. Quick wasn't my great-grandfather after all.

The senior librarian at the India Office took pity on me and sent
me off to the Public Record Office at Kew where, he assured me, I
would find musters and discharge details for just about anyone who
had travelled out to the subcontinent. I spent a week or two going
through boxes of enlistment papers. Still a blank. And then – at last! –

the eureka moment when I found Christopher. He wasn't among the Quicks, though his file was stored in a box marked 'Q'. Having gone through all the other files I idly opened this last and found Christopher there, lurking behind the pseudonym of Thomas Jones.

Now that I'd found him, after weeks of searching, the librarian at the Public Record Office told me that it was not at all unusual for soldiers to enlist under a false name; there was even an army order that permitted a soldier to reclaim his true name without prejudice, which was first introduced in 1835.[1] The date suggests that the Act was an expedient measure at a time when the expanding colony in India required a larger army, and in order to fill the quotas the military had to recruit without asking too many questions about a man's past. Lieutenant-Colonel Stanley Tullet of the Royal Artillery (himself a child of the ranks in India who had enlisted as a twelve-year-old trumpeter and rose to be in charge of the regiment) told that often a felon would be instructed by the judge to sign up or else go to prison.

I can only speculate what my great-grandfather might have been up to that had made him take on a false name – theft? Assault? A disastrous marriage? Manslaughter? – but, a few months short of his twentieth birthday in 1875, Tom Jones from South Wales signed up as an artilleryman. Neither father nor son was living near the mines of Calstock by now, and at some point, as I learnt later, the father Richard Quick took himself and the remaining members of his family off to settle in the new colony of Canada.

Christopher was five feet, seven inches tall, with a chest measurement of thirty-five inches, dark hair, brown eyes and a sallow complexion. He had joined the Royal Artillery for a term of service of twelve years, plus an extra year – called a buckshee year – that would be tagged on the end of his term 'if abroad'. His first four years were served in Britain and when he set off for India he cannot have imagined that he would be spending not just the remaining nine years he had already signed up for there, but the next twenty-two in the army and a further twenty-nine at Peshawar on the North-West Frontier. In fact he never returned to Britain.

Around the time my great-grandfather left England, there had been a great increase in the number of soldiers sent out to defend the jewel of the empire. Before the Sepoy Uprising of 1856–57 there had been a ratio of just one British soldier to nine natives but, fearing that more trouble was brewing and that they lacked the sheer numbers to deal with it if it came, the British government intervened. The East India Company had been in charge since 1600 when Elizabeth I granted them permission to trade speculatively in the East, but now, under Disraeli's leadership, Parliament passed the India Act in the summer of 1858, taking executive control away from the Company and vesting it instead in two sources, a Secretary of State for India answerable to Parliament, and a Viceroy in Calcutta who would preside over law-making and everyday administration in the country.[2]

One of the first actions of the government in London was to build up the military presence in India as quickly as possible. In the Northern Presidency of Bengal, where the trouble had started, they soon achieved a ratio of one to two, and one to three elsewhere. The Second Afghan War had been rumbling on for the two years before Christopher Quick travelled out in 1875, and at this time the British army in India amounted to some seventy thousand troops.

In fact at its peak there were never more than eight hundred thousand Europeans in India. For many new arrivals, and I am sure for Christopher too, the overwhelming impression would be how few white faces there were in a sea of locals.

In one way Christopher was lucky, for since the opening of the Suez Canal in 1869 the sea passage had been cut down to a mere two months; before this it could have taken the best part of six months. For a humble trooper, though, the sea journey was still pretty grim, and even fifty years later nothing had changed as Private Stephen Bentley recalls of the journey out to serve in India in the twenties:

> The whole administration just went to pieces. No one came round to see that the men were fed . . . that the men were really ill or just sea-sick . . . to sort the whole chaos of kit just dropped anywhere, no one to see that the latrines were working – and they weren't, so that the overflow from the latrines was swishing all over the middle deck. There was very little water. You couldn't get into a wash place, you couldn't get to your kit and worst of all, you couldn't get to your hammock after the first night. The hammocks were just thrown down into the hammock rooms . . . it was a really dreadful experience. The officers had got three parts of the ship anyhow for accommodation and the troops had only got the troop deck . . . I can honestly say that in the first five or six days I never saw a single officer on the troop deck.[3]

If Christopher managed to stay healthy on the way out he might well have passed the time by gambling. There was pontoon, whist and a particularly popular game called crown and anchor that could go on for days – all officially frowned upon, but impossible to limit.

Once he was serving in India the artillery regiments went through major re-organisations and in his record of service he seems to have been moved from unit to unit with quite dizzying frequency: from Bombay down to the south; then up to Bengal; from Calcutta across to the newly acquired territories of the North-West Frontier; and at one time being sent to Burma for a spell. But between these periods of intense military engagement time seems to have hung heavy for the other ranks. It would be at its most unbearable during the hot weather season, from April to June, and then during the monsoons of the following months to October. Anyone who could afford it would get away to the relative cool of the hills, but for the

private soldier this was not an option. The best he could look
forward to would be that parades and musters would be taking place
at dawn or sunset when the weather was not so hot. For the long
hot hours in between there was very little to divert him:

> You weren't allowed to go out, except to the latrine, and from
> then on you were incarcerated in your bungalow. It became
> dreadfully monotonous. The soldier sweated it out in one long
> torment of heat.[4]

For the officers it was quite another story. They had their messes
in which to relax for the evening, and the expectation of 'shikar' –
hunting birds or deer, wild boar or tigers – and polo, if they could
afford it, in their ample leisure time. All officers had horses, which
also made them mobile.

There was almost no provision for the other ranks. Soldiers were
expressly forbidden to go near the native town or the local women
in case they made mischief. In most places where the army had a
presence, the lines would be deliberately set well away from the
temptation of the bazaar. Lahore, where Christopher was to spend
the last few years of his military career and the first few of his civilian life, was a great exception, with the army lines close to the
town. They also had pitifully low wages – although I daresay the
sum seemed princely compared to local living costs – and the regiment quite deliberately manipulated their money to keep the men
on a tight rein. There would be stoppages against various expenses
and all misdemeanours were subject to fines; the hapless trooper
often ended up in debt year after year.

In the early years of Christopher's service in India, the young
journalist Rudyard Kipling was writing about the life of the lower
ranks in the *Civil and Military Gazette*, a newspaper for the British
population of Bengal, and he told of the bare horrors of the private's

life and the 'unnecessary torments' that he endured. Among the worst of these was boredom – for much of the time there was simply nothing to do. Even in the middle of putting down the Rebellion of 1857, when one might have thought he would have plenty to occupy him, Private William Guess of HM 95th Regiment begged his sister to find a songbook to send out to him, 'and if not just send the opera leaves or ballets if you would be so kind just to amuse me as we have not much here to amuse us'.[5]

Besides music, alcohol was a diversion from the sheer repetitive boredom of an average day on the cantonment. General Frederick Roberts, Commander-in-Chief of the army in India from 1885 to 1893, was the first to do anything to improve the lot of the ordinary soldier, campaigning for 'the abolition of that relic of barbarism, the canteen' and its replacement with more exciting facilities, to include 'a reading room, recreation room and a decently managed refreshment room.' He believed 'that it was impossible for any man to retain his self-respect if he were driven to take his glass of beer under the rules by which regimental canteens were governed'. His concern was not disinterested, though, for he had seen that the greater the efforts made to provide 'rational recreation and occupation in their leisure hours, the less there would be of drunkenness, and consequently of crime, the less immorality and the greater the number of efficient soldiers in the army'.[6] He oversaw the merging of various temperance societies into the Army Temperance Association, and by the time he left India in 1895 nearly a third of the British soldiers there were members. An officer who served forty-one years in India and was hugely popular with his men, Roberts was honoured by Kipling in a poem called 'Bobs' – his nickname – which included the following lines:

> 'E's a little down on drink,
> Chaplain Bobs;
> But it keeps us outer Clink –

Don't it, Bobs?
So we will not complain
Tho' 'e's water on the brain,
If 'e leads us straight again –
Blue-light Bobs.

For the two thirds of the BORs (British Other Ranks) who did not join the temperance movement there was still the daily ration of rum, and beer was available in the nontemperance canteens, and if that wasn't enough, it was pretty simple to organise a native bearer to bring some arrack* in from the native quarter; sometimes it would be boiled up with spices and green chillies to increase its potency, and all in the name of getting 'peggled'.

Tom Jones was a champion peggler: his military record shows that he rose from artillery man to Bombardier, but it also shows him to have been stripped of his rank on several occasions; whatever it was that he did, drink was probably a big part of it. I learned from my Uncle Basil (his grandson) that at the end of his life, and retired from active service first in the army and then as a police superintendant, Christopher was often the worse for drink. His son Bertie, by then a respectable private surgeon in Rawalpindi, would have to go over to Peshawar to pull his father out of a ditch with, he said, monotonous regularity.

It was common for soldiers to be involved in fracas, which, so long as they took place within the closed circle of regimental life, were treated lightly by the senior officers – a dose of solitary or square-bashing and, so long as you made it to parade next time, that was the end of it. The one thing that was forbidden was to shirk army duties because of a hangover.[7] But, later on in his army

---

* Spirits distilled from fermented fruits, grains, sugar cane or the sap of coconuts or other palm trees

career, Christopher was to go far beyond the acceptable drunken brawl, something so serious that neither family history nor his army papers have explained it in detail. He had just been posted from the 3/1st Scottish to the 1st Brigade, Lancashire Division and promoted to Bombardier for the first time when he was held for twenty days awaiting trial, then reduced to the ranks again and imprisoned for five and a half months. If it had been shorter it would not have been worth mentioning, for the heat drove everyone mad and no one offered any psychological help in how to survive it. When a soldier went stir-crazy, the response was standard: "'This is a breakdown of discipline . . . put him in detention for three months, four months, six months." That was commonplace.'[8]

It is frustrating not to be able to get at what it was he had done. Did he steal some property? Or assault an officer? Was it a repeat of the felony that had forced him to conceal his true identity under the risible *nom de guerre* Tom Jones? Whatever it was could be overlooked once he had served his time. He continued in the service as an acting bombardier in practice if not in title for nearly twenty-two years. When he was discharged the incident was long forgotten; the verdict 'Conduct: very good' was written on his papers.

Perhaps the booze defended Christopher from other ailments too, for, apart from drinking too much from time to time, in all his years as a soldier his only illness was a five-day bout of bronchitis. For most people, to survive at all was an achievement for it was commonly said that a career in India was two monsoons long. While the good health you brought with you from home might get you through the first year, many Europeans succumbed in the second to the diseases attacking them in the hot wet months between May and October. Lord Kitchener, a man who spent much of his career in hot climates – Palestine, Sudan, Egypt, India – had his own tried and tested defence against infection: 'Every British soldier should copiously drink tea, so that he should sweat and by that means he will never be laid out with fever.'[9] For fever was a constant hazard; another artilleryman described seeing the 2nd Battalion, Royal Artillery, leaving for home after some eighteen years' service in the subcontinent just as he arrived for his first tour of duty:

> The 2nd Battalion were all spick and span, upright, soldierly-looking people, lithe and suntanned, many of them wearing moustaches . . . However, on further inspection it was seen that two out of three of these fine, stalwart-looking, lithe fellows were in fact sufferers from malaria. This could be seen by their yellowish skins, their sunken cheeks and their fleshless limbs.[10]

Stanley Tullett of the Royal Artillery said that you got used to living with disease: 'It's a funny old country – death is nothing. There were always bodies from cholera or plague or smallpox . . . we used to bury twice a day . . . we had to bury them . . . that was life.' For those who survived, like Tom Jones, it must have been a case of what doesn't kill you makes you stronger.

Once back to the rank of Bombardier, Jones was posted to the Southern Division and he would have found himself in the desert a lot of the time, where the flies were a particular hazard – one soldier was 'almost covered from head to foot' – for if flies got into the drinking water they passed on dysentery. We now know that cholera also spreads in infected water, but in my great-grandfather's time there was a widespread belief that it was carried by a miasma that could sweep through a room, or a whole district.* The troops developed their own test for it, which involved attaching a lump of raw meat to a pole: if it turned black, you knew you were dealing with cholera. Stanley Tullett's father had a story of cholera sweeping through his camp one night, killing everyone who was asleep in their bed while any ne'er-do-well who had passed out on the floor, too drunk to make it into bed, survived beneath the level of the passing miasma.

So for Tom Jones and his kind, life was far from easy, but was life in service in India better than the life he had escaped? In India he faced disease, boredom, poverty and drunkenness every day. And there was no privacy, of course, since the bungalow in which he lived was the size of an aircraft hangar and was shared with perhaps fifty others. It must often have been a wretched existence, as Kipling evoked in his story 'In the Matter of a Private':

> All their work was over at eight in the morning, and for the rest of the day they could lie on their backs and smoke Canteen-plug and swear at the punkah coolies. They enjoyed a fine full flesh meal in the middle of the day, and then threw themselves down on their cots and sweated and slept til it was cool enough to go out. The men could only wait and wait and wait, and watch the shadow of the barrack creeping across the blinding white dust. That was a gay life.[11]

His bed became the centre of his life, not only used for sleeping, but as 'as writing desk, as a cleaning room, as a work bench, as a card table . . .' he lived in 'perhaps one hundred cubic feet for ninety per cent of his life.'[12]

---

* Though cholera can be transmitted on unwashed fruit and vegetables, the main cause of infection seems to be through infected faeces contaminating a water supply

Since 1827 all soldiers who could read had been issued with the
Bible and a common prayer book, and by the time Gunner Jones
arrived in India soldiers' clubs were starting to become more
common; the first had been introduced in the large northern cantonment at Meerut in 1843, offering 'a means of sober and suitable
recreation and refreshment'. But apart from the odd library book
and course of lectures most soldiers were stuck with the canteens
dry and wet (serving beer) for diversion. There were endless
parades – what we would call queues – to collect meals or stores or
ammunition or to see the doctor, and you could spend an enormous
amount of time doing Bull – shining up your kit. The company's
horses were polished up too, with their teeth cleaned and their
hooves oiled, even on the underside.

With so little else to do, training camp was always welcome.
They mixed with the rest of the regiment, officers as well as ranks,
and often trained in the jungle, which being green and full of
trees made a change from the dusty plains and the arid layout
of most barracks, which had barely a tree in sight. Many of the
regiment kept pets, and the comedian Spike Milligan recalled
that when his father's artillery regiment was on the move there
was a special wagon dedicated to the cats, dogs, parrots and
monkeys that were the regiment's combined pets. If he was sometimes a martyr to drink, Bombardier Jones seems to have avoided
one of the other great hazards of life in the ranks: venereal disease,
which sent around nine thousand soldiers to the military hospitals
for treatment each year. During my detective work in the Public
Record Office I came across another Quick – Robert, from
Leighton Buzzard – who was not so prudent, and the surgeon who
treated him had much to say on the prevalence of what we would
now call sexually transmitted infections, but were then called
contagion.

It was thought to be the native women who were infected, but it was not easy to meet European women, in any case. Many would return from a five year tour of duty having had virtually no contact with women except, perhaps, a glimpse of the officers' wives as they rode out on a dawn excursion before the heat of the day, or the warrant officers' wives in the married quarters. There was a rigid class structure in India, labyrinthine in its elaborate detail. The Code of Precedence ruled all social gatherings and much heat was generated by the niceties of the seating arrangements at any gathering. It began on the boat out although, stuck on the troop deck of an army transport and far below the social radar, the other ranks would not necessarily have been aware of the subtleties of this particular snobbery. Some thought the very word 'posh' had its origin in the desire of the returnees from India vying to get the best – the shadiest – cabins, which meant seeking to be berthed 'Port Out, Starboard Home' = P.O.S.H.

Once in India, it quickly became clear that white society reflected the four main divisions of the Hindu caste system. At the top of the social order was the civil service. Ever since the Uprising had been quelled and the new regime established, with India controlled from Whitehall, the civil service had proliferated on a fantastically elaborate scale. The 'politicals' who came out to administer it were called the 'heaven-born', its senior officers wielding enormous power, and often over gigantic territories. They were, of course, hand-picked from stiff competition; they had to be highly intelligent, resourceful and multiskilled to do their jobs, which combined judge, surveyor, clerk and governor. Being such an elite caste inevitably nominated them to be the Brahmins of European society. The army officers were the Kshatriyas, or warrior caste, and the planters and merchants were the Vaishyas or cultivators.

That leaves the Sudras, or servant class, for the British other ranks, who, though not strictly speaking servants, were mainly recruited from the working class. The only regular contact an ordinary soldier would have with the people of the subcontinent would be with the various wallahs who serviced the regiment – the bheestie who provided water; the nappy-wallah who, in some stations, came and shaved you in your bed before you were even awake enough to drink the tea brought by the char-wallah; the suppliers of provender to supplement army rations; the dhobhi who washed your kit and the chokra who pressed it. These were the people who meant India to the soldier boys. But my suspicion is that the BORs were not perceived as being even Sudras. Their proper station in the Raj was with the Untouchables – with the sweeper who emptied the latrines.

Lady Curzon (the wife, as it happened, of one of the most democratic of viceroys, around the turn of the twentieth century) thought that the two ugliest things in India were a water buffalo, and a British soldier dressed in his white uniform. And an editor of the *Statesman*, the important liberal paper in India, confirms that the soldier had no status whatsoever, so much so that if anyone was seen talking to a soldier they would be 'written down for speaking to a native'.

By now I had a much clearer picture of my great-grandfather's life. Confined to the lines for much of his time and forbidden social contact with other Europeans in India by a self-regulating system of class consciousness, a British soldier like Christopher Quick was 'less than the dust'. And, on top of that, what must it have been like for him to live as somebody else all those years? But then, perhaps, to live as Tom Jones was fun for him, a relief, or even the fulfilment of a fantasy. Perhaps he had an innate talent for impersonation, and it occurred to me that my acting skills may have been inherited from him, and I had already identified myself in his physical appearance. I had been much luckier in my younger years than him, however. While circumstances had caused him to flee, at nineteen, under an assumed name, to serve a long apprenticeship on the other side of the world, at the same age I was able to do just what I had always wanted, and act out a series of parts in plays.

5

How to Find a Wife

Necessity is the mother of invention, and the father of the
Anglo-Indian.

Anon

One of the most seductive things about acting is that you have
permission to fantasise. In fact, you have a positive mandate
to do just that in order to flesh out your character as fully as possible. As it happened, I became a professional actress while I was still
an undergraduate. The rehearsals and recording for my first job
fitted exactly into the Christmas vacation of my final year, so I was
able to squeeze it in, though I should have been starting my revision
for finals that summer. It was a BBC play by Hunter Davies and I
would be playing a student, so not too big a stretch.

When I graduated I started in rep, but when I found that there
was a state studentship available to me I decided to return to
Oxford to do a two-year research degree. It wasn't long before I was
again seduced by show business, and for the next eighteen months
I led a double life, continuing my postgraduate studies and being
president of the Oxford University Dramatic Society[1] while moon-

lighting in various television projects. My thesis was about reactions to the Industrial Revolution at the turn of the nineteenth century (they called themselves Neo-Paganists and much of it was about tearing up the railways and walking the ancient tracks of Britain, reviving the great god Pan and drinking real ale. It covered figures as diverse as W. E. Henley, Kipling (as writer of the whimsical *Puck of Pook's Hill*), Kenneth Grahame, Robert Louis Stevenson, D. H. Lawrence, Saki and E. M. Forster. Several parts later, I took the plunge of giving up my studies without quite finishing the thesis to come to London and commit to an acting career. I was twenty-one, and one of the first projects to come my way was a BBC adaptation of the Nikos Kazantzakis novel, *Christ Recrucified*. I was Lenio, the girlfriend of the boy chosen to be Christ in a passion play.

I had had no training as such for my new full-time career, but I took care to do a lot of voice work (which continued over the next five years) and many dance classes too, but no instruction in how to set about preparing for a part. Instead, I relied upon the text and the director.

I didn't think much about Lenio's Greekness, or the fact that she came from a peasant culture in the eastern Mediterranean, concentrating instead on her relationship with her boyfriend, which was threatened by her father's disapproval and the bigger events surrounding the staging of the Bible story. By now my dress in everyday life was late sixties hippy clothes: a mirrored and embroidered peasant blouse, a Rajasthani full skirt in vivid dark colours, a crocheted shawl I'd made myself. I felt the part of a gypsy even off camera, and as I spent a lot of time in the sun when I could I was very brown; people often asked if I was Greek/Italian/Spanish/Argentinian. After Rosa the Gypsy, it was the next phase of my fantasy of myself as being 'other' – and certainly not a grammar school kid from the suburbs from a respectable middle-class background. By now it was much cooler to be working class, and since I wasn't that I indulged my exotic side.

To my enormous excitement, shortly after appearing in *Christ Recrucified* I was cast in Edward Bond's reworking of *King Lear*. In Edward's version there are two Cordelias: one who is as bad as her sisters, and another Cordelia-like figure called Susan who nurtures and cares for Lear when all others have abandoned him. Susan wasn't a large part, but I adored everything about it and, more than anything, being part of the wave of new writing at the Royal Court Theatre, where I had been going to watch plays and workshops ever since I had seen the first British production of Beckett's *Endgame* as a twelve-year-old schoolgirl. I'd dreamed of one day getting to work there myself: I hadn't imagined it would fall into my lap so soon after coming to London.

I learnt a lot from being in *Lear*, above all how to focus and be still, using only the tiniest gestures to serve up the text in as clear a way as possible. I was still going to my voice lessons and dance classes, and I was lucky to have Bill Gaskill as my director. He had recently staged three Bond plays, *Narrow Road to the Deep North*, *Early Morning* and *Saved*. When first presented in November 1965, *Saved* had been refused a performance licence by the Lord Chamberlain unless substantial cuts were made, most significantly a scene in which some yobs stone a baby in its pram to death. The Royal Court then turned itself into a club theatre to put on the play, and was duly prosecuted and given a conditional discharge. The production of each of these plays was a challenge to the Lord Chamberlain's role as censor of theatre productions, and led directly to the abolition in 1968 of his office's power over plays. It had been an issue hotly debated by both sides, with many people still calling for the continuance of censorship. Looking back on those attitudes now makes me feel as if we were living in the Victorian age, and I do think that growing up in the fifties and early sixties was very much the last continuous development of those attitudes: prudery, stiff upper lips, observing the conventions of public as opposed to private

behaviour, knowing your place, trying to fit in and the impor-
tance of good manners. At the same time, of course, there was also
the emergence of the grammar-school generation and the rise of the
meritocracy, but many of the niceties of earlier, pre-war society were
still very much in evidence. The Bond plays at the Royal Court had
attracted much debate and Gaskill was by now a brilliant stager of
their spare, almost 'epic' style. He emphasised again and again that
an actor's job was to deliver the text, not to approximate it or
improve it but to bring it to life with all the accuracy and economy
one could muster. His most frequent note to me was 'Do it again; do
less, and do it better'. It is still a practice I try to follow.

In *Lear* I played the good girl, Susan, and when I returned to the
Royal Court a year or so later it was to play the sad girl, Rose Jones,
in Edward's *The Sea*; sad because the boy she was starting to love has
been drowned in the sea. In between these two Bond plays, I had
appeared in Howard Brenton's adaptation of Jean Genet's *The
Screens* at the Bristol Old Vic.

I was the Mother, a free-spirited outsider who lives with her son
on a rubbish heap. I made my own costume from a thousand different scraps of colourful material, just as Genet suggested the actress
should do in the notes he had supplied with the text: it took the
company weeks just to read his production notes. I thoroughly
enjoyed myself playing the Mother. It was the first major British
staging, perhaps because no one before Howard, and the director
Walter Donahue, believed it could be done. It was certainly a challenge, and when Bill Gaskill came down to see it, having already
offered me the part in *The Sea*, he said it was just as well he'd cast
me before he came to see *The Screens* as I was really bad in the part.

I made several forays into West End musicals but after a while I felt
that I wanted to work in a more alternative way, and so managed to
persuade an agit-prop company called Red Ladder to take me on
as a probationary member. They were far away from my previous

professional life, with its historic West End theatres like the Piccadilly
and Drury Lane, for Red Ladder played in non-theatrical spaces such
as trade union meetings and miners' galas, local community centres
and other venues that had never before seen anything like the pieces
presented by these twelve young socialists who were touring the country, and who chaired a discussion after the performance, which actively
encouraged the audience to question the political views of the play
they had just been watching. I was a feminist now, for the women's
movement had reached Britain around the time I had left university,
and at Red Ladder I was mainly involved in the writing, staging and
discussing of one particular new play, *A Woman's Work Is Never Done*.

I was very idealistic about this work, partly in reaction to my disappointment that the West End hadn't been more stimulating and
partly because I was only now, in my mid-twenties, discovering that
politics, especially personal politics, was about the world I lived in.
I'd only just realised that the world did in fact extend beyond my
personal ambitions and the circle of my relationships, but I soon
became a very vocal contributor to the after-show debates.
Eventually, though, I discovered that despite the idealistic hopes for
the transformation of society which had brought the group into
being and fuelled all its activities, the company was an average
mess. Person A was in love with person B who happened to be
married to person C, who in turn was in love with someone outside
the group: as socialists, they didn't believe in monogamy. In fact,
while we were on tour in Manchester I was loudly derided at a
women's liberation conference because, in the middle of a very well
attended session on sex, I seemed to be the only person who was
prepared to say that I thought a monogamous relationship could be
the ideal. When challenged by just about every other person in
the room, I defended myself by saying that I only had so much
energy and didn't want to expend it in managing simultaneous relationships; I'd rather use that energy for other things. People jeered

all round me. Meanwhile back at Red Ladder, the actress who was playing the put-upon title role in *A Woman's Work Is Never Done* seemed to be having a nervous breakdown.

It was clear even while we had been rehearsing that she wasn't happy, but she had managed to hang on until we were out on the road before collapsing at the end of the first show. I think it was in Bridlington Community Centre. In any case, she was a nervous wreck so the next day it was proposed that we cancel our individual tasks for the day (we shared the essential chores on a weekly rota; it covered everything from direction and administration to writing, chairing the nightly discussion after the show and driving the van) in order to manage the situation.

The group had a mechanism for dealing with unexpected crises that was known as a group dynamic. Like all major decisions, the motion to stop and hold one had to be proposed, then seconded, then voted on and carried by a majority. (The director of a piece had to direct in the same way, proposing a bit of direction and waiting for it to be seconded and then carried before it could be put into effect. It did make rehearsing a very slow process.) We were unanimous that we must suspend the major activity of the day, which was researching the lives of members of the National Union of Public Employees for a major rewrite of our play before taking it to their conference in Newcastle later on in the tour, and instead concentrate on discussing whatever was upsetting our leading actress so much that she was a shaking bundle of nerves by the end of the performance. We talked all day, and it was exhausting to be so seriously concentrated for hours on end and to talk through the group's political practice, yet to be no further forward by the time we had to go off to do the next show. She did say she felt better for the group dynamic, though, and so it was a shock as well as a disappointment to find her in a state of spasm behind one of the stage flats at the end of that night's performance.

The next day we had another group dynamic, which again took up the whole day; again she seemed better, and then the same thing happened. For a third day we held a group dynamic, and as the morning wore into another afternoon with no progress whatsoever I, the probationary member still, with no voting rights among the six men and five other women who made up the group, finally dared to express an opinion. I pointed out that while we were spending an inordinate amount of time on the practice of the group no one had mentioned the fact, so openly discussed in the kitchen or the dressing rooms outside the formal structure of our group dynamic, that the female lead was in love with someone who was in turn in love with someone else, who was raising a child with yet another person. As soon as I said it all hell broke loose. I had mentioned the unmentionable: ten of the twelve members of Red Ladder believed that to be a good socialist you must have socialistic sexual relations. Monogamy, or even the desire for it, was an absolute taboo. People started popping all over the place, in some cases coming out with resentments that had been festering for months, and as I went off to the kitchen to make tea for everyone I reflected that I might be the probationer but I had absolutely no intention of following their lead in relationships.

But at least I had a choice: it was up to me whether I got involved with a man, or even several men at once. A hundred years earlier, of course, I would not have expected that sort of freedom as a woman, but I was surprised to find out how very limited the choices had been for a man like my great-grandfather in the British India of the 1870s. However well he carried out his impersonation of Tom Jones, his acting skills were not able to help him much when it came to finding any sort of woman as a partner. It was always going to be a challenge. For a start, he was always on the move – in his first years he changed from the Southern Division to the Eastern, and by the late 1880s his regiment seems to have made the Punjab their area of operation. Lahore was one of the better cantonments, in that it was one of the few where the town and the bazaars were not off limits, but for much of his career the closest he might come to seeing any other people would be on a route march.

The British army in India was often used for internal security rather than aggressive action, and though the railways were expanding rapidly many areas of the intractable country could only be reached on foot. The distances covered might be huge – five hundred miles at a rate of fifteen to twenty miles a day. In an emergency, troops might cover a lot more than that, setting out early, resting for a few hours in the heat of the day and then carrying on through the night.[2] Drinking water on the march was taboo, and some developed a trick of sucking a pebble to keep the mouth moist. Troops would halt twenty minutes after setting out and would then keep going for fifty, before a ten-minute break.

For the artillery there was the additional complication of moving the guns. One gun involved twelve gunners, fifty drivers, and fifty mules – and this was after the improvements introduced by General Roberts, who had been shocked by the inefficiency with which troops had been moving, especially in the hostile western terrain. In autumn 1880 he travelled back along the 250-mile route from Kandahar to Quetta and on to Sibi, and said he could have picked out the road by the line of dead animals and broken carts left behind by the columns as they marched into Afghanistan. He replaced camels and elephants with the more versatile mule and held a competition to design a sturdier cart.

A report on the aftermath of the 1878 Afghan war had pointed out that a single train working a sixteen-hour day would have been able to transport as much as 2500 camels could in a fortnight. It seems incredible now, to think of the enormous complications of moving an army unit, but many old India hands confirm that the route march was something to look forward to: 'After the first day or two the blisters wore off and it was sheer enjoyment, and, of course, we saw much more of the country moving at a walking pace.'[3]

The army was aware that being out in the countryside held a threat for the ranks; when it came time to pitch camp for the night the NCOs would be on the lookout for the 'tree rats' or 'grass bhidis' who might be waiting to seduce the men in their charge. These were women from the villages, many of whom carried venereal disease. It was a serious problem for the army, although of course not confined to India; some men brought it with them from other postings. The figures for the middle part of the nineteenth century show that at any one time up to a third of the British army in India were infected. A friend's grandfather remembered that as a junior officer newly arrived in India,

> Amongst other useful knowledge [that I acquired from the Sergeant-Major] was that a campsite should not be chosen near long grass or other cover. This was not because there was any danger of attack, but in case some enterprising villager might conceal women who would lure the troops to almost inevitable venereal disease . . . one couldn't help feeling sympathy for the soldiers in the sexual desert which our prudery condemned them to live in.[4]

In earlier times the authorities had tried to establish some measure of control over the prostitutes by allowing regimental brothels and from 1800 'lock hospitals', where the women were regularly checked and treated for infection, were set up in each of the three Presidencies of India. But as the censoriousness of the Victorian era replaced the more libidinous mood of the previous century the brothels were closed down. In fact, the movement to shut them was led by the wife of General Roberts. No doubt the men found ways of getting back to the women of the bazaars, and there was an immediate rise in the rate of infection. Soon after General Roberts retired and he and his wife left India, some of the army brothels were quietly re-opened.

There was a more legitimate way to meet women, if you happened to be posted near a railway junction, for every medium-sized town would have a railway institute that was the social centre for railway employees. The trains were largely managed by the Anglo-Indian community, who welcomed the soldiers to join them at the institute.

The Anglo-Indian monopoly on the railways had come as a direct consequence of the 1856–7 Uprising. The unquestioning faith in the native population's loyalty that had characterised the British Raj had changed at a stroke to a deeply uneasy, untrusting atmosphere. In all three Presidencies there was a realisation that the numerically tiny British presence had survived the Uprising more by luck than by good management, and that part of that luck was the fact that throughout the troubles the mixed-race Anglo-Indians had, to a man and woman, remained steadfast in their loyalty to a homeland most of them had never seen. The fear was that there might soon be another and more catastrophic mutiny against the British. It was thus imperative that the lines of communication be kept open in the face of trouble and so as the railways and the telegraph system developed across the country both were put in the hands of this loyal group, the Anglo-Indians, who found for themselves a niche that was to define their lives right down to Independence. To an extent, the role of the Anglo-Indians was to define the social lives of the Tommies too. At the frequent socials given by the railway institutes the girls in particular were delighted to welcome British soldiers. Coming from a society that aspired to be as English as the English, if you could persuade a soldier to marry you it would mean that you moved up the social ladder. Private Stephen Bentley, serving in India some time later than Tom Jones, thought they were 'very very very attractive girls indeed' and said that

. . . they did everything they could, knowing the situation with the soldiers and their complete segregation from any sort of women, every womanly wile to make sure they married a European soldier and quite a lot of them did . . . You always saw them when they were made up at a dance . . . they were all wonderful dancers, because it was the only thing they had to do in India, was go to these dances and all their time was spent on making sure that at any hour of the day or night they were on parade. It was all their face painted and made up.[5]

When all who could went off to the hills to escape the hot weather, the Anglo-Indian girls became the target of the officer class too, though they always understood that there was little chance of being more than a hot weather plaything for an officer. Major E. S. Humphries particularly remembered that 'the aroma from their bodies was tinged with the wonderful scent of jasmine which made them probably far more attractive than they really were'.[6]

Others were more blunt: they called the Anglo-Indians B-class girls, even though they thought they were 'dears in every way and the greatest fun',[7] or they detected an aroma behind the jasmine: 'Whenever you were dancing with an Anglo-Indian girl the first thing she did was to assail you with a great puff of garlic and cheap perfume, but you stuck to her, because she was beautiful and in any case probably the only girl available.'[8]

There was a saying current in British India that went 'necessity is the mother of invention and the father of the Anglo-Indian'. Tom Jones was one of those for whom it was necessary to be inventive, and the more I found out about the world he was living in, the more convinced I became that he must have married someone of mixed origins. If that turned out to be true, it could begin to explain my grandfather's preoccupation with 'pureblooded Englishmen'. How did the Anglo-Indians come to be viewed so ambiguously, I wondered, when they were so necessary to the everyday functioning of the empire, so loyal to Britain, the girls so pretty and such 'dears', but ultimately not to be trusted or accepted into wider society in British India, except at the bottom of the hierarchy?

It was quite a minefield, uncovering the true social history of the British Raj. The Brits were supposed to be the enlightened ones, bringing the benefits of a superior civilisation to the caste-ridden natives, but during the period that I am interested in – the mid-nineteenth to mid-twentieth century, when three generations of my Quick forebears were making their way in India – prejudice against the 'blacks' and against the 'blackie-whites' got very much worse. It was the era of the Queen Empress, and British control of India brought a huge expansion of wealth and prestige; it also brought out increasing numbers of white women. Much of the blame for this prejudice lies with them. The trust that had existed before, that the weaker members of the conquering race would be respected simply because they were weaker, was destroyed for ever by memories of the massacres of women and children during the Uprising at places such as Cawnpore or Jhansi. It followed, then, that if there was a deep distrust of the native people there was a corresponding distrust of those who were thought to share any portion of their blood.

Women were coming out to India in greater numbers in the second half of the nineteenth century partly because, as Benedick says in *Much Ado About Nothing*, 'the world must be peopled', and as the colony expanded the old solutions no longer answered the needs of the menfolk. Earlier generations had gone in for interracial marriage, or had happily acknowledged their mistresses and their offspring – some maintained whole harems of them. Or you would pay a visit to the 'gay girls' of the major towns, or to the army brothels where they existed or would socialise with the Anglo-Indian girls when there was no one more 'suitable' available.

Up until the early 1800s the East India Company had resisted the presence of Christian missions in their territories, fearing – quite rightly, in my view – that to introduce a new religion into a land that had found an accommodation between its Muslim rulers and the mass of Hindus would destabilise the situation. The Company had managed to be pretty even handed in its treatment of the local religious practices – they left the people alone to follow their own religious observances – but now the force of evangelicalism back in Britain was to sweep that away. William Wilberforce championed a bill that allowed missionaries to enter the Eastern territories as long as they were licensed by the East India Company, though in practice anyone not connected to the Company's service was deemed 'objectionable' by the local government, and so many of the new pious breed of women whose mission was to 'enlighten' the native population continued on to Rangoon, where they were not so unwelcome.

By 1833 the need for a licence was done away with and missionaries came in increasing numbers, many of them women, bringing the high moral seriousness of the Victorian age to a society that in many ways still enjoyed the casual lustiness of an earlier era. Marriage was a holy sacrament to be witnessed by the one true (Christian) God, and as white society became more and more publicly Christian, with the apparatus of churches and schools and orphanages that developed, it was inevitable that the European women became intolerant of mistresses and harems. Such illicit liaisons were of course a sexual threat and a cause of jealousy, and putting some distance between the free and easy relations that had developed was an urgent need; the British Christian women had to insist that they were somehow superior in a society that left them socially marooned, with husbands away at work and their opposite numbers in the native community – respectable wives and mothers – unavailable because purdah kept all decent native women at home once they were married.

The most challenging task for these women was to manage their servants, for though hordes of cheap labour were available much time was spent in making sure the chores actually did get done. Children were raised from birth by a wet nurse and an ayah and sent home from the age of five or six; for their mothers this meant a further narrowing of their field of activity, and they rarely had the support of an extended family nearby to sustain them. In July 1845 the *Calcutta Review* published a survey entitled 'English Women in Hindustan', which observed how limited the range of female 'types' was, especially because disease picked off so many of the young and the old:

> The milliner's apprentice, deprived of her natural rest, that ladies may have their dresses to wear at some particular gala – the shivering mother who, by plying her needle all day long, barely earns six-pence for her hungry children – all the single women, living on a scanty annuity and endeavouring to relieve the solitude of her lodgings by the society of a cat, a canary bird, and a box of mignionette – the governess, to whom the bread earned by honourable labour is rendered more bitter than if it were that of abject indolence – all these classes are as rare as the wealthy dowager with her jointure and establishment; the rich and independent spinster, with tastes more akin to those of a country gentleman; and the dear old grandmother or great grandmother, who occupies her own snug arm-chair, by so many a fireside at home.[9]

No children, no grandparents. Cut off from their counterparts in the native community. No career, no skills and a climate that kept you indoors for the greater part of the day, often with servants who had to be chased to do their work properly. Husbands up to their eyes in pressing work or indulging in mannish pursuits such as hunting. The devil, as they say, makes work for idle hands and for many women of the Raj that was often the manufacture of racism, snobbism and class prejudice.

Such women were not, however, available to the likes of Christopher Quick, a mere ranking soldier. Far down the pecking order, he was unlikely to find a white bride – there were simply too few of them to go round. So when he had served enough time in the service as a mere 'other rank' to be eligible for marriage it was almost inevitable that he would look for a wife among the mixed-race community who were marginalised by those a little higher up the social order.

A Continent for Men?

It was becoming clear to me that the woman who rescued Tom Jones from his single state – and, incidentally, from his false identity – came from a family who had been in India for some generations already, and had emerged from quite a complicated historical background. She was born five years before the Mutiny, far from British India in the central state of Gwalior. There were many mysteries surrounding her life, and in order to understand what it meant to be a woman in that place at that time, I started to look into the history of the Company wives from the beginning.

It was not something we discussed when my father's childhood came up; in suburban Kent in the fifties, there was little interest in the social history of women anywhere, let alone in India.

In history lessons at school the idea of sexual politics, or even feminism, simply hadn't been born. The same with racism. We lived in the safe and conservative embrace of the *Daily Express* for print and the Home Service for broadcast news. Few of the women I came across had careers, and those who had served in the war as land girls or ambulance drivers did so out of necessity, in the absence of men who were away at the Front. I had been conceived on my father's first home leave at the end of the war, and so my childhood coincided with the return of women to their traditional role as homemakers.

I decided to find out just where the wives of colonial India had been coming from. When Western trade with India started in the early seventeenth century, there were of course no white women in the subcontinent. The agenda was conquest or trade, a rough, tough, speculative adventure. The Portuguese had been settling the west coast for a good few years before British merchant adventurers arrived and they intermarried with the local women, as they had already been doing in North Africa. These Portuguese communities along the Malabar Coast also received an annual cargo of 'poor, but well-descended' orphan girls who came out 'at the King's charge with a dowry . . . in order to further the peopling of the Portugal colonies in those parts.'[1] When the English came they settled where the Portugese had not – at Patna and Benares, for instance – and used the Armenians who were already trading there, and who spoke Persian, the court language under the Moghul emperors, as negotiators to secure trade for themselves. With this greater access to the Moghul court the English thrived and, in due course, they invited the Portugese-Indian mercenaries to work within the East India Company 'factories', the fortified stores that were used for trading.

Madras was the largest of these trading posts and soon included many of the Portugese settlers of St Thomas. These folk wore topis, the white-covered cork hats later adopted by all colonials to protect their heads from the fierce heat, and because of their headgear became known as 'topasses', a name that was to stick all through the centuries as a pejorative term for the dark-skinned descendants of these early experiments in mixed marriage. Others called them 'black mongrel Portugese'[2] or 'Firingees'.

Britishers married these Firingees, sometimes converting to Roman Catholicism, to please their part-Portuguese wives, who had been raised in that religious tradition. When the supply of suitable wives was used up, the Company directed that marriage with Hindus was now to be actively pursued in Madras. It was important that families remain loyal to the Company, though, and a handsome payment was offered to any mother swearing to raise her child a Christian – and that of course meant an Anglican. The financial incentive persuaded some Hindu women to choose a white man and ignore the powerful interdictions against marrying out of one's caste, let alone out of one's faith, but most Hindu women who stood to gain in status by becoming Christian were very low caste.[3] The exception to this was a widow, for traditionally she would perform suttee on the death of her husband, or else live in retirement, relying on the goodwill of her sons or living at the temple if childless. Job Charnock, then a junior member of the East India Company Council, who later became Governor of the Bay of Bengal and the founder of Calcutta, went out of curiosity to watch the ritual immolation of a widow at her husband's funeral. Struck by her charms, he snatched her from the pyre and later they raised four children together. After her death, he marked the anniversary each year with the sacrifice of a cockerel at her tomb.

From the earliest days of the Company there were always a number of Muslim widows and camp followers left on the battle-fields as well. Such women were, in the main, not so far removed from western culture as their Hindu contemporaries. They were exotic, but not alien. And one way for the company to reinforce trading arrangements in peacetime was to confirm the deal with another sort of contract: a marriage brokered between a company functionary and the daughter of a Muslim dignitary. For instance, Sir Charles Metcalfe, the resident at the Nizam's court in Hyderabad used his influence over a young military attaché in this way in the early 1820s, with the negotiation of his marriage to the

Princess Nasrat. In such marriages, the wife's religion would in most cases be her own affair.[4]

All through the seventeenth century and into the early eighteenth, when settlements were confined to the Presidency capitals on the coast, Bombay, Madras and Calcutta, and life in the mofusil* was still terribly isolated, there was an utter lack of self-consciousness on the British side about inter-breeding with the native peoples, whether sanctioned by marriage or not. An honourable tradition began to develop, passed on from generation to generation, whereby offspring felt doubly bound to the country in which they served – by both their native-born mother's and their colonist father's claim. The Anglo-Indians regarded themselves as British, aligned with the ruling elite, and never doubted their superiority.

In fact, by the 1790s there were more people of mixed descent than there were whites in India, but the tide was beginning to turn against them as more and more people from 'Home' – from Britain – wanted to take advantage of the rich pickings that came with an indentured post in the India service. Over the next decade the mixed race was to be effectively disowned by the very people with whom they had identified themselves and whose culture and values they aspired to: the white elite who ruled British India.

As the Anglo-Indian community had increased over the half-century before this, so had the presence of European women. They were finding their way there in small numbers by the mid 1750s, but there are many instances of women who turned up without a contact in the country being turned around at the port of entry – either Bombay or Calcutta – and sent home on the next boat. When 'there came eleven in one vessel' to Madras it was, thought the correspondent, 'too great a number for the peace and good order of a round house'. Few of the women had skills that could keep them in

---

* The parts of the country outside the Presidency capitals or, more generally, rural areas

the job market; if they failed to marry they might well drift into prostitution.

By the 1770s, though, the trickle of bona fide spinsters threatened to become a flood. They timed their long passage out so as to arrive at the end of the monsoon, and from October to March a social season began to develop around the presence of so many unmarried women in Calcutta. As the wretched heat that preceded the monsoon, and the damp of the monsoon itself, retreated and the cold weather began to make its welcome presence felt boat after boat would arrive from Britain carrying whole cargoes of marriageable women, from girls just out of the schoolroom to hopeful spinsters in their fifties for whom a husband in the colonies was perhaps a last, desperate hope. These shiploads became known as the 'fishing fleet'.[5]

All came looking for an advantageous match. It was possible in that age of nabobs* for a man to amass a huge fortune in speculative trade, and if it might well have taken fifteen or twenty years of unremitting work to acquired a fortune, what better to spend it on than a wife and family?[6] If not a nabob, there were increasing numbers of civil servants with handsome salaries and a pension for his widow if he succumbed to one of the many hazards of life in India. The army came lower in the social hierarchy than the civil service, but some of the fishing fleet were only too happy to ensnare an officer. He was likely to be in a position to marry at an earlier age than a civilian, while still relatively young and sound, and not so spoiled by pampering in India as to treat his wife like a servant. But there were drawbacks too: officers were poorer and likely to travel a lot and face the prospect of imminent death in a military engagement.

---

* 'Nabob' (from Urdu nawab, Arabic na'ib) = deputy. Originally used to mean a governor in Moghul India, the term was adopted in the eighteenth century to describe the many men who acquired substantial fortunes in India

If you married an officer you married his regiment; you would be vetted by his colonel to see if you fitted in to the family, the bhai-bund* of the regiment. For all, civil or military, the wooing season would kick off with a ball hosted by the ship's captain for his cargo of eligible women, which was advertised with posters around town before the boat docked.

There was, at best, five months in which to find a partner, and for those men who had had to get leave to travel hundreds of miles from their postings, find a wife, get married and return to work, it was a much shorter period, perhaps just five to ten days. A frenzied marriage market ensued, conducted at balls and soirées and picnics and riding expeditions. It was a hysterical time, in the true sense of the word. If a woman didn't get fixed up quickly there was one last chance at the end of the season, when all the remaining wallflow-ers pooled their resources and gave an entertainment as a last resort. After that, if you still weren't suited, you were shipped back to England, branded for ever a 'returned empty' or a 'jilt', and what an abject sense of failure that must have brought with it.

Travelling for half a year, braving the serious risk of disease or death in an alien climate and the condescension of the crew – 'it was no slight penance to be exposed during the whole voyage to the ½ sneering, satirical looks of the mates and the guinea pigs'† – to now find yourself rejected by these lonely colonials. One such unfortunate creature, travelling back in 1859 on the P&O mail steamer *Bombay* among the 'crowds of sick subalterns' and 'numer-ous ladies, sick themselves and bringing home children still more ill' was 'a young lady of most objectionable manners, and unwholesome complexion, [who] having failed in *la chasse aux maris* in India, made desperate efforts to ensnare each guileless subaltern whom she

* Brotherhood
† Guinea pigs = midshipmen

could get to listen to her never-ceasing clatter and discordant laugh, which might be heard at all hours of the day or night, all over the ship.'[7] What lay ahead for 'empties' like her on their return to Britain? A governess post? Tolerated and pitied as a poor relation? The workhouse or the streets?

It is hard to know, at this distance, how many of these hastily contracted marriages were happy; this correspondent discouraged her friend from 'the folly and impropriety' of coming out as a 'fisher' on the next fleet: 'I am married . . . but I have lost what I left behind me in my native country – happiness. Yet my husband is . . . richer than I could desire; but his health is ruined, as well as his temper, and he has taken me rather as a convenience than as a companion; and he plays the tyrant over me as if I was one of the slaves that carry his palanquin.' She thought that 'for every happy marriage, thousands more are married with no hope of comfort, and with a prospect merely of splendid misery.'[8]

But by the 1870s, when Christopher Quick was no doubt marooned in his cantonment, there was more chance of such marriages turning out well, if only because by now most of the fishing fleet had some connection with the subcontinent – a father who had sent his daughter home to be educated or a brother with a commission in the army – and so must have had a clearer idea of what life in the colony involved.

For the other ranks, however, the possibilities were very limited. The army deliberately made it hard for a trooper to marry, because wives and families made the whole business of moving soldiers around so much more complicated. Most warrant officers could marry, about 25 per cent of sergeants and corporals, and only 10 per cent of privates – and that after long and proven service. You had to be 'on the strength of the regiment', which meant at least seven years' service.

It is ironic that the British other ranks should have been so isolated, cut off not only from the life of the country in which they served but from their fellow expatriates as well, even though there were a lot more civilian Britishers about. In the north-east of the country the number of planters increased rapidly: indigo was the first large-scale export crop, soon followed by tea brought to Darjeeling by a doctor returning from China in 1841, and then jute in 1855; cotton, silk and rice production all expanded massively in the course of the century. So did the programme of road-building and canal-digging, and the laying of railways. All of these enterprises required skilled supervision over many years, and this vastly increased European workforce attracted women to the subcontinent in ever larger numbers.

There was also the Evangelical Movement, which brought a different kind of woman out.

One way or another, there were more and more women, most of them looking for a good catch; but few of these arrivals, if any, would consider marriage with a mere ranking soldier. So where was a wife for the likes of my great-grandfather to be found?

The main possibilities were either the Anglo-Indian community or other army families. For both groups, marrying off a daughter meant a welcome increase in income. One writer observed 'the anxiety of parents' when a European regiment was taking the field, that 'their daughters should be married before the corps marched', even if the daughter was a 'mere child' and her husband would have to leave her behind the next week 'because she can then draw wife's pay while he's away: and if anything should happen to him, she will get her six months' widow's pension'.[9]

But once her pension had run out there was no question of the army going to the expense of shipping her, and her children, back to Britain, so she was best to remarry as quickly as possible, since there was really only one other prospect if she didn't find a new husband:

. . . they know . . . one of two alternatives awaits them – either to be left utterly without means . . . or . . . marry. Under such circumstances, love or regard for the object of their choice is considered . . . by no means necessary; in fact there is good reason to believe that when soldiers are affected with illness, which appears likely to harm fatally, the affectionate wives are even then taking steps to render their . . . widowhood as short as circumstances permit.[10]

The regiment would often act as Cupid, arranging introductions for the newly bereaved. With the heavy losses through illness that all European families experienced in the hostile climate, this pattern of marrying several times over was not at all unusual for both men and women, and they would bring the children from previous arrangements with them. Thus a state of affairs that we think of as peculiar to our times – extended families of half-siblings and step-parents – was the prevailing state of affairs in India more than a hundred years ago.

One woman, asked about her career as army wife, replied: 'At that time I was in the Light Company, the next husband I got was a Canteen Sergeant and the man I have now is only a Lance Corporal.' She clearly lost status as she became less marriageable. Tom Jones finally found a bride who was an army widow. Margaret Kerr's first husband had been a Sergeant-Overseer, so in marrying a Bombardier she was more or less maintaining her previous status.

By now, Tom had reclaimed his true identity as Christopher Quick, and acquired a family of five step-children long before he had his own two sons. My grandfather Bertie was the younger of the two sons, and his eldest step-sister, Mig, was married with children by the time he was born.

The picture becomes clearer. Family life for my great-grandparents wasn't going to be a rosy vision of high Victorian rectitude.

Drunkenness and venereal disease were routine; so was death in childbirth or infancy.[11] Cholera could wipe you out just hours after a slight feeling of queasiness, and malaria and other fevers were hardly worthy of comment as they were such a fact of life. One man sat through dinner quaking with an ague, as it was often called, and shrugged it off, saying he'd be better in the morning, but not everyone survived the night.

Fevers of all sorts were just one of many hazards that might bring a life in India to a premature end. Bereavement was a constant companion, and new family connections almost to be expected. If the army wives were hardboiled about lining up their next husbands, did their children take on bereavement and new parents in the same matter-of-fact way?

If a new step family wasn't to be your lot, then separation was almost sure to be. The children of those who could afford to send their offspring to school in England might be estranged from the rest of their families for up to twelve years. A child's early years were spent with the ayahs, and there are many accounts of the disastrous effects on children who were left too long in native hands, such as the case of Mary in *The Secret Garden*, with her imperious, sour manner, or these on the same England-bound boat as the unhappy 'returned empty':

> The children were what only children brought up by native servants can be – rude, dirty, and disagreeable to the last degree, and most of them (and indeed the great majority of passengers of all ages) suffering from boils and prickly heat, which gave the company the general appearance of being convalescents from the small-pox hospital.[12]

Children returning, like Mary, to England would usually be officer class, however ill-bred their manners, but children of the other ranks used to be left in the lines, growing up around the barrack rooms with precious little education and no concessions to the fact that they were children. Christopher's children were fortunate to be born when they were, for by the 1880s children like them had the chance to be sent off to the new schools for army children in the hills for the best part of the year, away from the heat, and from the unregulated drinking of life in the lines. But still this meant separation from the family for much of their childhood.

For the wives there was a sense of hierarchy and an urgent need to be accepted, and to rise in status if it could be contrived. Wherever you were on the social scale, though, you felt superior to the native peoples around you, as well as holding a memory inherited from your elders that the native was not to be trusted, however intimately they were involved in the day to day management of your life. I have looked at how the white women were regarded in the earlier days of the British Presence in India, and by inference, how the natives were regarded as – well, as natives, with all the sense of otherness and inferiority and exploitability that colonialism brings wherever it gains a foothold. But it wasn't until I came across my great-grandmother Margaret's name in the records that I started to be aware of another feature of British East Indian settlement, and that was the zenanas – or harems – where so many of the mixed-race community were born. Margaret Kerr had been born a Johnstone. In Calcutta there were quite a few Johnstone brothers, and they each had a zenana full of their offspring.

7

Margaret's Mutiny

By 1755 four Johnstone brothers were serving on the Bengal council in Calcutta. John Johnstone was a thorn in the flesh of Robert Clive – Clive of India – and it was said that all four brothers were instrumental in driving Clive to suicide by hounding him in Parliament for treason.[1] The Johnstone brothers, like Clive and many others, made a lot of money in India, some of it through pretty dubious transactions. It was common for employees of the Honourable John Company – as the East India Company styled itself – to make liaisons with local women, establishing houses with a zenana or bibi* compound for their women and (illegitimate) children on the Indian model, and the Johnstones all did this. But when the last of the brothers finally left India in the 1790s the children were left behind in Bengal to make a new kind of life for themselves. Had they been born in the previous century, the Johnstone sons might have expected to live in reasonable comfort, being the children of successful Company members. They would have been educated in order to take their places as army officers or

---

* Bibi = Hindustani name for a woman, usually applied to women of a lower social rank, and native mistresses

writers (executives) in the John Company, even travelling to Britain to attend school or to graduate through the Royal Military Academy at Woolwich. Their sisters, often beauties, would have married well in the European community. But attitudes to mixed-race offspring, who now vastly outnumbered the Europeans in India, were changing.

A look at the names being used for the mixed-race children of India is significant; to the old terms topass and Firingee new ones were added. The politer of these names were 'Indo-Briton', 'East Indian' and 'Eurasian', but not until 1911 did the Viceroy, Lord Hardinge, officially sanction the term 'Anglo-Indian' for those of mixed race.* Up to that time, an Anglo-Indian simply meant anyone who had been born in India of British stock, whether white or of mixed race. Meanwhile there were plenty of slang words: 'blackie-white', 'black and tans', 'calla-firingees', 'twelve annas in the rupee' (a rupee was generally sixteen annas), 'kutcha butcha' or half-baked bread and, depending on the shade of your skin, 'teen pao' – three-quarters of a pound – for those who were dark or 'adha seer', meaning half a pound, if you were nearly white. Also 'chica-boo' and 'chi-chi'. These names started to appear in the second half of the eighteenth century, and chi-chi especially was to stick, down to Partition in the forties. An 1874 guide to British India for the newcomer explained the name's derivation:

The general ill effects of an Indian bringing-up on children of pure English blood, are very forcibly implied in the term 'chee-chee', which is commonly applied to them in Bengal. Without lending any approval to its use, I may explain that 'chee-chee' is an ejaculation of disgust, used by the natives of India upon all

---

* In the context of this book, Anglo-India is used to denote a person of mixed race

occasions; and the origin of the application of the term to
Europeans born and brought up in India, is probably their constant habit of using it themselves in the same manner.[1]

There, again, is the phrase that my grandfather had used: 'pure
English blood'. That it was used so unselfconsciously is a sign of
how deep the obsession with race had been planted. Many years
later, a soldier interviewed about his time in India gave some very
unguarded replies, not least on the subject of relations with the local
people. He felt there were unwritten rules about how Europeans
treated them. The first was that you must 'never exhibit any liking
for Indians; the second was that you should always treat Indians as
subnormal children'. He commented that 'of all the unrealistic attitudes that I ever met in India, this was the most unrealistic'.[2]

Why were attitudes changing so noticeably? I wanted to try to
understand why, from the 1790s onwards, those who had once
shared in the bounty of the expanding colony found themselves
excluded. One reason was that more British, aware of the profits to
be made from a career in the East Indies, were willing to travel out
and many of them were Evangelicals with an immovable belief that
the 'heathen' natives – or half-natives like the Johnstone children –
were cast out from the light, so they had little compunction in oust-
ing them from jobs they wanted for themselves.

On the other side of the colonial world, an uprising in Haiti in
1791 set off alarm bells for the Company's Council in London and
led to a review of their attitudes to their own colonial population in
India. A wave of independence struggles across the world – in particular the American War of Independence and the French
Revolution – had inspired the slaves of Haiti (which was already
being administered as a *departement* of France, so that, in theory if
not practise, the same laws applied as in France) to seek a similar
freedom. As citizens of the New Republic they too felt entitled to

liberty, equality and fraternity, and appealed to the *gens de couleur* to make an alliance with them against the French masters. Like their counterparts in British India, the mixed-race population of Haiti had been educated to European standards and had been given real power back in the land of their mothers. As fortunes fluctuated during the struggle this mulatto population, here born of French masters and Haitian slaves, found themselves caught between the rival claims of black and white.

Disastrously, they changed their allegiance from one side to the other and back again, embracing their black roots when it was advantageous to do so, then quickly declaring they were French when it seemed the European force would win. As a result the conflict in Haiti was chaotic and bloody, and lasted some thirteen years. In the end the slaves were victorious – and France lost its colony.

Back in London, this turn of events confirmed what the Company Council already feared, namely that the mixed-race would rise against British colonial power, and they were swift to institute a number of edicts to limit their autonomy. At the Upper Orphanage in Calcutta, which had been set up to educate the issue of officers and their Indian partners, the children were banned from travelling to Britain to further their education. In 1791 people of mixed blood were excluded from holding officer rank in the civil, military or marine services of the Company, and since a Company law already forbade anyone of British or Anglo-Indian descent from living more than ten miles away from a Company settlement it was impractical to consider a career in commerce or farming and so they were left almost destitute.

The Council now sent Viscount Valentia out to India to report on the situation in the country. He made it clear that the potential threat came not from the Hindu or Muslim peoples of the subcontinent, but from the mixed-race offspring who had once been acknowledged as members of the British family. He believed that the 'increase of half-caste children' was the most rapidly accumulating evil of Bengal, and set out to disempower the very offspring who had once been cherished. He said, 'In every country where this interme- diate caste has been permitted to rise, it has ultimately tended to its ruin. Spanish America and St. Domingo are examples of this fact. Their increase in India is beyond calculation . . . what may not in time be dreaded from them? I have no hesitation in saying that the evil ought to be stopt . . .'[3] He wanted to send all people of mixed parentage to Europe and ban them from ever returning. But others felt that their very presence would contaminate the Europeans 'because the imperfections of the children, whether bodily or mental, would in the process of time be communicated by inter- marriage to the generality of the people in Great Britain, and by this means debase the succeeding generations of Englishmen'.[4]

No one who did not have two parents born in Britain could wield power in the Company any longer. Jacob Johnstone – son of one of the Johnstone brothers – was the grandfather of Margaret, the future wife of Christopher Quick. The only way he and his kind could serve in the military was as fifers, drummers, bandsmen or farriers. Perhaps the thinking behind this was that if you were playing an instrument or looking after the cavalry's horses you could not be wielding a gun or a knife.[5] Jacob became a drummer in the 68th Regiment, Bengal Native Infantry, and in the records of the pension fund his rank is given as a matross – the name, now obso- lete, for a soldier of artillery ranked below a gunner. His duty was to assist the gunners in loading and firing the guns, then sponging them down to stop them overheating. They carried flintlocks and marched with the store wagons, acting as guards. Jacob saw active service around northern India and when he died in 1828 his fifteen- year-old son James inherited his post in the 68th. The native infantry liked its drummers to be married, unlike the British army, so James complied by marrying another fifteen-year-old, Isabella;

neither of them could sign their name in the marriage register at Myanpoorie.

What was their marriage like? I can never know, but the *Calcutta Review* of this time suggests that some young wives were scarcely ready for it, like this one, already both a mother and a widow at thirteen:

> 'You had a good husband, then?' said we, 'Indeed I had, my mother thought he was not kind to me because he used to beat me; but I deserved it well, for I was a great scamp.' 'A great scamp!' we repeated, in some dismay. 'How?' 'I used to be playing marbles with the boys, when he wanted his supper ready.'[6]

I pursued Margaret and her forebears through the registers of baptism, marriage and death in the India Office records at the British Library. On the pages of the marriage registers are only the bare facts – place, date, age at marriage if under twenty-one, husband's occupation, name of the bride's father. Baptisms and deaths are even more meagre, but it is by these skeletons that I have built up my family background. It seems that Jacob Johnstone, Margaret's grandfather, was married to Lakshmi, a native from Calcutta, and her name was Anglicised to Lucky. There is no other information about her, nor anything about her daughter-in-law Isabella. I am convinced that both Lucky and Isabella were not of 'pure English blood', though – their circumstances, married to bandsmen, would mean that they were at most of mixed race, or they could even have been Indian foundlings, Christianised and raised in orphanages in Calcutta, such as Mrs Wilson's Native Orphan School, where the girls were raised as Christians and married off at fifteen to native converts.

I don't know if Margaret's grandmother and mother were, like the child bride described in the *Calcutta Review*, forced by circumstances to be hardboiled in their attitude to love and marriage, but I do know that by the time Margaret was born in 1853 her parents

Isabella and James had lost two children in infancy, but included a fifteen-year-old girl and a thirteen-year-old boy, as well as the newborn Margaret, in their family. They were living during a time of aggressive expansion and consolidation for the Company. There had been the long campaigns early in the century to subdue the Marathas, a warrior people whose territories stretched in a wide band across the whole of India below Bengal, and who were themselves masters of a number of tribes, Bheels and Pindarees as well as Rajputs. The native regiments were also kept busy with a series of military campaigns to acquire native sovereign states.

Wealthy Hyderabad had been annexed in 1843, and the Punjab was wrested from the Sikhs in a series of campaigns between 1846 and 1849. The new Governor-General, Lord Dalhousie, implemented what he called his Doctrine of Lapse, which meant that wherever a native ruler died without a direct heir, the succession was deemed to have lapsed and the Company claimed the right to annexe the territory, flying in the face of tradition whereby the incumbent ruler could nominate his heir. Soon, four territories in Central India had been annexed in this way.[7] There were often angry claimants in the wake of these acquisitions, and when Oudh was taken from its deposed nawab four years after Margaret's birth, the last of these takeovers brought a near-catastrophic reaction. The fierce residents rose against the outrage, becoming one of the main factors in the Sepoy Rebellion of 1857 and found willing collaborators all over the north, where the East India Company had been most active.

Much of James and Isabella's early married life was spent crossing vast distances as the regiment moved on to the next conflict. Before Margaret's birth the family were not even stationed in the Company's territory. Her father had left his old regiment to join the 2nd Native Infantry of the Gwalior Contingent as a drum major, and they found themselves posted to 'Hindu' India. The Contingent had been formed after an ambitious Begum had tried to manoeuvre the succession away from the ten-year-old heir to Gwalior. In 1843 the Company sent in two armies to secure their own interests and Gwalior became the largest Princely state in the Central India Agency, under the supervision of a Resident who reported direct to Calcutta. A force of around eight thousand men, to be known as the Gwalior Contingent, was stationed in the state and paid for out of its revenue, rather than from the Company's coffers. There were to be seven regiments, of which James's was the most senior.

A native regiment had about twenty bandsmen, who played the regiment into battle and conveyed instructions to the troops in the heat of the fight, and the *Calcutta Review* observed that: 'There is not a native regiment that does not reckon, besides its non-commissioned officers, a number of drummers, who ... bear the Christian name, but are distinguished from the pure heathen by little except their indiscriminate diet, and by coming to the Padree Sahib to be "*Shadi-kur'd*" or "*Christian-kur'd*" – married or christened'.[8] There was only one drum major to a regiment, however, a non-warranted rank who earned the same as the paymaster sergeant[9] and I imagine James was not such a 'near heathen'. As a zenana child, surviving the fall from grace of his kind, he was no doubt jealously guarding the quasi-hereditary rank that had come his way through his father. The 2nd Native Infantry was formed by Sir Robert Clive soon after the Battle of Plassey, and was considered the cream of the Bengal troops; for James to be appointed its drum major was a reassuring promotion both in rank and in status.

Sindhia of Gwalior* needed the support of the Company. A

---

* Jayajirao Sindhia, Maharajah of Gwalior 1843–86, also called Srimant Maharaja Jayaviro or Maharaja Jayajirao Sahib Shinde

Maratha himself, he ruled over several groups – Rajput, Aleer, and Goojar – whose leaders were watching for any opportunity to seize power. During a long visit to Calcutta in 1857, when trouble was already rumbling in the north, the twenty-two-year-old Maharajah entertained lavishly, but public opinion was far from favourable. *The Times* called him 'an irascible, self-willed lad, very difficult to manage' and thought that 'it seems horrible that a boy of this description, without principle or restraint, should exercise, by our favour, power of life and death over some millions of people'.

At his side, however, was a remarkable adviser, his Dewan Dinakar Rao, and though Sindhia sometimes tried to ignore his advice the Dewan steered him through turbulent and dangerous times. The British Resident, Major S. C. Macpherson, thought him a 'great native statesman . . . from whom the best of our English administrators have learnt many lessons of wisdom', not only benefiting the once run-down state of Gwalior, but improving the character of Sindhia himself.

The Resident was a remarkable man, who early in his career had studied the local non-Hindu tribal peoples and then persuaded them to give up their practice of human sacrifice. During much of his residency at Gwalior, Macpherson found himself alone in making life-or-death decisions, for the Political Agent, with whom he might have conferred when the chaos of the rebellion started, was away on furlough from April to December, just the worst time from the point of view of those left behind to face the music. Macpherson managed to keep in touch with Sindhia and the Dewan long after he had had to flee from Gwalior, constantly urging them to keep things on an even keel. It is thanks to his advice that when the Contingent finally rose Sindhia managed to keep many of them, as well as his own palace guard, contained at the fort in Gwalior, earning precious months' respite for the

Company's forces while they dealt with the mutineers in Delhi and elsewhere.

Had he not, the outcome could have been very different, with rebels to the east and south moving freely across Gwalior to join forces with other troops. They might then have swept unchallenged through the Ganges Plain, subduing the whole of the north from Delhi to Calcutta. Bengal would have been lost to the East India Company; it could have been the end of British dominance, kicked out like so many conquerors before them, but Sindhia was steadfast and the rebellion remained a series of scattered campaigns. After the chaos had subsided, Sindhia's restraining hand on the Contingent forces during those crucial early months was recognised and he was hailed as 'the saviour of India' and 'the firm friend of the English'.

Drum Major Johnstone had been posted to Mhow, a garrison town in the Central Provinces, about eighty miles south of Gwalior in the heart of Maratha India, and it was here that Margaret was born in 1853. When she was four, the family experienced a particularly bloody episode in the Sepoy Rebellion. As the troubles spread from the north and news came in of the mutineers in Meerut and Delhi to the north-west, and Ferozepur to the east, troops started rising in their own part of Central India. It became unsafe for families to remain in the outlying posts, and all who could made their way back to the protection of the Contingent's headquarters in Gwalior.

The British officers in Gwalior believed that the Contingent troops would remain steady, trusting to an old-school loyalty that had been eroded in many other regiments as the Company's force had grown ever bigger.[10] But if none of the European officers believed that their men's loyalty might waver, Gwalior's court had other information and there was to be considerable disagreement between the military leaders on one side and the court and the

Resident on the other as to how to react to the rising tide of unrest. In late May the Dewan had gone to the cantonments to investigate the source of a widespread rumour that the flour for sale in the bazaar had been deliberately contaminated by the British with the ground-up bones of cows and pigs, thus defiling both Hindus and Muslims. The Dewan tracked down the people responsible for this unfounded rumour and in doing so made himself very unpopular with the men of the Contingent. Fearing for his own safety he abandoned his carriage and left the cantonments on horseback, returning to the lashkar – the centre of military operations – by back roads. He reported to the Maharajah that nightly meetings were taking place between palace troops and the Contingent, at which they pledged to exterminate the Christians, taking oaths of fealty on Ganges water if Hindu or the Koran if Muslim, and received emissaries from troops in Delhi and Calcutta that had already mutinied. The court passed all this on to the European officers, urging them not to trust the sepoys under their command and advising them to send all the women and children left in the lines at Morar to the Residency some six miles away, where Marathas from the palace force would replace the unreliable Contingent guards, and to command all officers to mount their horses at once and ride away from danger. However Brigadier Ramsay, commanding the Contingent forces, and his senior officers would not believe that the traditional trust between officers and men could be broken, any more than did the senior command in the Red Fort at Agra, who continued to requisition out parts of the Contingent to quell trouble in the districts.

In a native regiment with few warrant officers, the drum major was usually close to his senior officers, and would have been at the beck and call of both the adjutant and the commanding officer. Before the troubles began, the officers stationed in Gwalior were busy putting their own musical band together and I like to think of them calling on the expertise of Drum Major Johnstone for advice, possibly even breaking the social taboos and allowing him to play with them. But then came the present crisis, and as his regiment, the Second, were mainly at Gwalior through the troubles, and as one of the drum major's duties was to administer the lash to miscreants, James would have been busy during this time and not very popular with the troops. Though the band's main duties comprised playing for parades, musters and route marches, James might well have been involved in the security and operation of the regimental treasury, too – which was a tempting prize for the sepoys who were going to need money to feed and arm themselves if they succeeded in breaking loose.

It was May and the temperature had been rising to an unbearable pre-monsoon heat. By the middle of the month there were fewer than twenty officers left in command of about five thousand native troops. A number of unprotected wives and children were also left behind in the lines when officers were sent out on missions to the trouble spots. They were all stuck, the temperature rising to 120 degrees, the wind blowing furiously and whipping up a storm of dust. In a letter from this time the regimental chaplain, the Reverend Coopland, wrote to his sister, 'I would leave for Bombay at once, but it would be death to be exposed even for an hour to the sun.'[11] Trouble was bubbling all over Central India, with rumours and horror stories coming in from all sides until the telegraph wires were cut, leaving them isolated and nervous.

If the Brigadier ignored the advice of the Dewan, the Resident did not. Thirteen officer's wives, four sergeants' wives, all of their many children and Mr Coopland accompanied Macpherson to the relative safety of the Residency under the protection of the Maharajah's 'wild Maratha horse and infantry'.[12] The officers did not heed the palace's warning to flee from the district, nor did they accompany the womenfolk; instead they thought to calm the threatening eruption by all sleeping among their sepoy troops that night. The next day, the sepoys 'loudly declared' that removing them from their guardianship of the Residency showed a loss of faith in their loyalty and pledged that they would protect all treasure (presumably the treasury) from falling into the hands of the Maharajah's men. The 4th Native Infantry volunteered to serve against the rebels, and similar promises were made by the Contingent forces at Mhow, Bhopal and Lalitpur. Ramsay believed that, by trusting what his men said and allowing them back on guard duty, he was encouraging them to think he feared danger from without and not from them.

Sindhia had been making almost daily visits to the European lines and he warned the Contingent officers that even his own state troops were more hostile to the European presence than he had realised. It would be better for those at the residency to come under his direct protection at the palace. He offered fifteen carriages for the women and children, who made a dash from the residency to a building he had set aside for them near his palace. Major Macpherson fired off a telegram to Agra, asking for Sindhia's personal bodyguard, who had been sent to Agra at the suggestion of the high command to demonstrate 'in an unmistakable manner that he [Sindhia] had identified the British cause with his own', to be allowed back to Gwalior in order to escort all of the women and children to the safety of the Red Fort. But the Brigadier was feeling a renewed confidence in his men after the night in the lines and effectively neutralised the urgency of the Resident's request by sending off a telegram of his own which said that all was now quiet, and that Sindhia's advice was motivated by a desire to 'enhance his own services at the expense of the contingent'. An order came back that no one should attempt to get to Agra until the regiments actually mutinied. Sindhia urged the families to stay on at the palace where he could protect them, but two of the wives returned to the lines at

Morar despite this and 'the most urgent solicitations' of Major Macpherson. All of the others followed the next day, believing that this return demonstrated their faith in the *esprit de corps* so beloved of the officers and would in itself prevent any further threat to their safety from the sepoy troops. In reality it meant that, when the crisis came, most of the unmarried officers were able to flee but all who were married stayed to protect their families and were massacred.

Almost every day brought fresh details of 'horrible outrages and massacres', as the Reverend Coopland put it. During the first days of June rumours circulated that the Commanding Officer at the assault on Delhi had died of cholera, and then that the troops in Lucknow had burnt the beautiful garden city and were in open rebellion. Stories came in from all over the Punjab, even from as far east as Peshawar. It was said that, up in the hills at Simla, hundreds of invalids and women and children – the usual escapees from the heat of the plains – had been crowded into the magazine, and those who fled into the jungle faced a forty-eight-mile trek to the hill station of Kasauli, where cholera had already broken out.

Some of the rumours reaching the cantonment at Morar, about six or seven miles from Sindhia's lashkar in Gwalior, were falsely hopeful, such as the news that Delhi had been won back from the mutineers[13] but most of it was bad. People seldom left their houses for fear. The Europeans were eleven officers, three surgeons and four sergeants, with their families and those of four other officers on duty elsewhere. The serious violence at many of the outposts meant that only two of the seven native infantry regiments were left in Gwalior itself, the 4th and James Johnstone's regiment, the 2nd, with two companies of artillery and perhaps a hundred cavalrymen as well. The mixed-race families in the lines, who are never mentioned in the official accounts of what happened, were lost in a limbo between the white officer class and the native forces, who were by now regarded as the enemy.

What must it have been like for the Johnstones? Isabella, with her mixed descent would have been fluent in at least one of the Indian languages, and it is likely that James would have been too: one of his jobs would have been to liaise between officers and sepoys. Margaret, at four, would probably have been comfortable in both Marathi and English, and would have found her playmates on both sides of the divide. Not that anyone apart from the children would have been in the mood to play. The most chilling news came on 8 June from Jhansi, a mere sixty miles away, where the implacable Maharani had promised free passage to the two hundred European inhabitants and then allowed all to be slaughtered.[14] 'It stirred the capital of Sindhia to its inmost depths. All believed that the foundations of the British Empire in India were crumbling into dust,' said a report of the intelligence department to the army. When the news reached Captain Murray, who was on his way to Jhansi with a wing of the 4th, he retraced his troops to Gwalior, fearing that they would not remain loyal despite their earlier pledges. He got back to the city on 13 June, just in time for the events that were to explode in the lines at Morar.

It was difficult to know who would remain loyal to the European force and who would not. When chaos finally broke out in the Contingent's lines, every officer's house in Morar was torched and raided, and most European men (and their sons) were executed, but the rear guard of the 4th – 'that fearsome regiment', as one lady called them – defended Captain Murray and a fellow officer against an attack from the 2nd. A guard from the 1st protected the family of the Commandant, even though most of their regiment had taken part in a particularly vicious uprising at Etawah. When Captain Stewart of the artillery was badly wounded, he was tended through the night by two of his own battery, only to be taken out and shot in the morning. And, right at the beginning of the outbreak, Major Blake of the 2nd – a man 'as good as he was brave'[15] – galloped to the lines and was shot through the chest as he sat on his horse before the main guard. Hundreds of the sepoys of his regiment then expressed profound grief and blamed his death on men from the 4th, and gave him a decent burial.

Lieutenant Pierson witnessed the scene around Major Blake's death as he made a dramatic escape of his own. Riding down to the lines, he met two escapees from Jhansi and the three men were 'regularly hustled down to parade by crowds of sepoys'. Four volleys were fired at them and the lieutenant's horse was shot from under him. He struggled free of the fallen animal, leaving one of his boots behind, and hurried to the fallen Blake on the parade ground, trying to make him as comfortable as possible and witnessing the distress of the sepoys from the 2nd at the attack on their commander. These sepoys urged the three men to flee. The two from Jhansi made good their escape on horseback, but Pierson had no horse and only one boot. Three of the sepoys took charge, stripping him of his hat, trousers and remaining boot, and unceremoniously wrapping him up in a horse blanket. They slung the blanket from their muskets and, pretending he was the dead wife of one of them whom they were going to bury, carried 'her' across the river to safety. Pierson would not go without knowing his wife's fate, however, and sent the sepoys back to his house where they found his wife alive and terrified.

They brought her out wrapped in the blanket and eventually carried her slung between them for the seven miles to the residency, with Pierson, half-naked and barefoot, at their side. There they found three other fugitives and an elephant. The elephant being a little like a tank in more modern warfare, the five of them mounted it and attempted to make their escape, until they bumped into one of the palace search parties who conducted them to the safety of the phool bagh, the palace gardens.

No one knew whom they could trust. One or two managed to

flee across the small river, but soon that was patrolled by the sepoys too. The officers' families hid where they could: in their gardens, and in the ranks' lines, which lay behind the officer's residences. It must have been chaos. A number of sergeants' wives turned up the next day; they had been savagely treated and their clothing torn away, and perhaps raped.

Isabella and Margaret survived the uprising, but what became of James is not clear. The registers show that by the time Margaret was a fifteen-year-old bride her father was dead but, frustratingly, the relevant file is one of the few that are missing from the India Office, lost no doubt in the aftermath of the troubles. There was every likelihood he had died in the bloodbath; but then, how on earth had Margaret and her mother survived? In order to flesh out the story I had to rely on general reading, and by good fortune came across a first-hand account of what happened to some of the women and children written by Mrs Coopland, the wife of the chaplain. These were the wives of officers and white civilians, and though she does mention that some sergeants' wives and their children attached themselves to the convoy of women who fled Gwalior for Agra, there was no mention of a Margaret or an Isabella Johnstone. I feared that the next part of the story would have to begin with unsatisfactory conjecture, the inevitable outcome of piecing together scraps of information about a family who were, at this stage, pretty well illiterate and thus incapable of leaving any written record of their own. But then a wonderful thing happened: so unexpected, so thrilling, that it sent a shiver down my spine and for days I didn't sleep for the excitement.

Out of the blue one of my brothers forwarded an e-mail to me, asking if we were the Quicks who were descended from Margaret Johnstone. It had come from Basil Thyer, a great-grandson of Margaret's, not Uncle Basil, my father's half-brother. This Basil had also been raised in India and now lived in New Zealand. In his retirement he had busied himself with constructing a family tree and had now reached some of the cadet branches. He knew that the Quicks were a medical family who had gone to England, and had simply searched the Internet for doctors called Quick. The search turned up my brother, a surgeon in Cambridgeshire, who instantly sent Basil's e-mail on to me. I began a correspondence with Basil, who told me that as a boy he had often visited Rawalpindi, where my grandfather Bertie – Basil's uncle – lived and worked. Basil was the grandson of Margaret's oldest child, Mig, and my grandfather was Margaret's youngest. Margaret died when Bertie was a small boy and he was more or less raised by Mig, who told him many stories about their mother to help him feel close to her. In turn, Bertie passed these stories on to his young nephew whenever he was visiting and Basil told me that one of the most vivid of these tales was how Margaret and her mother had been part of a ragtag band of women and children who fled for their lives from Gwalior and had survived to reach the Red Fort above the river in Agra. And so a story from a hundred and fifty years ago, about a Eurasian woman and her four-year-old daughter, people who had lived below the radar of government reports or historic narratives or personal papers, marginalised by colour and rank and gender, came down to me by virtue of people simply telling it to each other. It was a thrilling moment.

8

To the Red Fort

As Margaret and Isabella were mere appendages to the drum major, himself a minor figure in the tumultuous events of 1857, it was not an easy matter to pin down the details of their escape, even armed with the exciting confirmation that I was absolutely on track with my hunch about how they had survived. In Morar they knew they were in trouble on the afternoon of 14 June, when an empty house in the heart of the cantonment went up in flames. Soon the mess and the bathhouse next door were alight, and when Captain Stewart's bungalow started to go too no one could tell if the sepoys of the 2nd were feeding the flames or attempting to put them out. The first buildings that had been fired burnt to the ground, and after months of searingly hot weather it was desperately important that the flames shouldn't be carried along the lines to the other houses. Once they were razed, everything went quiet and there was a fierce divide in the opinion of the residents: many were frightened, but others insisted it had been an accident; no one knew where it would explode next – in the artillery lines, or the magazine or up at the fort near the palace. The result was that again no plans were made to get the women and children out, and everyone stayed indoors, fearing that the trouble they had dreaded for months was upon them. Nothing happened for the rest of the day, the nine o'clock gun – the usual signal to retire for the night – was fired and everyone was on their way to bed when the chaos engulfed them.

It happened in the same way as had happened in the other outposts: a cry came along the lines – 'the Europeans are upon us!' – started no doubt by some agent provocateur, like putting a spark to dry tinder, and at once there was a panic all through the lines. Most of the families were roused by their servants or the sound of bugles and cries. Most of the domestic servants then melted away, leaving the Europeans to defend themselves as best they could. Officers' houses had a nightly guard in place, often fourteen or so men, and some of them persuaded the inmates to stay inside with a promise that they, the guard, would protect them. The infantry and the artillery armed themselves, with no one sure who was on which side; regiments were divided by personal loyalty to their officers even when they knew they were in principle against continuing British rule. One who was there described how, amid the flames and sound of gunfire about a hundred sepoys of the Contingent descended on the officers' houses first and, 'shouting, yelling and bugling . . . in the wildest confusion, under the influence of a great fear . . . roused themselves to the work of mischief',[1] going from house to house, looting and burning. Other parties went behind the row of officers' houses to find the batteries and the magazine, and into the cavalry lines to prevent anyone taking the horses. What few officers were left went to their duty; Major Blake of the 2nd then Major Sheriff of the 4th fell 'amidst the volleys which flew everywhere'. Four sergeants died and so did two pensioners of the regiments. At first it was thought that anyone connected with the artillery would inevitably be killed, but Captain Stewart, though wounded, was concealed and attended by his bearer.

Meanwhile other artillerymen offered to help Captain Hawkins leave the artillery lines to rescue his four older children, but he thought it more prudent to hide in the battery and send for his wife, who had given birth to their fifth child only three days earlier. Mrs Hawkins and the baby were carried down to the battery on a bed, with the servants bringing her other four children, while Mrs Stewart arrived there by coach with her boy and her girl, fearing the worst for her husband as his horse had just returned to her compound riderless. The party hid in the battery overnight, but the next day some infantrymen came in, furiously looking for Europeans, and killed Hawkins and, by accident, Mrs Stewart – with the same bullet as she clung to his arm. Her son and the Hawkins' son were also killed, and the nurse who was holding the new baby died in a volley, as did the baby girl, by falling from her arms. Captain Stewart survived in hiding for one more night, but when he learned of the death of his wife he said that he no longer wished to live and was shot by the mutineers. His faithful bearer then assisted the one surviving Stewart, six-year-old Charlotte, to escape with Mrs Hawkins and her three remaining girls. This small party eventually arrived in Agra concealed in a bullock cart.

Another officer, Lieutenant Proctor, remained in his house to take care of Mrs Gilbert, the heavily pregnant wife of an absent colleague, who was unwell and had been in the care of the Proctors for the past three weeks. There was no chance of her fleeing and so they stayed with her. The servants persuaded Mrs Gilbert to hide in a hut in the garden with her other child and the nanny, but Mrs Proctor would not leave her husband. They heard the rampage going on around them and some hours later the servants returned with news of the death of the artillery officers Stewart and Sheriff. The Proctors then hid in the hut with Mrs Gilbert, with the lieutenant hidden under a cover as his wife lay on top of him. Three hours later small groups of six or seven sepoys at a time entered the hut and searched around, still too respectful of the women to move them and find Proctor hiding under his wife. In time however, the sepoys first removed Mrs Gilbert, her child and the nanny, sending them to join other women they had rounded up in the lines of the 2nd, and then led Mrs Proctor away by the arm. She turned back to see her husband running for his life; he got a good forty yards from the hut before she had to turn away, unable to bear it. She heard shots and then heard them say '*girghea*' – fallen. A similar end befell the senior surgeon, Dr Kirke, and the Reverend Coopland, literally smoked out of other huts where they hid with their families and shot in front them. Of the women, besides Mrs Stewart, three others died that night: Mrs Pike, a sergeant's wife, Mrs Burrows, the widow of a conductor who had managed to save a considerable amount of money and refused to reveal where it was buried, and Mrs Hennessy as she fled across the river. I name them here since they are otherwise lost in the dusty accounts of the nineteenth century, and I am moved by the random way in which fate took them, when Mrs Proctor and all the other females – including Margaret Johnstone – survived.

Eleven men survived the chaos in Morar, including a Sergeant Quick, who managed to ride off with another officer, crossing the Chumbal River to the safety of Dholpur, where the sympathetic Rana Bhagwant Singh helped them on their way to Agra. (This Quick, and his wife, who appears later in the story, were nothing to do with Margaret or Christopher, but I was struck by the coincidence of their shared name.) Everyone was trying to get away from the lines and find their way to the protection of Sindhia in the palace at Gwalior.

Over at the Residency six miles away, Major Macpherson decided it was time to get out and so took his sister and another officer by carriage to the palace, escorted by Sindhia's Muslim guards and about forty Mahratta horsemen. They were stopped on the way by a band of Ghazis,* implacable anti-British Muslims. Their leader was Jehangir Khan, a former Contingent havildar (sergeant) who would not let the carriage pass until the guards convinced him that the Resident was their prisoner whom they were taking to Sindhia. Once at the palace, they found Sindhia in his flower garden guarded by armed troops and with a motley band of refugees already there, including Brigadier Ramsay, a few officers, lots of women and children and Lieutenant Pierson's party, who had come there from the residency on the elephant. Margaret and Isabella may well have been among those refugees in the phool bagh gardens. Parties of the palace guard had been sent out in all directions to bring in whoever they could find, and it was feared that anyone who had not made it to the safety of the flower garden by now must be dead, for the sepoys had lined all the roads through the cantonment at Morar as well as both sides of the river and had started to go through the parade area and artillery lines as well.

By now struggling to protect the Christians in his own service – mainly brigade commanders of Portuguese or Italian descent – Sindhia felt that he could not harbour the refugees for even an hour longer, least of all the Resident who, as the British political agent in Gwalior, was the man the rebels most wanted dead, and so he insisted that they must all leave for Agra as soon as possible. The Maharajah had already ordered carriages and palanquins for those who were unable to walk, and would send an escort of his own bodyguard with them at least as far as the halfway point, the Chambal River, and if necessary all the way to Agra.

Sindhia feared that the rebels were expecting him to lead them against the British at Agra, or at least to hand over the wealth of his treasury, and that if he resisted they would attack Gwalior, incite his own troops to join them and so gain access to his powerful artillery

* Warriors of the faith

and magazine. If the strengthened troops did then get to Agra it would be all over for the British there, for they had pitifully few troops or arms available to them by this stage, and no chance of reinforcements as the Company's troops were stretched to the absolute limit all over the north and the west.

Macpherson saw that he must try to lead his band of waifs and strays to safety, however much he would have wanted to stay and advise the Maharajah and his Dewan. He urged them that at all costs they must keep the Contingent in Gwalior for as long as they could, paying them for their 'service' until such time as a European force could be mustered to crush them. The rebellious Contingent were agitating to move on the offensive to Agra and then Delhi, but Sindhia and the Dewan were to persuade the mutineers that the court was with them in spirit and simply waiting for kinder weather before moving out; Macpherson assured them that however treacherous that might seem, the Governor-General would understand the plan and would reward them for their support later. That they managed to restrain the Contingent for four months was against all the odds, and later Macpherson paid tribute to their 'firmness, courage and skill'.

Sindhia managed to contain the sepoys by sowing dissent between Hindu and Muslim so that they could not agree on a plan of action, and to prevent the troops from mustering at one point the palace had to confiscate all the Contingent's bugles, remove all wheels from the gun carriages and hide them, disperse all the elephants and camels to distant jungles where they would not be easily found, and sweep the Chumbal River of all boats to prevent their movement between Gwalior and Agra. That was later, though, and Sindhia and the Dewan were by then again being advised on strategy by Macpherson from the safe distance of Agra.

Meanwhile, the party of refugees had to get on their way to Agra. Macpherson led them, some thirty in all, away from Gwalior towards the Chumbal. As they neared the river the landscape

changed dramatically from the open, almost treeless plain to deep
ravines that to this day provide cover for robbers. Twelve miles
from the river, the party reached the village of Hingonah, where
they were stopped by Jehangir Khan, the same havildar who had
challenged the Resident as he made his way to the palace the night
before. He had been a serving native officer with the Contingent,
and had then transferred to the Maharajah's service where he had
been one of Sindhia's favourites. Now, in the rebellion, Jehangir
had emerged dressed in his true colour – green, the colour of the
prophet Mohammed – and fingered his prayer beads ceaselessly as
he negotiated with the party of European fugitives. He had with
him two hundred other Ghazis, who were distinguished by their
religious zeal and their intolerance of the decadent ways of the
'Nazarenes' – Christians. They were the most implacable foes of the
British during the Sepoy Rebellion, and many had already sworn
jihad – holy war – against all who did not follow their fundamentalist
view of Islam. They were also known as the Hindustani Fanatics, and
my grandfather Bertie was later to meet their kind face to face on
the North-West Frontier. Many later said that the Ghazis were the
prime force behind the rebellion.

Jehangir Khan insists that he means the refugees no harm, but the
Captain of the palace bodyguard points out 'a body of plunderers' in
the ravines ahead, who will no doubt strip them of any valuables.
There is a stand-off and Macpherson secretly makes a plan to abandon the Maharajah's carriages and take what horses they can from
their palace guard to send all the women and children – the bulk of
his party – off to find a point further down the river where they can
cross safely, away from the ravines and the danger that lurks there.
It is a desperate plan and, luckily for them all, as they are about to
put it into effect the local warlord Thakur Buldeo Sing arrives with
a strong band of followers. He is the leader of the Dunouteeah

Brahmins and a vassal to the Maharajah. The Dewan has alerted him to the desperate flight of the Resident and his protégées, and the Thakur has come to say that he and his people owe the Resident a debt of gratitude because he had once intervened with the Dewan on their behalf, convincing him to build some water tanks and wells for their use. The Thakur and his men will defend the refugees with their lives. The women and children are spared their headlong flight and the whole party sets off for the river at first light, leaving a rear guard to watch for Jehangir Khan.

When they reach the ravines Sindhia's bodyguard turns back with their horses and the palanquins, but the coachmen continue on. The Chumbal is a mighty river, still some fifty feet deep even during this, the driest season, and getting everyone across safely costs Macpherson sunstroke from exposure to the fierce pre-monsoon heat. Once on the other side they are in the territory of Bhagwant Singh, the Rana of Dholpoor. Macpherson had managed to send a message across to his court the previous day and the Rana came magnificently to their aid, sending an escort and elephants for them to ride on. Spying brigands waiting to attack them in the ravines, the escort change the refugees' route and stay with them for the rest of the journey to Agra, where they are welcomed into the giant Red Fort, so far safe from the troubles besetting the whole of British India.

They are reunited with others who have arrived before them, among them Sindhia's personal guard and the troops from the Contingent force who had been sent to Agra in the preceding weeks and unmarried officers who had managed to flee from Gwalior at the first sign of trouble on 14 June, as well as a number of waifs and strays who fled other troubled outposts in the Central Provinces. Macpherson's party believe that they are the last from Gwalior to have survived; they have no way of knowing that, in fact, a number of other wives and children had been left in the lines, hiding as best they could in gardens and their servants' quarters. Gwalior was one of the few places where the women and children were spared. In many others – Delhi and nearby Jhansi, and later at Cawnpore, for instance – even where there was a gesture of sympathy towards them the women and the children usually died. Some said that the fact that so many were spared at Gwalior was because of the stern injunctions of Maharajah Sindhia.

The escape of this remnant who had been stranded in Gwalior after the main party had left was recorded and published the year after the mutiny, and became a best-seller – there was a hunger to know just what had happened during the chaos of the rebellion. The account was written by Mrs Coopland, the wife of the chaplain of the Contingent; she was new in India, having arrived in the autumn before the rebellion. Her husband was English, but Mrs Coopland noticed at once that nearly all the officers and their wives in Gwalior were Scottish like her. She was very struck by how young her companions in the lines were; the average age was well below thirty. At the time of the rebellion she was pregnant, like many of the wives: one of her companions in flight was at full term and likely to give birth at any moment. Mrs Coopland herself was at least seven months gone and Mrs Stewart had been delivered only three days before the troubles broke out. Victorian sensibility forbade her to dwell on this delicate fact, however: she does not mention the fact of her own advanced pregnancy until she is describing her life in the Fort at Agra after her safe arrival there. Her account suffers from the usual prejudices of her class, so that she is only concerned with the other officers' families, telling how they listened terrified to the rampage through the cantonment. Miraculously, there was one servant who had stayed loyal when all others had fled, and he was Mirza, the kitmutghar* of Major Blake.

* Butler (literally 'worker')

When the sentry on duty at the Blake house came and reported how, as the Commanding Officer of the 2nd, Blake had already been shot at his main guard in the lines, where his own men wept over him and bitterly blamed the 4th for his death, it was clear to Mirza what to do. The two loyal natives – the kitmutghar and the sentry – urged the Europeans to flee into the gardens and to hide themselves somehow from the brilliant moonlight and the sparkling stars while pandemonium was unleashed around them.

They heard the smashing of glass and china, and of untold numbers of bottles of wine and beer and brandy. The rampagers included the badmashes* of the town, released from jail by the rebels and intoxicated by bhang lassi, a narcotic drink made from hemp, as well as the alcohol they found in the European lines. Somehow they elude the sepoys hunting for them through the gardens, and Mirza then takes some of them first to his own modest house at the bottom of the compound and later moves them to the hut of the bearer. They find it 'very low and small' – I am sure none of them would have been anywhere near the servants' quarters before – and there they are left cowering. The other Europeans have scattered to hide where they can, but soon another woman arrives at the hut with her small son and his ayah. When the sepoys finally come there the baby's cries give them away and the bearer's wife tries to placate the sepoys by taking out the kitchen utensils to give to them. The sepoys believe that the officers who have eluded them must be hiding there and dare not go into the hut, fearing the revolvers that they believe the party will have trained on them. Instead they smoke out the fugitives, taking the roof off the hut and setting fire to it. The chaplain says to the women, 'Let us rush out, and not die like rats in a hole,' and the women surround him as they come out, crying 'Mut maro, mut maro!' – 'Do not kill us.' The

* A bad lot, a criminal

sepoys tell them, 'We will not kill the memsahibs, only the sahib.'
The Reverend Coopland, who until now has been unknown to the
sepoys, has a rifle and makes a run for it, shooting two of them dead
before they bring him down. The women hear volley after volley of
gunfire. A young sepoy of the 4th tells them that their lives are safe
but they must give up their jewellery, for the rule of the Firingee is
over, and they are dragged to the sweeper's hut – the home of the
one who is the lowest of the low in the caste system, the untouch-
able who cleans the latrines. They are so horrified by it all that they
lie there in silence, and a mouse creeps out to look at them. Later
they are joined by three more survivors: Mrs Campbell, the wife of
the captain who had escorted Sindhia's bodyguard to Agra and a
great beauty who was known as the Rose of Gibraltar, and Mrs
Kirke, the wife of the senior surgeon, who has seen her husband
murdered in front of her. Her arms are bruised and swollen where
her bracelets have been torn off but she is cuddling her four-year-old
son, who has been saved from death as his hair is in long curls and
he is dressed in petticoats, as was the custom with small children of
either sex; the sepoys had thought the child a 'missie baba' and thus
spared him.

The women take some comfort in being together, for some of
them have been hiding alone all night. A crowd of natives gathers
at the hut and passes comment on them all, but some of the 2nd
Infantry escort them to the native lines, saving them from being
shot as trophies by some cavalrymen on the way. In the native lines
they are paraded and taunted by the sepoys, then left on a charpoy
under a tree where more women join them, one of whom is heavily
pregnant and with her a small daughter and an ayah, and another
who, like most of the women, has just seen her husband killed.
Left alone, the women tell each other what they have seen and
been through, and try to work out who is still alive. All of their
menfolk are dead or away on duty at other posts, or have fled to

Agra. They have no way of knowing for sure who has survived, but they do know that they must get to Agra too. The men of the 2nd allow them to take a landau that belongs to one of the wives. The sepoys put beer, camphor water and plain water in the carriage, and two of them escort the women halfway to Sindhia's lashkar. A landau has a capacity of six to eight, and there are now at least six women in the carriage, and three of those pregnant, as well as a newborn baby and a little boy who must not reveal that he is male. As they try to leave some other women, 'sergeants' wives' as Mrs Coopland describes then, also cling to the carriage – though Mrs Coopland cannot understand how they manage to do so. The landau crosses the small river that marks the boundary of the cantonment and, a little way from the station, the group come across more sergeants' wives and their children, 'some of them nearly naked, and in great distress'. This may be where Margaret and her mother come into the tale: perhaps they had not yet reached the safety of the palace, nor joined the first party that escaped to Agra with Major Macpherson. 'Poor things, their distress was very pitiable,' said Mrs Coopland. 'Their feelings being less under control than ours.' And perhaps these women down the social scale had good reason to be less in control of their emotions: perhaps they had been roughed up more than the officers' wives – they were, after all, nearly naked.

They stop at a chowki hut – a staging post – where some of the mutineers taunt them with the news that Mrs Hennessy has been shot as she tried to escape across the river by the cantonment, and so has Captain Murray. Two more women join them, one with a small child and her ayah, and they try to press on but the horses, no doubt frightened by all the noise and confusion of the night before, become very difficult to control. The traces keep breaking and can't be mended – hardly surprising with so many women and children clinging to the one small carriage – so the whole group decide that they must go to the Rajah and beg him for sanctuary. When they have struggled to the palace they are appalled to hear that Sindhia refuses to see them. Mrs Coopland suspects he is watching them from behind a screen, but my own feeling is that by now he is so preoccupied with handling the Contingent's demands that he simply dare not be seen to be sheltering the Europeans; later he said that he could barely save the lives of the Christians he had in his own employ. He does, however, provide the women with bullock carts that, though painfully slow and without any protection from the glaring sun, do at least have the royal arms emblazoned on the side, which will perhaps command some respect for the desperate passengers within.

So the party of women set off through the jeering, threatening crowd, their only chaperone the faithful servant Mirza. They are told that it is pointless to try for Agra, since it has already fallen to the sepoys and been burned to the ground, but they have no other choice. Some of them are barely clothed, and the only provisions they have are the beers and the camphor water to purify drinking water on the road given to them by the sepoys. Mrs Coopland had also brought some vinegar and a bottle of opium, which she had managed to grab as she fled from her house the night before. There are bands of men everywhere on their route, and when they stop at the Chomedale dak bungalow* on the second day – their first rest since fleeing from Gwalior – they are joined by the heavily pregnant Mrs Gilbert with her child and nurse, Mrs Proctor and the wife of the Sergeant Quick who had bolted on horseback across the river in a desperate attempt to get help. These four women have had a difficult time, turned away from the palace by officials, forced to abandon the rough hackery because their bullocks would go no further and then, as they attempted to

* Rest station

walk back from the palace to the residency in the gathering night, with Mrs Gilbert unable to go for more than five minutes at a time, they were surrounded by a large crowd of armed men who told them that they were to be taken before the 'Biza Bhie', where the men will cut their throats. In fact they were taken to the post office, where the postmaster, a respectable-looking man, warned them in English that they must get out of the city at once. He found them a dak cart and the last horse in town, which was lame, and the four women were once again escorted out onto the road to the residency. Once out of the city the Maharajah's chuprassies,* who have escorted them all the way from the palace, warn them that there is danger from dacoits. When Mrs Proctor asked where these robbers were, the man seized her by the throat and drew his tulwar, saying, 'I am one: give me all you have or I will kill you.' Not satisfied with the small things the women gave up to him, he and his companions felt under the women's clothes as they searched them, tearing off skirts, petticoats and puggaries (long Indian scarves) before they made off. Soon the women reached the chowki hut near the residence of the Lalla Sahib, where there was a guard of the Maharajah's sepoys, but the groom leading their horse refused to find them a fresh horse or to carry on through the night. The four women did not know what to do, and the Maharajah's men were divided in their advice when asked: some said to go on, others that it was not safe. Eventually Mrs Proctor got a message to the Lalla Sahib, who would not see them but allowed them a blanket and some water in a field full of cows, where they slept deeply despite their fears. They awoke surrounded by local people who brought them plenty of milk to drink, and a message that the Lalla Sahib was granting them two rupees and two bailles,† and an escort to get

* Attendants
† Baille = four-wheeled ox cart, from Hindi 'bahalii'

them to the next dak bungalow. They travelled on through the hot day, Mrs Proctor and Mrs Gilbert and her child in one cart, the lower class – Mrs Jones, the nurse and Mrs Quick – in the other. They were offered chapattis as they travelled through the villages but no one felt able to eat them. Two of their escort abandoned them en route but at last they reached the dak bungalow, just moments before Mrs Campbell's party set off from it to travel on through the cool of the evening. If they had been five minutes later they would have missed each other and Mrs Proctor, herself five months pregnant, would probably not have been able to lead her band out of danger alone. Now the two groups can travel on together, in the hope that there will be safety in numbers, though Mrs Proctor's party will have to leave their tired oxen at this dak.

Mrs Quick is a vastly fat woman; she makes a huge fuss about how she cannot walk and the others explain there is no room for her in the bullock carts, for priority has to be given to the pregnant women, especially Mrs Gilbert who is at full term. Her noise eventually forces them to make room for her somehow, but the cart then collapses under her weight. They are now one cart down, baked and boiled by the sun despite the large white chuddars – veils – that Mirza has managed to find for them, and with no food but they struggle on as best they can. The group reaches a large village, where they fear the locals with their tulwahs are very threatening. People crowd round discussing the women and Mrs Blake and Mrs Campbell, who speak the local tongue, translate for the others; the villagers declare that none of the women are worth a pice – not much more than a farthing – except for Mrs Campbell, the Rose of Gibraltar, who is worth a whole anna. Suddenly more men are heard arriving on horseback. Mirza makes the women get out of their carts and lie on the ground, pretending to sleep. The women hear him pleading with the men that the women are exhausted, and at least to allow them a good night's sleep before they are killed. Grumbling, the men withdraw a certain distance, though all of the women are convinced they will die before the night is over. (In her account afterwards one of the women described how at this moment she thought that theirs would be a particularly horrible and long drawn-out death, since the blades that the men were wielding looked very rusty: but, exhausted and defeated by circumstances, she no longer felt frightened.)

Then they hear the sound of more horses galloping towards them and fear it will be more implacable Ghazis on a mission to kill them, but it turns out to be the palace bodyguard returning from escorting Macpherson and his party to the Chambal. The women are overjoyed and beg for protection but the guard refuse because they have no orders from Sindhia to help the women, and they soon gallop off back to Gwalior, leaving the women and children desolate. The men in the village are, however, subdued by the visit of the palace guard and the next day they allow the women to make their way to the Chambal River. The villagers here are very hostile and force the women out of their carts, telling them that they are now out of Sindhia's territory and can no longer rely on his protection.

While this is going on, a mounted policeman arrives from Agra on a camel. He is on his way to Sindhia with a note from Captain Campbell at the Red Fort, which begs that all the victims of the rising, including, he has assumed, his own wife – who is now reading the note – be given a Christian burial. The policeman tells them that Campbell has ventured out as far as Munnia, to the first dak bungalow from Agra; he dare not risk coming further on the road, but ventured that far to try to learn of his wife's fate. None of the women trust the policeman but he does order the villagers to allow the women to leave. They all get on to the old flat-bottomed boat, little more than a raft, that Mirza has found somewhere. The villagers threaten the women with their tulwahs and as the boat begins to make its way across the huge river some of the men suddenly rush into the water after the escapees, shouting and attempting to rip planks from the boat. The women and children scream – most of them cannot swim – but the men are only threatening them and know better than to swim out into the deep water in the middle of the river, so everyone in the boat makes it to the other side. They have great trouble walking up the muddy bank, and most of them have long since lost their shoes so they tear the hems off their dresses to bind their bleeding feet. Unlike most of the others, Mrs Kirke and Mrs Campbell have no hats and they lift their hems so their skirts can make a parasol above their heads. Mrs Quick, weighed down by her bulk, fares worst of all and keeps up a steady stream of cursing.

Now on the Agra side of the Chumbal, the officer sent by Campbell tries to convince Mrs Campbell to mount the horse he has kept on this side – Campbell's own horse, in fact – and return to her husband with him. She refuses to leave the rest of her party behind for they all rely on her skill in the local language as well as her strength, for she is the only one whose spirit has not been broken by losing her husband. Mrs Campbell uses a pin to prick out a message to her husband on the back of his note to Sindhia – 'We are here, more than a dozen women and children, send us help.' – and sends the officer back to Campbell.

Bhagwant Singh, the Rana of Dholpur, meanwhile, sends them an elephant, but as there is no howdah to sit in the women keep falling off it. It has made them laugh, though, and they struggle on up through the sandy banks to await the return of Mirza, who has gone to beg for carts from the Rana. Mrs Quick finds it harder and harder to keep going and suddenly has what Mrs Coopland describes as an 'apoplectic fit' and falls by the roadside, black in the face. She is dead within fifteen minutes but the rest of the party

Graham Finlayson

hotographed with my flatmate, the painter Vivi Rothwell, for the *Observer* colour
pplement, January 1966. I was asked to find more student-like clothes than the
erringbone double-breasted coat and caramel velour hat I had originally chosen.
he bike was borrowed, mine having long since vanished.

Escort of the 20th
Bengal Native
Infantry.

The walls of
Gwalior Fort.

The Red Fort at
Agra. The Taj
Mahal is visible in
the background.

35A Ellenborough Crescent, the 'best house in Rawalpindi'.

Ashburnham Cottage, Murree, where they were still waiting for my grandfather's return in 1999.

he family and their servants at Ellenborough Crescent, *circa* 1932. Back row, from ft: Akbar, Umar Khan, Suleiman, Muni, Bhati, Ashraf, Khalu. Middle row, from ft: Leonard, Nora, Esme, Bertie. Basil is seated in the foreground. The servants and separated by religion on either side of Muni, the ayah, who was married to the rdener Bhati: the Muslims are to her right, the Hindus to her left. Akbar had been y grandfather's batman during his army medical career, and stayed with him for the st of his life, while my grandfather stayed on for some years after Independence to ake sure that his family were treated properly for TB.

Leonard as a small boy,
before his mother's death.

Bertie, Esme, Bas
and Nora prepari
for a trip up to
Murree, 1933.

St Joseph's College Nanital, winners of the Culhane Cup, 1932. Leonard is at the
back on the far left.

Left:
Pop Brise.

Right:
Nana Brise,
who brought
us up, as a
young nurse.

Above: Heathside, the Brise family home, where
also grew up.

Right: Joan, aka Freckles.

Joan with
Leaping Lena.

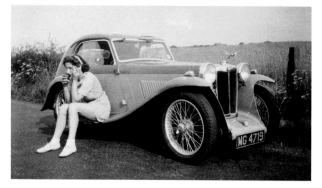

Leonard in 1937, age 22.

Joan in 1937, age 23.

Wedding day. The bridesmaids were Poppy Bryant and Joan's younger sister Betty.

he Quick family. Children, from left: Julie, me, Clive, Richard.

s Rosa the Gypsy (far left).

The Oxford Line, a revue at the Edinburgh Festival in 1966. With, from left, John Sergeant, Michael Sadler, Nigel Rees and Simon Brett.

dare not linger in the ravines to bury her, even if they had had the tools to do it with. They ask some locals to bury her and leave a small payment for them to do so, but have to move on without waiting to see it carried out, hurrying on to shelter out of the sun in a lane and await Mirza's return. Soon a whole fleet of bullock carts arrive with the arms of the house of Dholpur blazoned on them.[2] The women make their way to the next dak bungalow, where they find some refreshments ordered for them by Campbell – bread, biscuits and beer. Early the next day they set off for Munnia, once more travelling in open carts with no shade from the sun. Finally they arrive to find that Campbell has procured for them 'every conceivable comfort' and, at last, Mrs Gilbert gives birth to a healthy child. After a few hours' rest and their first proper meal in five days the party hurry on their way to Agra by back roads, accompanied by a cavalry escort from Dholpur.

They travel all night and it is only when they join the large and motley crew of waifs in Agra that they realise that they are, for the moment, safe. But they have to inform Sergeant Quick that his wife has been left at the roadside. A few days later, when it was judged safe to travel, a rescue party went to find her body. It was still where she had fallen, unburied but not mutilated by humans or dogs. Her rescuers soon discovered why she had been so incredibly heavy: she had stashed all of her household wealth – silver and jewellery, cutlery and plate – into her bosom. No wonder she was described as hugely fat, and no wonder she didn't survive in the heat. She must have been roasted by her own household goods.

Return to Gwalior

The Red Fort at Agra was one of the few places that did not fall to the mutinous regiments of the East India Company's army during the Uprising. It was to here that the officers of the Gwalior Contingent made their way under escort from the palace guard when chaos threatened to engulf Gwalior, and it was the only haven the women left behind in the cantonment could make for when it did. The story of their flight from villagers and native soldiers alike had caught my imagination, and when I knew that my great-grandmother Margaret had managed to get there as a child of five, against the odds, I wanted to see it for myself.

The Taj Mahal gleamed across the Yamuna River, and as my uneducated eye went from the Moghul masterpiece to the buildings around me inside the Red Fort it seemed to me that there was a jumble of architectural styles here. I struggled to make sense of this fantastic richness of building and decoration, but as I moved from monument to monument I noticed how the Moghul rulers had borrowed from the cultures they had come to rule as Muslim overlords. For instance, the golden pavilions that flank Shah Jahan's palace were inspired by Bengali village huts, though I thought them similar to buildings I have seen in Thailand. And Jahangir's Palace is

Hindu not Islamic in its decoration, with flat roofs, lotus flowers and dragons. If the Moghul style was a synthesis of other styles – from Central Asian to the Delhi Sultanate, from Persia to the Deccan – their own particular signature was an obsession with perfect symmetry and for buildings to have a discreet symbolic meaning for those who can read it.[1] I felt again, as I had so often in trying to uncover my family's history, that the subcontinent defies any simple narrative that attempts to define it.

I intended to trace the route that Margaret and Isabella had taken, but we found ourselves travelling the eighty-five kilometres in reverse, from Agra back along the Trunk Road towards Gwalior, 'we' being me and my daughter, just as the earlier two were mother and child. Like them, we were accompanied by a faithful servant, who we felt confident would protect us if the going got even a little rough, though we were comfortable tourists, ensconced in a four-wheel drive rather than a buffalo cart.

Raju had collected us from Delhi and brought us to Agra, and would be with us for the next couple of weeks. He came from a Kshatriya family who farmed their own lands, he told us with pride. He had spent much of the last twenty years in the army and was now well used to driving tourists from Europe to support his wife and young daughters back on the farm. His usual beat was the so-called golden triangle – Delhi–Rajasthan–Agra – and he was pleased by the prospect of a trip down through Madhya Pradesh visiting some sites he had not been to himself. He had an impeccable formal manner, referring to me as 'Ma'am' and to my daughter as 'Miss Mary', which only lapsed once in the three weeks we were travelling.

Some time later, high up in the hill station of Pachmarhi where we had gone to see in the new year in a place that might remind us of a European winter, we invited Raju to join us for dinner at the only hotel in town. Pachmarhi turned out to be a garrison town and was therefore full of soldiers; it didn't feel like a good place for two unaccompanied English women to be roaming late at night. On the way back from dinner Raju made several stops while attempting to buy a bottle of champagne, which he eventually found in a shop downtown. We couldn't find a cab back and in the end I persuaded a party of young men to give us a lift – for a fee – in their very cool white convertible. Raju sat stiffly between us in the back, clearly not liking this turn of events. The young men chatted gaily all the way back to the bungalow of the brahminical Rao family where we were staying, cheerily waved a goodbye and took off to party. As we said goodnight to Raju he presented us with the champagne and solemnly wished us a happy new year. Thanking him, we wished him a happy new year back, went off to our delightful room, made a roaring log fire, put on some music, cracked open the champagne and tucked ourselves cosily in to what felt like the best place to be at midnight. Meanwhile Raju hadn't informed us of his plan to come over to our rooms and see in the New Year with us and promptly at five minutes to midnight knocked on our door. I drew back the curtain to unlock the door and wish him happy new year again but the door lock was jammed. Poor Raju: we could only raise our glasses to him from the other side of the glass door that separated us. We really were locked in, and next morning had to telephone the main house for someone to come over with a new set of keys to get us out.

That bungalow in Pachmarhi was to be the only one we stayed in. As we followed the route from Agra down to Gwalior we wanted to go and look at the dak bungalows where the women had sheltered, if they still existed, but we planned to stay at the Raj Niwas Palace in Dholpur, the halfway point of their journey, which had only just opened as a hotel. Still a residence of the former royal family, it was being built as the last word in European style by Rana Bhagwant Singh, in the very year that Margaret and the other fugitives from Gwalior were passing through his territory on their way north to safety.

The countryside around Dholpur was once loved by the Moghuls, who appreciated its natural beauty, the dense forests and abundant game. Little of that had survived even down to Margaret's time, with the fugitives suffering terribly on their journey from the lack of tree cover in the heat. What had survived, however, was the lotus pool at nearby Jhor that lay at the centre of the very first garden made in Hindustan by Babur, the founder of the Moghul dynasty, who has been called 'The Prince of Gardeners'. When we found that the palace was in darkness because of the daily two-hour power cut, we set off in search of Babur's garden, with someone from the Palace as a guide. It was a short car ride back up the motorway connecting Gwalior to Agra, following the route of the Grand Trunk Road that has stretched across northern India since at least the sixteenth century. As we crossed fields the sound of traffic faded and the modern era fell away. As soon as the car stopped in the village we were surrounded by the first of many gaggles of children fascinated by the fairness of my daughter's skin and the curliness of her hair.

They all accompany us up the street where we meet a man who proudly tells us that he owns the pool. It lies behind his modest house and is indeed lotus-shaped, and fenced off from the village goats and chickens and children, but there is precious little sign that this was once the centre of a pleasure garden. It looks like a neglected garden pond; apart from its shape, there is nothing to indicate its elevated origins. We walk around it and try not to stare in through the open doors of the surrounding houses. The women cover their heads as we wander past, but as soon as we greet them they respond with palms together and 'Namaste', their faces breaking into smiles. They offer us a seat and refreshment, which makes me remember the fugitives' encounters with village women when

they stopped to shelter: of how the women brought Mrs Proctor and
Mrs Quick, and the pregnant Mrs Gilbert, plenty of milk to drink
even as the mayhem roared around them, and how, though men
were wielding their tulwahs all along the route, women in the villages they passed through offered the white women chapattis,
though they were too wretched, too parched and frightened to eat
them. I wondered if there is always some fellow feeling between
women, however disparate their cultures.

Returning to the palace hotel I noticed the high metal gates
that swung open to admit us, and the drive that led us through
immaculate green lawns and herbaceous borders to a portico, where
we are warmly welcomed by Bubbles, the widow of an army man
now managing the hotel where we are the only guests at present,
and led into a vast dark red salon with imposing pedimented door-
ways. It is all very grand, a two-storey building of the celebrated
local red stone with a curving bay window pierced by three sets of
French windows. With the electricity restored, I can now see the
extraordinary splendour of what the Rana had commissioned 150
years earlier. Every room has double-height ceilings, stretching up
maybe twenty or thirty feet, to allow for the circulation of cooling
air. The walls are tiled from floor to ceiling in elaborate patterns,
one below the dado rail and another above. The tiles were imported
from Europe at the behest of Rana Baghwant Singh, in the rich
colours beloved of the Victorians: forest green and ochre and bur-
gundy and turquoise. It is a building frozen in time, at the exact
period of the Uprising, and what it represents is not any indigenous
style but the current taste of 1850s England. We take tea with
Bubbles amid wall sconces and chandeliers, tiled floors, huge
Chinese vases and overstuffed three-piece suites, and she tells us
that Dushyant Singh, MP,[2] son of the last maharajah, though absent
in Delhi for the whole period that we are going to be at his palace,
has sent a message that we are to take advantage of his library and

staff to help us in our quest. In the library we find exquisite Survey of India maps from 1850, which show every building along the route from Gwalior to Agra, and Bubbles introduces us to a palace retainer who knows every inch of the surrounding country. I decide that the next day's task will be to find the Jaju Serai, which was probably the women's last overnight stopping point before they knew they were going to be all right, and is about thirty kilometres south of Agra.

Our vast bedroom makes us gasp, encompassing as it does the whole width of the bay. Soft grey-blue below the dado and above, a four-tile repeating pattern washes the walls in a sea of leaping fish and waves in blue, silver and amber. All the furniture is dark polished wood, beds, wardrobes and occasional tables that look as if they must have been selected from the catalogues of John Harris Heal.[3]

Beyond, in another vast space, is the most fantastic bath and shower arrangement we have ever seen, an assembly of chrome and brass pipework arching over the bath with six dials on each side and levers and shower heads galore. When Mary has a shower the water jets upwards with great force from six feet away in the middle of the floor. We spend some hilarious hours trying to make this Heath Robinson contraption work, but every dial sends a whoosh of water up from an unexpected direction and not always within the bath itself. It's fun, but not very effective for ablutions.

Our drawing room is the only part of our suite to reflect Indian taste. The armchairs we collapse into after our hysterics are upholstered in horsehair and embroidered silk, and the room has a marble fireplace inlaid with lapis, cornelian and agate, the same kind of exquisite work as Shah Jahan had commissioned from Persian-trained craftsmen to adorn the Taj Mahal. Here the wall tiles include laden orange trees and between them large medallions showing Friesian cows and sheep and ducks, windmills and bucolic views of sailing boats on very English-looking lakes.

The final part of our suite – oh joy – is the veranda that runs along the building from our rooms, and as I gazed out from it, far across the landscape, I found myself trying to make sense of the curious juxtaposition of India and England here. The fact that the Rana of Dholpur was busy building this epitome of the British country house while the uprising seethed around him was nothing less than startling. I looked out from the veranda, conjuring all those benighted young mothers from Britain who had passed so close to this haven of British civility. There they were, shut out from sanctuary with their babies – born and unborn – surrounded by the violence unleashed among the Indian population after witnessing their husbands' murders and their son's murders and then, just down the road from where I am standing, the apoplectic seizure that finished off Mrs Quick. I went to bed wondering if they still thought that they might make it by the time they were crossing this part of Dholpur, or were they so exhausted by all they had witnessed that they had started to despair?

The next day I found a ruined canal officer's bungalow near to Jaju Serai. The pattern of such buildings is a standard one, and would have been pretty much the same for the dak bungalows that had provided shelter for the women every fourteen or so miles along their route to Agra – three main rooms, a central veranda with a small room on either side at the front, and a longer veranda with two small rooms at the back. It reminded me of my Grandfather's house at Murree in the Himalayan foothills, which I had visited seven years earlier, at the beginning of my quest. The canal officer's bungalow is set back from the road with trees lining the approach, though many of them are now only stumps as they have been chopped down for firewood. Inside the gate there is a temple to Shiva, great god, destroyer, but also lord of the dance and source of all knowledge. As you enter there is Nandi, the bull who is Shiva's gatekeeper, transport and foremost disciple, and opposite, the head of Shiva rises from the floor of the shrine, a black cobra coiling up the right side of his face. To his left is his consort Parvati and to his right is their first son, Ganesha the elephant god, lord of learning, peace and success. Behind Shiva is Hanuman, the monkey god, protector of students and, in the centre, a lingam. All of the figures are chrome yellow and Shiva's lips and the markings on his forehead are red. I wondered if I should make an offering, but there was nothing to hand. Outside, as at all temples, a pennant flutters.

As we made our way on foot to the village beyond the fields we were soon engulfed by the usual crowd of children and menfolk, all instantly experts on the splendid ruined serai, which still has two towers and a gigantic portal, perhaps twenty-five feet high. It feels as if few visitors come to this small village, which gets on with the business of growing crops and raising a few animals. The fact of the ruined serai in their midst must usually seem an irrelevance to the villagers, and we two visitors from Europe might as well have dropped in from the moon. Once I have seen and explored one of the buildings my ancestors had camped in, my imagination is set alight: this is more than I could have hoped for and I decide that I will track down as many of their refuges as I can.

The following day I set off to find the site by the Chambal where they took shelter once they had crossed the mighty river. It is a dramatic place: there are many ravines near the river and a bumpy track through scrubby vegetation leads to a great rampart and a gateway in to what must have been a fort. Now there is a grassy field with a few buildings, a temple in the distance and the ruins of Shergarh – the fort whose name means 'abode of lions' – visible over on the top of the next headland to the west. We come to another mighty ruined serai and scramble up to the very top, from where we can look out across the river. It is a spectacular sight, with the sun low in the sky and the ravines folding in on themselves in both directions. Down on the banks are the ruins of the royal sanctuary, where the women of the palace would have descended to their private ghat* to bathe. When I start to walk down the track towards the sanctuary, Raju pulls me back – 'No madam, not safe. Too many dacoits.' – so we go back through the village and make our way down by car. I borrow a boat as the sun is going down, the sky strobed with pink and coral, the ravines dark and lowering, and out on this river, fifty feet deep and a kilometre wide, I am moved to tears at the thought of those poor straggling women and children making their crossing in a flat-bottomed boat pursued by tribesmen who tried to drown them. Before I came to India I'd no idea of the scale of the Chambal and the enormity of their undertaking.

The river crossing, so momentous for the women from the cantonment, was long a site whose strategic value was well known, guarding as it did the route south to Gwalior. Many years before 1857, the British had sought to control Dholpur because they could see its value as a buffer state between their northern territories and the often unruly Princely states beyond. In Margaret's childhood, of course, the strategic import was the other way round: the river was the great barrier that had to be crossed going north, whether you were a mixed-race fugitive, a European or an ambitious Ghazi in pursuit.

In the ravines beside the river you could quite literally get away with murder, and though there is no longer any sign of the 'small Maida Hill-like villa'⁴ where the women had sought refuge while they waited for Mirza to return with help from the Rana before attempting the climb up through the ravines to the serai, the atmosphere is heavy. I am reminded of what Kipling wrote about these wayfarers' huts:

* Steps leading down to a river

Seeing that a fair proportion of the tragedy of our lives out here acted itself in dak-bungalows, I wondered that I had met no ghosts. A ghost that would voluntarily hang about a dak-bungalow would be mad of course; but so many men have died mad in dak-bungalows that there must be a fair percentage of lunatic ghosts.[5]

Somewhere on this northern bank is where Mrs Quick died. I look around quietly for a moment, in reverence to her untimely, and perhaps slightly lunatic, end and then, as night falls, I return to the palace. I spend the rest of the evening reading about the female dacoit leader, Phoolan Devi, who was terrorising villages in the neighbouring state of Uttar Pradesh during the eighties. She was caught and imprisoned for a decade. Two years after she was released, in 1996, she was elected a member of parliament; Phoolan Devi was assassinated in 2003.

Next day we crossed the Chambal by the road bridge and, leaving the ravines behind, travel along a high open plain all the way to Gwalior, with what look to my untrained eye like acacias and other tall trees dotted about in the fields. We seek out several more dak sites en route. At Noorabad, the circuit house, established here 150 years ago, is still in use, mostly by visiting ministers and government officials. It is very simple and clean, and built on the same pattern as the dak we had seen by the ruins at Jaju. The Gwalior light railway passes nearby, and the Sawa River used to be crowded with traffic, mostly steamers; it would once have been a local hub of commerce and law-giving, thronged with people, but today the only sign of life is from the chickens scratching in the dust of the yard. There at least is continuity, for all dak bungalows kept chickens, known to one and all as 'sudden death', since they were there to provide a meal for anyone staying overnight.

We can't find any sign of the next bungalow, nor of the serai two miles after that, and so head on towards Gwalior. North of Banmur there is suddenly a long ribbon of palms and, as we proceed south, groves of silver birches along the route. The Sadak-e-Azam – the route initiated in the sixteenth century by Sher Shah Suri, the Pashtun emperor of northern India, to link the furthest reaches of his empire, which later became the Grand Trunk Road – once had trees planted along its entire length to provide shade for travellers. It takes us no time to reach the city by car – we could have done the whole trip from Agra to Gwalior in an hour and a half – and again I think how different our journey is from the five painful days it took the women fleeing.

I am sorry not to linger in the bustle of Gwalior and visit the Jai Vilas Palace, which is stuffed full of European treasures and a carpet over forty metres long, or the sixteenth-century gem that is the tomb of Mahommed Ghaus, who helped Babur conquer the city. I am not here as a tourist, though, and only glimpse the Jain colossi cut into the rocks on the climb up to the Arwarhi gate into the fort. Months after Margaret and Isabella made it to the safety of Agra, the English had attacked the vast fort in Gwalior from a hill to the west. It was here, too, that the celebrated female ruler, the Rani of Jhansi, had holed up to prolong her resistance to English conquest in the later stages of the Uprising.[6]

There are many other exotic tales in Gwalior: the ceramic frieze of peacocks, elephants, crocodiles and tigers outside the Man Mandir Palace made me shiver at the idea of incarceration in its depths, where prisoners under the Moghul conquerors endured a long drawn-out death brought about by a diet of boiled poppy heads, or 'poust', which left them addicted and starving. There is also the Jauhar Pond where, in 1232, seven hundred Rajput women committed suttee after their husbands had been defeated in battle rather than falling into the hands of the Turkish conqueror Il Tut

Mish, and the Suraj Kund, where the tenth-century ruler Suraj Sen was cured of leprosy by the hermit Gwalipa, for whom the city is named. And then there is the Gojira Mahal, a palace built by Man Singh, leader of the Tomars, in the late fifteenth century. He built it for his adored ninth wife, a Rajput peasant girl nicknamed Nami or 'gazelle eyes', who made three demands of her consort: she was to be allowed to live unveiled; she was to be allowed to go into battle with him; and she was to be allowed to drink the water of her own village of Rai, north of Gwalior, which she held to be the source of her radiance. In my brief time in the city several people told this story; they liked its romance, I dare say. The British, however, chose not to live amid all this exoticism; their lines were about eight kilometres away at Morar.

Morar is still recognisably a cantonment: the roads are in straight lines and a lot of the old bungalows and villas survive. It was hard to find the cemetery and when we eventually did the graves for Christian burial were in a terrible state, buried under long grass and scrub, with goats foraging in the branches of the shrubs. Among the unkempt graves there is a row of large monuments. On the second is the following inscription:

The Revd. George William Coopland
late fellow of St Catharine's, Cambridge,
and HEICS Chaplain
This monument was erected by his widow
after the retaking of Gwalior in June 1858

This was the same widow whose account had led me to understand how my great-grandmother had survived. There were others too, to Kinloch Winlaid Kirk, Superintending Surgeon, who was 'shot by the mutinous sepoys' and died next to Coopland, and to Archibald Proctor, 'Lieutnt. 39th regt NI', whose wife had vainly tried to save him by concealing him under a cloth and lying on top of him. The widows of these men had returned to Morar two years after the rebellion to commemorate the husbands they had seen die in front of their eyes. And then there was another gravestone:

> Major Muirson Trower Blake,
> Comdr. 2nd Regt. Gwalior Contingt.
> who was shot by the mutineers
> at Gwalior
> His remains were interred here by
> some Sepoys of his Regt.

This was my great-great-grandfather's commanding officer, but there was no sign of James's tomb; too lowly, I suppose, or simply lost in the mêlée. The landscape – tranquil, with a river running through flat fields – is curiously like Suffolk, where I now live.

Back in Morar town at St Peter's Church, where the cantonment residents had attended their last service only hours before the troubles broke out, someone tells me that the temperature in mid June is a sweltering 38 or 39 degrees, so the women really had trekked in boiling heat when they escaped to Agra. Poor Mrs Quick; poor all of them, though at least the others escaped with their lives.

10

How Tom Became Chris

When Margaret Johnstone and her mother Isabella finally reached Agra the city was still relatively untouched by the troubles that beset all the other major garrison towns of the Bengal Presidency. Fugitives were pouring in from all over the Central Provinces with tales of hostility and slaughter, divided loyalties and sudden flights. Stories were starting to come in from Delhi of how hand-to-hand fighting through the streets had led to the crucifixion of some Anglo-Indian women, their bodies pinioned to the walls of their homes; of the rape or kidnap of others; of the feet of a six-year-old girl that were cut off, still wearing her bootees. The women of Gwalior, on the whole, had been lucky, for though many had lost the husbands who had stayed at their sides to protect them as best they could, somehow an innate respect for women had prevented the sepoys of the Contingent from finishing them off. They now found themselves part of the 'great carnival of the dispossessed'[1] thronging Agra. Sooner or later they found their way up to the mighty Red Fort on a citadel built by Rajputs, past the ramparts added by the last effective Moghul emperor, Aurangzeb, through the gates thrown up by Akbar, one of the first Moghul rulers, and into the exquisite collection of ornately carved and decorated buildings erected by Shah Jahan, builder of the glittering Taj Mahal, which could be seen a mile away beyond the Yamuna River.

These masterpieces of Moghul architecture were now overrun by fugitives as regiment after regiment mutinied in the North-West and the Central Provinces, and Agra became the Western nerve centre of the Company's response. Telegraphs poured in and directives poured out until the lines were cut, and then the news was conveyed by cossids, highly paid messengers who were risking their life as soon as they ventured away from the purlieus of the town. Agra held precious few troops of its own,[2] and there were few regiments within easy reach to call on for support. In any case there were more pressing claims on their services for the moment – above all, Delhi needed to be won back from the rebels – and so long as the five thousand or so remaining Contingent forces and the ten thousand of Sindhia's palace troops could be contained at Gwalior they had a breathing space in the fort on the Yamuna.

Margaret and Isabella would have spent the last week of June making themselves as comfortable as they could under the circumstances. The fort was like a beehive thronging with all of humanity, as an officer later described:

> Nuns from the banks of the Garonne and the Loire, priests from Sicily and Rome, missionaries from Ohio and Basle, mixed with rope dancers from Paris, and pedlars from Armenia. Besides these we had Calcutta Baboos, and Parsee merchants . . . the circumstances of the multitude were as varied as the races . . .[3]

At its peak, there were close to six thousand people living in the fort, of whom a thousand were European men, just over nine hundred European women and children and the remainder 'natives and half-castes'. Another account says that there were fifteen hundred children among the inmates. The fort was divided into living quarters for all these groups of people, each with numbered compartments, and soon stars were painted up on every gateway and arch to help the new inmates find their way around. The Pearl Mosque, with its jewel-encrusted walls, was turned into a hospital and tented cities pitched on the gardens became the barracks, with single men in one area, those lucky enough to still be with their spouse in another. The former residents of the Agra cantonment moved into the gardens of the Diwan-i-Khas, the Hall of Private Audience which was inlaid with lapis lazuli and jasper, while the newcomers from Gwalior were sent to Block F, the roof terrace of the Diwan-i-Am.* They soon christened it Trafalgar Square, and the officers took to it more readily than their womenfolk. The men called it 'the kennels' and said it reminded them of their army quarters when they had been training in England. For the mixed races and the natives who started to come into the Red Fort to service the growing population within, it was a question of finding space where you could. For Margaret and her mother that probably meant down below the Gwalior widows on the veranda of the Diwan-i-Am. The standard joke among the officers' wives was they lived 'stables above, and pigsties below' – they, of course, being the horses, and the regular soldiers' wives and the mixed races being the pigs. Mrs Coopland, the chaplain's widow, had this to say:

> The half-castes, or 'Kala-Feringhis', as the natives call them, who are uncharitably said to have the vices of both different races, and the virtues of neither, were in immense swarms, and had to accommodate themselves anywhere. A large number of them lived in our 'square', just beneath our balcony: the rest lived in holes, tyrconnels [escape tunnels to the outside of the fort], or on the tops of buildings all over the fort. Poor creatures!

* The Hall of Public Audience

They must have had a miserable time of it; for their habitations were very wretched.[4]

The children were not aware of these distinctions of colour in the same way, of course. Though many of them were traumatised by the violence they had seen, in the cool of the evening great swarms of children, both European and half-caste, would gather on the large terrace before the marble hall to play; encouraged by the servants, a favourite game was fighting out battles as sepoy versus Firingee.

Soon more dreadful news started to come in. In late June they learnt that over two hundred died in the Satichaura Ghat massacre at Cawnpore after they had been promised boats and a safe passage out by Nana Sahib, and at the beginning of July the Residence at Lucknow was besieged, entrapping the European population against impossible odds for months to come. Even more urgently for those in Agra, the Indore Contingent rose against their officers and drove all Europeans out, and the same thing happened in nearby Mhow. This had serious implications for Agra; these native troops, based only a few days' march away, might well stir up more trouble at Gwalior, and if they were successful in destabilising the sepoys there it would be only a matter of time before a mighty army up to twenty-five thousand strong might set its sights on Agra.

Meanwhile, the weather was terrible, with a week of thunderstorms and torrential rain as the monsoon broke, bringing in its wake the almost inevitable cholera. Worst of all was that on 4 July some mutineers who were on their way to Delhi made a detour to mount an attempt on Agra. They were a mixed group: the 72nd Native Infantry and the 7th regiment of the Contingent, who had mutinied outside Gwalior at Neemuch, the 1st Horse Artillery, four troops of the Mehidpore Horse and part of the 1st Native Cavalry.

Seven hundred troops from the Kotah Contingent had been stationed in Agra, guarding the gaol, and they joined the rebel force too. Against them, the fort could only muster 816 men to oppose a rebel army of perhaps seven thousand infantry and fifteen hundred cavalry with eight heavy guns. The defenders included five hundred of the 3rd Bengal European Regiment and a scratch cavalry of two hundred volunteers – everyone who could find a horse and knew how to ride it. There were European officers whose regiments had already mutinied or been disbanded, members of the Civil Service, clerks from public offices and others who had never before served in this way, as well as a number of 'pensioners, Christian drummers, musicians, &c., from Native regiments'. Perhaps James Johnstone was among the last.

It was a debacle; the defenders lost forty-nine men and a further ninety-four were wounded, and they were pursued back to the fort by the enemy. The next day, instead of guarding Agra gaol, the Kotah Contingent liberated the thousands of prisoners it contained. Agra was overrun; more than eighty of the Eurasians and Portuguese who had fought with the Agra volunteers, but who had then returned to their homes in the city rather than enter the Red Fort, were ravaged by the released prisoners. The civil lines were burnt down and from their vantage point in the fort the fugitives looked out across more than six miles of flames as the city was ransacked below them. For John Russell Colvin, Lieutenant-Governor of the North-West Provinces, who had been stretched to breaking point for some time, it was too much. Some of the officers in Calcutta complained to Lord Canning that there were 'screeches from Agra'; one said 'there are the Agra-Wallahs howling again!'[5] Though afflicted with mental illness for a period, Colvin actually died of cholera and was buried in the fort, and his tomb is still there to this day, a solitary, perhaps incongruous reminder of the former British presence in the midst of the Moghul buildings.[6]

After the attack on Agra the mutineers moved on towards Delhi and life gradually returned to more normal lines in the Red Fort. Colvin's deputy, Reade, took over as acting Lieutenant-Governor, but the Brigadier who had commanded the Agra force against the rebel attack lost his professional reputation. Reports condemned his 'vacillation and bad choices'. His second-in-command replaced him and, together with a Brigade Major of Engineers, set about reinforcing the Red Fort properly. The two new civil and military commanding officers made a point of taking a turn round the hospital together each day and became very popular as a result. There were several energetic ladies who made it their business to organise employment for the native Christians, of whom there were about eight hundred. History does not relate what, exactly, they were encouraged to do. Some at least would have been supervising and teaching the children, and meanwhile the wounded were cared for in the Pearl Mosque hospital by 'a goodly staff of gentlewomen who supported the work of the numerous East Indian females who had no other occupation'[7] – Isabella was perhaps among them. Mrs Muir was one who, with her five children about her, was 'cheery as a sunbeam'. Another was Lady Outram, wife of one of the leading generals, who shrugged off her achievement in walking the many miles from Aligarh to the relative safety of Agra barefoot as she busied herself with the day-to-day running of life inside the fort.

A bazaar grew up between the walls of the fort and the new entrenchments, facilitated by a commisariat lieutenant and a celebrated local purveyor and fixer, 'the great and well-known Jootee Persand', and everyone was grateful for the semblance of normal life that the market brought into their world of enforced isolation. Though by now the hot weather was unbearable, making life 'stuffy, stewy and vermin-infested', everyone found pleasure in the cool of the evenings, the children meeting to play, the men retreating to their improvised messes and the ladies gathering in the cool of the marbled terraces overlooking the river to stroll and catch the long view across to life on the far banks, with the Taj Mahal in the distance. Captain Campbell, husband of the Rose of Gibraltar, was a colourful figure around the fort, with his improvised costume of a sallu* and white trousers, two pistols stuck in his black belt and a little Scotch cap, and accompanied everywhere by his assistant, a tall, muscular, half-caste ex-pirate. It seemed that the only ones who felt unable to make the best of life inside their fortifications were the Roman Catholics, whose bishop was generally regarded as so troublesome and uncooperative that an intermediary, Father Lewis, had to be appointed in his place, but still the clerics did not help in any of the charitable works set up to keep the fort running as smoothly as possible under difficult circumstances. Charles Raikes thought that 'their inner life was a sealed book. Their outward demonstration was a long promenade of pale, sad faces, headed by two monks whose jolly visages afforded a curious contrast to the rest.'[8]

During July the rains and thunderstorms of the monsoon season arrived, and with it cholera really took hold. The limited diet and cramped quarters started to take a toll on everyone, especially the children, who suffered a troublesome fever and eruption of the skin. Medical supplies were starting to run out, especially of the all-important quinine. Then bad news started to reach them from elsewhere. On 20 July they learnt that the women and children of Cawnpore, who had survived the slaughter of a month before, as they took to the boats at Satichaura Ghat and had been held prisoner ever since, had now been massacred when Nana Sahib realised that the town was about to fall to the European force sent to liberate it. Soon after, they heard that Sir Henry Lawrence, hero of Lucknow and founder of the Lawrence Military Asylums – where

* A kind of sari made from red cloth

most of Margaret's children and grandchildren would later be educated – had died of his wounds before the residence at Lucknow
could be liberated.

But they hung on in the fort at Agra. Major Macpherson, the
Resident, managed to remain in constant touch with Sindhia and
the Dewan in the lashkar at Gwalior, and was able to send them
tactical advice for their handling of the Contingent. Luckily for the
British, when the Indore rebels did eventually arrive in Gwalior
town in August, they quarrelled with the Contingent troops about
where to attack next, thus delaying their next sally; the Indore
force wanted to head for Delhi, the Gwalior Contingent for
Cawnpore and Agra. Macpherson encouraged Sindhia to fan the
flames of the quarrel, for they understood that the best chance of
containing the rebels was by dividing them. This strategy worked
for a time but eventually Sindhia had to pay off six hundred of his
cavalry, who were Muslim, and much inspired by what the
Europeans called the 'fanatics' amongst the Indore rebels – Muslims
who had sworn jihad against the Christian colonisers. Sindhia's
cavalry set off with the Indore rebels to cross the Chambal River
near Dholpor, bound for Agra and Cawnpore. It was at this moment
that the Maharajah managed to impede the rebels' progress by
hiding all the wheels, pack animals and boats that would have facilitated their passage. He also managed to keep the rest of his own
men in Gwalior until October, and by the time they did move out
to join the massed rebel army on its way to attack Agra the East
India Company was in a better position to challenge them. By
pulling together troops from wherever they could – significant numbers of Sikhs and Gurkhas from their newer territories in the north
and west among them – the Company's forces had by now won
back Delhi and sent their victorious army on a forced march north
to the defence of Agra, skirmishing and battling on the way, but
covering sixty miles in only thirty-six hours.

After the threat to Agra was repulsed the sepoy army, swelled now by the thousands of Gwalior forces, turned to attack Lucknow. When the rebels were finally routed there, and the four-month siege of the residence was lifted, Agra could breathe easier too. The threat to the Company's rule was diminished. Fighting did of course go on in the Central Provinces, in pursuit of the Rana of Jhansi and of Tantia Topee, until well into 1858, as they were chased from Jhansi to Gwalior and round again, and Sindhia himself had to abandon his lashkar for a while and take refuge with his courtiers at Agra. But while he watched anxiously over developments in his kingdom, the Europeans were preparing to repossess Lucknow. Once it was secured, the Company sent a gigantic trail of people and property on their way back from Delhi towards Lucknow. En route it stopped at Agra, and by that time the trail was more than fifteen miles long. Margaret and Isabella joined the convoy and made their way back to the city where James and Isabella had been stationed before their posting south to Mhow and Gwalior. It was in Lucknow that Isabella would watch her daughter grow up, and also live out her own life to the then ripe age of sixty-one.

It seems unlikely that her father James, the drum major, returned to Lucknow to be reunited with his family. He may have been dead by then, but there is a persistent story among his descendants that he surfaced some years later as a batman to a retired Indian army officer in Canada. Any officer attached to a Bengal regiment that had successfully mutinied would afterwards have been in disgrace for failing to control his men so I cannot imagine that if James did indeed survive the rebellion – and that in itself is a big if – he would be able to pursue a military career in India afterwards, even though the army had been the only way of life he had ever known. Owing to the prevailing attitude to Indo-Europeans, it would have been difficult for him to find attractive alternative employment and leaving India for a new colonial territory was perhaps a more appealing proposition than a menial job.

The commanding officer of the 2nd Bengal Infantry had been Lieutenant-Colonel Atkins Hamerton, who after standing down from active service went as consul and Foreign Officer adviser on slavery to Zanzibar where the Sultan of Oman had moved his capital. The story goes that he may have taken James with him as his batman, and on his death he passed his batman over to his brother-in-law, Major Thomas Atkins of the 75th Foot, who also left the service in India and returned to the estate he owned in Dundas, Ontario. Certainly this Tommy Atkins had with him a dark-skinned man called Johnstone, who spoke fondly of having a daughter in India.

It is a little far-fetched, this futher adventure of James in Canada, especially since the dates do not quite fit, the Atkins brothers leaving India in 1841, when James was still deeply involved in life in the native infantry, but there are no convincing records for him anywhere in India. I spent months searching, and so had Basil, my newly dis- covered kinsman in New Zealand. There are a few James Johnstones recorded in all three Presidencies, but none fits my James's dates or known military record. He may indeed have been swallowed up in the chaos of the mutiny as I first thought, but if he did go off to other colonies, leaving his wife and children behind in India, he would not be the first of his kind to do so. In any case, by the time Margaret was wed, ten years later, her marriage lines said 'the late James Johnstone' and she was given away by her older brother Alexander.

Unlike her parents, Margaret seems to have been educated. Nowadays Lucknow is one of the centres of educational excellence in India, with many schools and colleges and an important teaching hospital. In 1858, in the ruins of the siege, the city would have had little to offer in the way of regular classes for a five-year-old. Perhaps, however, she had already started to benefit from the super- vision of the gentlewomen or the clerics in the Red Fort during her six months' enforced sojourn at Agra; Isabella may well have developed some nursing skills in the improvised hospital of the Pearl Mosque under the supervision of Lady Muir and Lady Ottram, which she could now put to good use in Lucknow as the city began to recover from the long siege. She may have passed these skills on to her daughter too: certainly it was the case that in due course many of Margaret's children chose to go into the medical professions, three of her sons studying medicine and one of her daughters becoming a nursing matron.

Margaret was fifteen when she married and may have been a product of the asylums that had been springing up for children of the ranks whose job, as far as the girls were concerned, was to raise them to be fit wives and mothers, skilled in 'needlework, housewifery, attention to the sick, management of children'. If her father had disappeared from her life she may have qualified for a small government allowance as an orphan, even though her mother was still alive, but it was of limited value:

> Small as it is, they only receive it until they reach the mature age of fourteen years, when the boys have no alternative but to enlist, unless, as sometimes happens, they obtain apprenticeships in the subordinate medical department. The girls, however, less fortunate than they, have only one of three alternatives – namely, to become wives, and in due time mothers, at an age when neither their bodily formation nor their mental development fit them for the functions, duties, and responsibilities they are called upon to perform; secondly, they have the alternative of starving and dying of want – and thirdly, that sad and terrible resort of the abandoned of their sex, to minister to the depraved passions of the debauchee.[9]

Margaret may have been sent to an orphanage; perhaps she was among the last little ones to be sent to Kidderpore, which had been going since the previous century and whose senior school had until just before Margaret's birth been 'a sort of harbour of refuge for bachelors in want of wives. Balls were given expressly for the purpose of securing matrimonial engagements for the pupils. Persons in want of wives frequently made their selection of an evening. Officers in the upper provinces sometimes travelled a distance of 500 miles to obtain a wife in this way.'[10]

But then Margaret did not go on to marry an officer, only a Sergeant-Overseer, the equivalent of a Sergeant-Major; I had hoped to find her securely placed in the Sanawar Military Asylum, which had a deliberate policy of reserving places for children of mixed race, but there is no mention of her in the records of the school. So her next ten years, from five to fifteen, are a closed book and the next trace of her is as the teenage bride of Sergeant Charles Kerr of the 6th Royal Regiment. He was a man much older than herself – the marriage register calls him 'full age'. They married in Ghazeepore, near Calcutta, and Margaret followed her husband as his regiment moved around from Calcutta to Lucknow, Allahabad and Bombay, and then back to Lucknow again. She produced five children before her husband passed on, leaving her to find a new husband and father for her brood. It took her four years, but in 1886 the thirty-three-year-old widow met Bombadier Tom Jones of the Royal Artillery.

He was a bachelor of thirty-two, and she had the advantage over him in the marriage stakes: she was already a veteran of thirteen years as a wife. Tom Jones must have been smitten to take her on with her five children, but perhaps he knew of the advice Kipling gave in 'The Young British Soldier':

> *Now, if you must marry, take care she is old –*
> *A troop-sergeant's widow's the nicest I'm told,*
> *For beauty won't help if your rations is cold,*
> *Nor love ain't enough for a soldier.*

It is hard to know how they met. Perhaps Tom had known Margaret's brother Alexander, or perhaps, somehow, Christopher met her through the Sergeant Quick whose wife had died on the flight from Gwalior. Whatever the circumstances, he cared enough to go through the hoops to reclaim his true name: Tom once more became Christopher George Quick.

II

Acting it Out

Once I knew all this about my great-grandmother and her mother, and what their life may have been during the Uprising, it became a fascinating exercise to go back and think about the first play I was in that was set in India, and set, as it happened, in the time soon after the Sepoy Mutiny.

Soon after the tour with Red Ladder had ended I was invited to audition for *Phaedra Britannica*, the National Theatre's production of Racine's *Phèdre*. All I knew about it at this stage was that it would be set in India, and I was being seen to play the part of a young Indian woman. I had to excuse myself from a group writing session at the Red Ladder HQ, promising that I would make up the time I missed. Hastily and secretly I changed into a pretty Indian smock, put kohl around my eyes and rouge on my cheeks and hurried across London to audition. I was offered the part on the spot by the director John Dexter, which was fantastically exciting for me as he was someone whose work I had admired ever since I first saw the National Theatre on tour as a student. But when they said I had to return at the end of the day so that Peter Hall* could have a look at

* Then artistic director of the National Theatre Company

me before Dexter's choice could be confirmed, I was in turmoil. I'd managed to excuse myself once from Red Ladder's working day, but however was I going to do it again?

I scrubbed my face clean of make-up, changed back into my dungarees and went back to resume the day's writing. Then, at five, I excused myself again, swearing that I'd explain on my return, and crossed London a second time to repeat the transformation from socialist feminist to Rajput prisoner of the Raj. Peter Hall approved my casting and then, back in my dungarees for the last time that day, I returned to Red Ladder and shamefacedly had to confess that I had been arranging my return to the heart of the bourgeois theatre. Several members of the company said they felt utterly betrayed and others that they would be coming to the first night at the Old Vic armed with rotten tomatoes.

Racine's play, following the Greek myth, has Phaedra fall for her stepson with tragic consequences. Hippolytus is her husband's child by an Amazon queen; Phaedra's desire breaks the taboo on incest and she incurs the wrath of the god Poseidon, bringing death upon herself, her stepson and her confidante Oenone. At the end of the play her husband has lost both wife and son, but how, in twentieth-century Britain, was an audience to be drawn into this tale of a classical hero brought low by the forbidden desires of his wife? How could the gods be made a real force in the play, in order to avoid presenting a museum piece? Was it possible to find a historical context that would allow the tragedy to unfold? Tony Harrison's inspiration was to set the play in British India, a few years before the Mutiny of 1857, when society was in transition from the free and easy heroic stage of the early settlement to the stricter social mores of Victorian Britain.

Theseus, mythic adventurer and bringer of civilisation to Athens, became the colonial governor; his son became Thomas, the half-caste child of a Rajput woman with whom the Governor had been involved before his marriage to Phaedra, who in our version was called simply the Memsahib. Her confidante the ayah who has looked after her since she arrived in the subcontinent. And Aricia, the girl who loves Hippolytus (Thomas) became the Rajput princess Lilamani, whose father and six brothers have died at the hands of the Governor and the last survivor of her family, is living under house arrest at the governor's palace. By the play's end she has lost the man she wished to marry, and as the curtain falls the Governor makes the first uncomfortable moves towards an alliance with this young woman. I was to play her, little realising how I was being drawn into the world of my forebears. Thinking about the content of *Phaedra Britannica* now, more than thirty years later, I can see that, had I only realised it at the time, it was full of hints that could have helped me understand Grandfather's preoccupations with obeying parents and with pure blood. I had no idea of the close parallels between the world of the play and my great-grandmother's first-hand experience during the uprising.

Before I could tackle the history there was a more immediate challenge: to find a way of managing the verse. The formal structure of Racine's original hadn't been successfully translated for an English audience since the time of Sarah Siddons; the long line of the French Alexandrine, with its twelve syllables, does not sit comfortably in English; our ear has become accustomed to iambic pentameter – the ten-syllable line – that since the time of Shakespeare has been our preferred metre. Those extra syllables were making us all stumble or run out of breath. We spent the first three weeks of rehearsal reading English plays and poems from the eighteenth century – Pope, Dryden and the like – to practise getting our breath in order to accommodate the spirit, if not the form, of Racine's text. For half of each day we worked on our voices with the National's voice coach, Kate Fleming. For me, that alone was worth leaving Red Ladder for. I had had no formal training as an actor, although I had already been taking private lessons with Kate for about three years, ever since coming down to London to commit to acting, but this was different, like boot camp. Four hours' voice every morning, then twenty lines of Augustan verse to work on at home and perform to the rest of the company in class the next day. John Dexter was a fierce judge, giving us marks out of ten. I was his whipping boy for some time and regularly scored minus fifteen; my scores eventually began to improve and in the end, like the rest of the company, I was awarded ten out of ten, then fifteen out of ten and finally twenty out of ten. Only when trained up to manage the Augustans were we allowed near the play itself.

In the end, Harrison wrote his version in the ten-syllable line that is close to our natural speech pattern and in his skilled execution it became like a heartbeat, pounding under the story. But all that immersion in the eighteenth-century certainly helped us sustain the long speeches and the heightened style that the play demanded.

The Governor is missing: in his palace there is speculation that he has gone on an adventure beyond the frontier of the territory that he governs, probably in pursuit of a woman. It's not the first time he has done it – his half-caste son Thomas, who lives in the palace, is testimony to that – and Thomas's tutor speaks freely of the Governor: 'Spreading his plausible empty love vows everywhere, / Oudh, Hyderabad, Kabul . . .'

Oudh was famously cosmopolitan well into the nineteenth century, long after Victorian convention frowned on a mixing of the races elsewhere, and Hyderabad was a Muslim kingdom where the political officers of the East India Company made long-lasting relationships with women within the Muslim court circle.[1] As for Kabul, it was then, as now, a thorn in the side of anyone who attempted to colonise it. I did not yet know that both Oudh and the

North-West Frontier had figured so large in the lives of my forebears, the first as the place where my great-grandmother Margaret
lived after the Uprising, and the latter as the homeland of my
grandfather and my father.

Everyone comments on the Governor's womanising, but while
he notoriously strays outside the strict code of Victorian family
values, he is, nevertheless, the Governor, bringing the rule of law to
unruly India. He is a person of almost legendary achievements and
appetites, from time to time assuming native ways and dress to seek
new experiences. He is called Richard, perhaps in a deliberate echo
of the explorer Richard Burton. We learn that he has had many
encounters with wild beasts, which have earned him a heroic reputation, and of course the great pastime for the officer class in India
was shikar, or hunting.[2] But it was not just the jungle beasts that
had to be brought to heel: many accounts of the early British
colonisers emphasise the near-mythic quality of their exploits in
subduing the savage elements in the people too as they tried to
establish the rule of law in India – for example in suppressing
thugee, infanticide, suttee and cannibalism. Both adventurer and
law-giver, the Governor is at the same time the upholder of conventional morality and its flouter. When he returns it is clear that
he has been taking too many liberties in a native state, pursuing the
wife of an Afghan grandee, and has been languishing for some time
in a native jail before making a daring escape – 'a season spent in
Hell', as he later describes it.

For Racine there was a tension between the monarch reason
and the democracy of the senses. This is largely lost to us in the
modern world, but in India at the height of the British Raj, that
conflict is re-energised as a friction between Victorian values and
the sensual country on which they were imposed. Tony Harrison
also made sexuality dangerous again; the Memsahib's passion for her
stepson made the more shocking by the taboo on inter-racial sex in

a world that was only too aware of differences in colour and creed and by this means the downfall of Thomas and the Memsahib became clearer.

In the original myth, Phaedra is the child of Minos, the king of Crete, and Pasiphae, who had been cursed by Poseidon to fall in love with the Cretan Bull, a liaison that produced the Minotaur. She thus inherited a dual nature, split between reason and sensuality, and her life was a battleground of propriety versus illicit desire. In Harrison's version, Phaedra (the Memsahib) is appalled by her desire for her half-caste stepson, even as she is helplessly drawn to act on it, and blames India and its gods: 'The Gods of India possess / My darkened mind and make it powerless.'

The coming of the memsahibs in the early nineteenth century was one of the main reasons why cheerful intermarriage with the local women came to an end in British India. Indeed, it was one of the reasons that my great-great-grandparents Jacob and Lakshmi had led a life in the army band instead of as members of the officer class, and why James and Isabella, the next generation, have become lost in the accounts of the uprising, rendered invisible by their colour. Had they been living even fifty years earlier their life would have been so much more free in every way as someone in the play says of life in India: 'Paradise it may have been / Until the memsahib came on the scene.'

The Memsahib in *Phaedra Britannica* becomes more and more helplessly conflicted, and India itself becomes a malign presence: she exclaims 'Ravenous India', 'I felt you mocking, India' and 'It's India! Your cruel gods / Athirst for victims'. The room in the governor's palace where the play unfolds comes to feel like a prison, and there is a powerful sense of India, its jungle and its gods outside, ravenous, sensual and remorseless. It must have felt more than a little like that for those women trapped first in Gwalior and then sheltering in the various dak bungalows and caravanserais on their desperate rush cross-country to Agra.

The action takes place just before the Mutiny and, like the
events in Gwalior, just before the monsoon breaks, so tensions are
already running very high and the audience is brought right into
the contradictions that life in the British Raj threw up. Everyone is
affected; no one escapes unscathed. By the end of the play Lilamani,
the native princess, is the only shred of hope left for both the
natives, who hope she will become a figurehead to rally them
against the whites, and the Governor, who woos her as he realises
that the only hope for his administration lies in a reconciliation
with the native forces.

Before this attempt to forge new bonds, the Europeans have all
equated the native with the animal. When Thomas refuses her,
the Memsahib calls down India's revenge on the 'halfbreed'; he is an
animal fit for nothing but to be hunted down and 'mounted along
with all / The monsters on the Sahib's study wall.' She even turns
on her only confidante, her ayah, calling her a reptile who has
brought 'her ladyship' down to the level of her 'blackness' – and
after this the ayah does disappear, swallowed up in the jungle.
When the Memsahib learns that Thomas loves the Rajput princess
she denigrates Lilamani – 'The charms of any native concubine /
Are no doubt more agreeable than mine' – and tries to imagine
what 'native sorcery' has protected them. Not an unfamiliar view
among women after the uprising, perhaps, for whom it was a short
step from suspicion to racial hatred. Even the Governor's feelings
for his son are tainted by a knee-jerk racism. When he thinks that
his son has incestuous feelings for the Memsahib, he calls him a
beast in human shape who should have gone 'Running back to the
jungle and its savages / Beyond our influence and aged laws, / Back
to the world of bestial lusts like yours' and exclaims, 'How could his
kind absorb our discipline / It's in his blood.'

Thomas is to be banished from British India to the 'far north-
west' across the Indus, 'the forbidden river'. He refuses to tell his

father the truth and feels he has no choice but to flee. He urges
Lilamani to join him and fight but though she knows she would be
leading a just cause, to 'set free our subdued people from white
tyranny', she will not contemplate any hint of shame in the eyes of
her people. Far from being 'bestial', it is the 'natives', Lilamani and
Thomas, who are the morally pure. Both invoke the nobility of
their parentage, its purity, chastity and courage. The moral order is
reversed: it is the Governor and his Memsahib who are devilish and
depraved. Lilamani tries to convince the Governor to revoke the
curse on his son, warning him that 'Our gods may well give ear to
your wild wish / Because they find you brutish, devilish.' But it is too
late; the Memsahib dies by her own hand and the hero is destroyed.
On his journey, Thomas comes face to face with a monster ram-
paging out of the jungle. The native people say it is Shiva in his
avatar of monster and Thomas, inspired by the heroic exploits of his
father, decides to challenge it alone. But Shiva prevails. He thrusts
a trident[3] into each flank of Thomas's horse, Thomas is thrown
and the maddened creature drags him along the ground until his
head is a bloody pulp. With his dying breath he asks that Lilamani
be looked after and begs that his father 'treat her kindly and
restore . . .' – he dies without finishing his sentence.

The Governor loses both his wife and his son. He knows that he
has 'murdered his own future' and he takes the first tentative steps
towards reconciliation with Lilamani as the monsoon breaks and the
rains pour down. He knows that she must see him as 'some savage
brute', but finds common ground with her in that both of them have
'borne the cost of crossing certain bounds best left uncrossed'. The
play's sliding scale of transgression has brought the two survivors, on
either side of the racial divide, to the point at which the Governor is
left pleading with the young Rajput princess, though the times force
them apart, to 'ford those frontiers of blood into my heart'.

*

The hoped-for reconciliation between the colonisers and the subdued rebels in the closing lines of Tony Harrison's play was never
to develop in real life. After the Sepoy Uprising had been quelled
there was to be no going back to the carefree associations of the
eighteenth century. The rigid separation by race, class and caste
became an irreversible fact for the generations that came after. My
great-grandmother was born just before the Mutiny, on the cusp of
change from tolerance to virtual apartheid. By the time she bore
her last son, my grandfather, in the early 1880s the strictness of the
Victorian age had pushed out the inclusive ways of the time before
the memsahibs. While her father and grandfather may have found
a way of life that allowed them to acknowledge their dual heritage,
by the time Margaret Johnstone was marrying for the first time,
ten years after the Mutiny, her choices would have been severely
limited. By then the 'halfbreeds' had sided with the British, and
their reward in the aftermath of the Mutiny was to be given a
defined, if somewhat ghettoised, place in society, running the newly
expanding railways and the telegraph service. The aspiration among
those of mixed race was towards white society – natural enough,
one might think, in a society where the white man was so often the
boss. On the whole the Anglo-Indians looked down on the natives,
while the white community looked down on the Anglo-Indians,
but this pecking order was to backfire disastrously when, finally,
independence was granted to the subcontinent. The Anglo-Indians
did not find it easy to have a voice or even a power base; not for
them a return to the easy social customs of the eighteenth century,
when my forebears, the Scottish Johnstone brothers, each kept a
zenana in Calcutta. But even for the Johnstones the times were
changing: they retired back to Scotland once they had made their
pile, and the offspring they left behind in India had no choice but
to hang fiercely on to that very 'Britishness' which was the only real
legacy their white fathers had left them. If Margaret wanted to find

a white husband it was going to have to be an English soldier from the ranks. And that's what she did find, twice over, and the second one was Christopher Quick, also known as Tom Jones.

No wonder that by the time Grandfather was growing up it was as well to downplay any hint that native blood, however dilute, might run in his veins, for he would be marked by that 'touch of the tar brush', put down as a 'country-born' if not a 'blackie-white' – by definition emotional, irrational, unreliable and not capable of holding any position requiring authority or serious responsibility. No wonder Grandfather was such a stickler for good manners and obedience too. Apart from his accent, which he was never able to lose, there were to be no tell-tale slips to reveal his origins. His status, in the shifting values of Indian society as history left the Mutiny behind and moved on towards Independence, relied upon not being found out. The price would be too high.

Many years later – about thirty, in fact – I came to play another person caught in that ambiguous middle ground between two cultures and two races, the Dominican-born writer Jean Rhys. She had been a favourite writer of mine at university – I had devoured everything she ever wrote, mostly tales of women surviving or attempting to survive in a world of men where they had no skills but their femininity. I loved her spare, elegant prose, her forensic wit. It was not until I came to play her that I appreciated how much her writing was a masterly exercise in transforming the painful experiences she kept in her own dark cupboard into art, often giving an unflinchingly ironic take on her own inadequacies. When I was first reading her I had not really registered that she was herself an outsider from a former colony far across the sea making a life of sorts in Europe. By the time the Shared Experience Theatre Company asked me to play her I had been piecing together the history of Christopher Quick and Margaret Johnstone for a while and was starting to understand the effect that their situation must have had on my grandfather's life, and, in turn, on his attitude towards his youngest son, my father.

Shared Experience work very much in a collaborative way: although scripted, the work is based in physical theatre so that a huge input is demanded from the cast during the rehearsal process. (Some of it went almost too far: I certainly wondered what we thought we were doing one day in rehearsals as we trotted around the room on all fours, pretending to be dogs in a pack, sniffing each other's bottoms and baying at the moon.) By and large it was a marvellous way to work, allowing one's imagination to roam over the given material and bringing one's own experience to bear. I felt the connections with all that was in my family cupboard very strongly, and it helped me to overcome the reservations I had about playing a historically documented person. It is a very different ball game from playing a fictional character, where one somehow has permission to let one's imagination free; but then, as Edward Burne Jones said, one tries to work always 'in that strange land that is more true than real', and *After Mrs Rochester* allowed me to enjoy the attempt to be 'true' as much as any role I have ever played.

Like my father, Jean Rhys became a Catholic as a result of her schooling and, like him, was sent far away from the place of her birth to the other, unknown, place the family called home – England. Once there she felt for ever an outsider, and for ever unable to return to where she was born. Her last, and some say greatest, novel was *Wide Sargasso Sea*, named for a mythic sea midway between her birthplace and Europe, in which seaweed was thought to entangle ships and prevent their passage in either direction; neither forward to a new identity, nor back to what had been home.

After Mrs Rochester opens with the sixty-year-old Jean living alone in England, drinking too much and frightened to open the door to her daughter who has come a long way to visit her. In an attempt to explain her fears to her girl, she goes back in memory to her own childhood on the Caribbean island of Dominica, long before she had transformed herself into the writer Jean Rhys. She meets Ella, the small child she then was. This child self is fleeing from her mother who is going to beat the daylight out of her, and Jean tries to explain to her young self why her mother would do such a thing: the mother had been beaten herself as a child, beaten because her family were frightened. 'Imagine living thousands of miles from home on a tiny West Indian island. Imagine twenty thousand people and only one hundred of them white. It was terrifying.'

This rang many bells with me. I thought of my great-grandmother Margaret Johnstone fleeing as a small girl from the mutineering natives in Gwalior. I thought of the fate of the mixed-race society to which her family belonged, who in former times had enjoyed a much higher status in the land of their birth and were numerically superior to their white 'mother race'. Of the huge anxiety among the whites, later, that they would rise against their masters. And of their subsequent confusion about where, exactly, they belonged in the colonial scheme of things: still calling England home even though they had never been there; preoccupied with their status, insisting it was higher than that of the native people, but never accepted by the whites; for ever suspended in a limbo that would eventually lead to their alienation from both whites and Indians.

In the play, Ella is told in no uncertain terms how far she and her kind have fallen by her only friend, a black girl from the island: 'Real white people . . . don't come near you. They don't even look at you. You nothing but white nigger now. And black nigger better than white nigger.'

Her mother is a woman obsessed with keeping up appearances, and fearful that she is losing status in front of the natives. She refuses to hear her daughter say that 'half the village [are] my brothers and sisters' and, despairing because the girl will 'never learn to be like other people', she sends her away to a Catholic convent on the other side of the island. It might as well have been the other side of the world – or the Himalayas. Ella learnt to make her school a refuge from all the ambiguities of her life at home, and I found myself making many connections with what I was starting to learn about my own father's childhood. There was his ambiguous position as a country-born person who adored the land of his birth, but never completely belonged there, who feels at home in the jungle and forest but must soon leave it behind to enter the decorous, disciplined and guilt-ridden world of a Catholic school far from home and family then complete his education a continent away, in England, where he is always conspicuous, with a voice that marks him as an outsider, and where the very landscape confounds his fantasy of what the mother country would be like. And there is a parent – remote, forbidding and violent, but who somewhere loves the child – from whom the child becomes estranged for ever.

Ella – young Jean – had described England to her island friend before she ever got there: it is white with snow and freezing cold, and one day she will go there to be a lady. My father was to be sent to England to be turned into a proper medic, not a sub-assistant like his father had been, and, just as happened to Ella, he was to be abandoned by his family before he was properly able to support himself because they 'cannot afford to keep' him. As she sails away from Dominica for ever, Jean feels that there are some words that are too sad to say, 'like mountain . . . or . . . mother'. I thought of my father, a year older than Ella, leaving the Himalayas, and the grave of the mother he lost when he was five years old. I am getting ahead of myself here, but all this happened and it all made an eerily accurate fit with what I knew of Jean Rhys's experience.

Jean's particular demon is that she has brought with her the 'beast' – Bertha Rochester – who has been her *Doppelgänger* all her life; her native self, a creature of passionate feelings, needy and raging, who can never hope to fit into polite society. She is Jean's guilty secret and Jean wants desperately to get away from her, but wherever she turns Bertha is there. She is at the drama school which expels her after telling her that she sounds like a 'nigger', and there with her first lover, a gentleman who is happy to keep her for a few years but who then dumps her without ceremony, destroying her fantasy that they will live happily ever after. She is by her side in her life as a prostitute in London, and later in her marriage to a half-Dutch man who gets busted for currency dealings in the aftermath of the First World War, just when their life has taken an upswing, leaving her destitute in Paris, her adopted home. Wherever her bohemian life casts her, there is Bertha, her secret self, who sabotages all Jean's efforts to transcend her colonial, Caribbean life, to fit in and be normal . . . and English.

Jean seeks a haven through her affairs, and though greatly loved by men all her life she fails to find enduring love. In real life Rhys married three times and had a daughter whom she adored after her own fashion, but who spent much of her childhood in Catholic orphanages and schools – sometimes because there was no money to care for her, but later because her mother was incapable of sustaining a normal family life. At the end of the play the daughter shows that, despite everything, she loved her mother; she has always understood that Jean was a special case and forgave her for it.

Jean Rhys was above all a special case because she was a writer. She attempted to make sense of her life by writing about it, believing that, 'When you've written it down it doesn't hurt any more . . . but you're finished.' And the great conceit of Polly Teale's play is that Bertha, Jean's native self, became the heroine of her last book, published when she was seventy-six, which finally brought her fame, recognition and her own money for the first time, really, in her life. Jean felt the irony of all this success coming, as she felt, 'too late' and in the play she is asked which she would choose if she could: to be successful or to be happy. Without hesitating she replies, 'To be happy, of course. To be happy.'

For Jean Rhys, Bertha was an emblem of all that she could not ignore about the accident of her birth: a Creole – a hybrid, if you will, of the native place and the aspirations of the European colonists. It is when Jean Rhys transplants her to Europe as the wife of the English gentleman in her prequel to *Jane Eyre* that the catastrophe occurs. Bertha goes mad, has to be incarcerated in the attic and burns the house down, dying in the process and blinding Mr Rochester.[4]

I cannot help wondering whether my great-grandmother suffered anything of the same tension between native ways and European aspirations. Growing up, as she did, in the aftermath of the Uprising she would have known in her marrow that to be native was to be considered untrustworthy. Married to an English non-commissioned officer from the age of fifteen, she would have learnt a certain discipline, and her children would have had the benefit of the new schools for the offspring of ranking soldiers. They must all, mother and children alike, have been Anglicised to some degree. But then Margaret was widowed at twenty-eight with five living children, and others who had died of the usual enemies to the young, such as diarrhoea, malaria and fever. She would have had at most six months' support from her dead husband's regiment. Somehow she managed for four years, unmarried; perhaps her experience at her mother's side in the fort had encouraged her to become a nurse of sorts. It was often the sergeant's wives who became the midwives and nurses to officer's wives: they were not as crude as the ranking soldiers' women, nor too grand to lend a hand to the senior officers' wives in labour and in the early stages of recovery from childbirth.

In any case, Margaret must have been very used to the ups and downs of life in the married lines of the cantonment. It was a far cry from the pampered domestic life of even quite lowly civilian wives, who could count on a battalion of servants – the bearer, the cook, the kitmutghar, the masalachi who, as underling of both the cook and the bearer cleaned up the kitchen and did lamps, fires and bath water, the dhobi for the laundry, a dherzi to do any sewing, a sweeper to do the dirty jobs and a mali or two to tend the garden, as well as a wet nurse and an ayah to care for the children. In fact the main problem for civilian wives seems to have been how to fill the day when, apart from issuing instructions and housekeeping money, their traditional role was admirably – amply – filled by others in their household. Flora Annie Steel, who was to prove herself an exception to nearly every rule of female behaviour on the subcontinent – she travelled about with her husband rather than fleeing to the hills in the hot weather, she took the trouble to become fluent in several local languages: and, above all, she was interested in the culture of the people around her – wrote *The Complete Indian Housekeeper and Cook* with Grace Gardiner to pass on her strategy for domestic survival. In her book she prescribes the following formula to the wife keen to avoid ennui and to enjoy 'a healthy, comfortable hot-weather day':

Rise at five o'clock, or half-past, after a night spent under a thermantidote, or on the roof with a punkah. Take tea and toast. Then, on some pretence or other – if possible with an object – stay out of doors riding, driving, or walking until half-past seven or eight o'clock. Take some porridge and milk, or some other light refreshment, remembering that in the hot weather it is a mistake either to feel empty or to take a full meal. Then bathe, either in a shower bath, or in a tub of really hot water. Look after the house, either before or after your bath.

Not later than ten o'clock, breakfast and work steadily on
something till noon. From twelve till two lie down and read, or
sleep. It is a horrible mistake to sleep after a heavy luncheon; you
wake unfit even for your own society. Lunch at two, or half-past.
Work till four, bathe, dress and go out. So, as Pepys says, dinner
at eight, and to bed about half-past ten.[5]

Margaret's life was far different from that of the officer's wife
which was found by some to be 'excessively boring, trivial, claus-
trophobic, confined and totally male-oriented. The army wife
was not expected to do anything or be anything except a decora-
tive chattel or appendage . . . Nothing else was required of her
whatsoever . . . riding . . . horse sports . . . looking after her children and running a fairly decent dinner party, there her role
ended.'[6] Lower down the ranks, the wives had to graft; small wage
packets meant there was not much of anything: no facilities nor
people to help with domestic chores, very few educational opportunities for the children, and no one even to complain to. There
was only the most limited provision of married quarters: in some
postings whole families might find themselves having to muck in
with life in the barrack room, with its drunkenness and ennui and
time-wasting and routine violence. Not a good place, we would
now think, to raise a family. Fortunately Margaret's children, the
Kerrs, were able to get away to school at the new Lawrence
Asylum in the hills for much of the year, and from there the boys
could gain entry to the medical school in Calcutta, but the urgent
thing for Margaret was to find herself some means of support. It is
likely that she survived the next four years by making herself
useful as a nurse-cum-midwife, and then she found her protector
in Christopher Quick. It must have been a relief to have found
him, and he must have seemed quite a catch – the newly elevated
bombardier with no attachments, healthy, hearty and with only

a few years' service to go before he could be discharged on a pension.

It must have been a very big deal for him too. After sixteen years in the service of the artillery as Tom Jones, he was not only finally able to marry but he was now able to reclaim his true name, no questions asked, so that the marriage would be legal.

Not that marriage would be easy for either one of them. One of the most graphic descriptions of what it meant to be a bombardier's wife came from Spike Milligan, who described his mother's life in a desert cantonment, where she waged a constant battle to maintain safe drinking water, by swatting flies and attempting to keep sand out of the chatti, the stone water jug. He thought the life was 'a very great stress for her, and we were comparatively well-off'.

A particular source of stress for Margaret must have been her new husband's drinking for though Tom, now Christopher, had a real stab at respectability, over the first years of married life he was promoted to bombardier, demoted, reinstated and then screwed up spectacularly, ending up in jail for five months and deprived of the prospect of promotion for another six years. Margaret's fortunes fluctuated alongside those of her husband, but luckily for them both they survived and, five years later, he was able to leave the service for good with an honourable record, more than twenty-one years after he had enlisted back in Newport.

The army turned a blind eye to drink so long as the soldier made it to parade, and after the life she'd led Margaret must have been tough too. She makes me think of another woman I played, who was married to a battle-scarred soldier and chose to take the consequences of his war experience without comment or complaint. Based on a historical character, her name was simply Madam, and she was created by Phyllis Shand Allfrey, another writer from Dominica, the island that had been home to Jean Rhys. She made her returning soldier an addict not to drink, but to opium.

Filming *The Orchid House* for Channel 4 meant spending quite a few months in the Caribbean. It was my first time in the West Indies; I had yet to travel to the East Indies of my father's childhood but I found many echoes. Like my father, Madam is the child of a doctor, who was respected in the local community and who had a more than averagely intimate connection with the local people who were his patients.

Her brother Rufus, proprietor of the local newspaper, has taken this intimacy further and made babies all over the island. Although Madam has hidden herself and her household away on a remote estate and 'was never one to spend the year waiting for a Government House *at home* or a bridge-party', she is not unsympathetic to the looser native ways. Each time her cook Christophine has a new baby by a different father – six in all – Madam attempts to discipline her: '"I don't mind you not being married . . . but I do think it rather unfair to the children to have these incessant fights over the various fathers . . ." But Madam could not keep from smiling when she made these speeches . . .'

The secret at the heart of her life is that her husband is addicted to opium. Absent for six years, fighting in the First World War, he has returned from the Far East an addict, and his habit has been serviced ever since by regular visits from Mr Lilipoulala, the Haitian drug vendor. Left with three little girls to raise while her husband was away, Madam now runs a matriarchal household together with Mamselle Bosquet, the children's governess and Lally, their former nanny, and all enable the master's drug habit; no one will acknowledge that there is a problem.

Sadness is not in Madam's nature, and she is brave. But this strength has also been the undoing of the family: 'Now if Madam for once would be the weak one, and throw a fit, and need to be cherished; if Madam had been the weak one right from the start . . . all of her life and the children's lives would have been different.'

In fact, Madam's denial about her husband's abject dependence on opium makes her send away the one friend from his past who comes to propose taking him away from the island in order to allow him to recover from his addiction. She just does not allow them to meet, telling the visitor that her husband is not available.

The story follows the family over twenty years, and the crisis hits with the return of the grown-up daughters, all of whom have left the island and married. One daughter believes that she is helping her father when she exploits the island's reputation for spirits and frightens Mr Lilipolala, the drug dealer, into falling to his death off a rope bridge. Another returns from her passionate leftist life in London to stir up the dispossessed natives, and the third, who has married money, whisks her father away by helicopter to the Bahamas for treatment for his addiction only to find, when they land, that he has died during the flight. Through the years Madam has come to an accommodation with the governess, who has always loved the Master; time has outlasted jealousy and the two are united by their love for the same man.

I loved being on Dominica. I loved its green fecundity and the high volcanic peaks of the interior, the 365 streams and rivers, one for each day of the year, the rainbows that appeared with the showers every afternoon, the long tradition of independence from the time when runaway slaves would make their way there from other islands to find safety in the lush forest hills. I loved the fact that the only remaining settlement of Caribs exists on the island, and I also loved that I was playing a real person, one who was still remembered by islanders, and that this created a curious overlap of art and life which resulted in me being treated as if I actually was Madam. The forest made me dream about the jungle of my father's childhood, the ambiguousness of being of a place but in a colour minority; perhaps being of mixed racial heritage there, and certainly of being in a lowly social position. The father being a doctor, respected by the community and the sense of time moving things on so the old social hierarchy no longer works, and, even though you are isolated and surrounded by a native people who are not necessarily going to respect or even remember the old times, feeling that this place is home.

I felt curiously at home from the moment I got to the island, and have been back several times. The first visits were for old times' sake but when, ten years on, I was cast as Jean Rhys – who by coincidence had known and encouraged the younger writer of *The Orchid House* – I began to see some sort of pattern. *After Mrs Rochester* was to take me to places I had never been before, in my imagination and in my acting, and around the world to meet my ex-India relatives now settled in Australia and New Zealand, who were able to fill in some of the gaps about the family in India. It was through them that I pieced together Margaret's story. So life fed into work and work back into the family's history.

12

To the Frontier

Margaret Johnstone's first marriage, to Charles Kerr, brought her a reasonably comfortable life. She was to spend her early years as a wife in Lucknow, the town where she and her mother had settled after their period of siege in the fort at Agra. It was here in 1866 that they met when Charles was stationed there as a Sergeant Overseer in the public works department. Charles was originally from Sheffield, the son of a fender-maker, and had trained as an engineer in the army engineering college at Roorkee, to the west of Lucknow in the state of Uttar Pradesh.* After several years the young Kerrs moved into the north-west, where they were to spend nearly all of their life together. There was plenty of work for a man with Charles's training: roads to build and railways to connect up, canals to dig and aqueducts to construct all over the Punjab in order to irrigate these potentially fertile lands.

If Christopher had not met the widowed Margaret Johnstone Kerr, born and bred in India, it may well have been that he would have headed home to England on his discharge from the army. By

* Now in Uttarakhand

then he had served twenty-two years altogether, including the extra
Buckshee year tagged on the twenty-one-year life contract. He had
done the first five in Britain, and since arriving in Bombay in 1880,
he had served four years in Bangalore and two in Hyderabad; in
other words, so far what he had seen of the subcontinent had been
southern and central India. When he met Margaret he was a veteran
with eleven years' service; he was 'on the strength' of the regiment,
and thus finally considered eligible for marriage. When Margaret
was widowed in 1882 she was the mother of four daughters and two
sons. By the time she agreed to marry Christopher four years later,
she was double bereaved for her last child, Charlotte, had died at
the tender age of three. It is not clear if any of her Kerr children
were to live with the newly wed Quicks. The eldest, Mig, was just
turning eighteen and within the year was married and went on to
produce nine healthy children of her own. The next, Ernest, was
about to be seventeen and would have been nearing the end of his
studies in the hill station school before going off to train as a surgeon in Calcutta. Lillian and Archie were fourteen and twelve,
and must have been safely parked at the Lawrence School. That
left the youngest surviving daughter, Daisy, now six. She would
be joining her older siblings at school early in the new year. So
perhaps it was not such a daunting prospect for the novice husband
Christopher – just one small girl at home to get to know as well as
his wife.

They married in Ferozepur, the cantonment outside Lahore, on
29 September 1886, a month after Christopher's thirty-second
birthday. Within a year their first son Frank was born and
Christopher was posted south to Tamil Nadu and promoted to the
rank of bombardier. Soon after this there was a massive reorgani-
sation of the artillery regiments, which meant that the family had
to move again to the other end of the empire: Roorkee, in the
foothills of the Himalayas, which for Margaret at least would be

very familiar as it was the place where she had spent a number of years as a new bride the first time around.

In 1888 Margaret gave birth to her last children, twin boys called Bertie and Eric. Perhaps it was in the way of celebrating their birth, or perhaps it was the huge shift of regiments – whatever the reason, now lost in unrecorded time, Christopher got himself into serious trouble and ended up on a charge, demoted, confined, away from his new family for some months. It must have been a bleak time for Margaret, for within six months of his birth one twin, Eric, was dead – he had been a blue baby. So there she was: her husband on a charge, a little one dead, her bigger Kerr children off her hands.

Ernest was now well into his medical studies and was to be the first in what was to become a family tradition of working in medicine, although being born and educated in India he and his brothers after him would find that as country-born – and country educated – all that was open to them was the Sub-Medical Department. What lay ahead for Margaret's doctor sons was a slow crawl upwards, from fourth to third to second and finally to first sub-assistant surgeon in five-year increments. Unless extraordinary circumstances arose they would always have that limiting label of 'sub' defining them as second-class. Nevertheless, Ernest set a precedent that both of his half-brothers would follow, and his sister Daisy was to marry a doctor too, but all that lay in the future and Margaret must have been passing lonely days with two-year-old Frank and her remaining infant, Bertie. Christopher was confined for nearly six months and came back to her demoted and disgraced. It took him three years to regain the rank of bombardier and he spent those years, and then the remaining four of his time in the artillery service, in the northwest of India, first at Ferozepur and then at Delhi. When Christopher was finally discharged at the end of August 1897 he decided to remain in the country he had lived in for more than half

his life. Like many other long-termers from Britain who had married
in India, he stayed on in the land of his wife's birth: perhaps
because it would be more comfortable socially than the strangeness
of an Anglo-Indian partner back in Britain; perhaps because
Christopher's own family had in any case long since abandoned
Britain for Canada, so there was really no one to go back to; or perhaps, simply, that he, as well as his extended family, were too deeply
embedded in the life they had made in India to think of moving
and of calling a small North European island home.

For the next sixty years – the remainder of their time in India –
the Quicks were all to stay in the north-west. Christopher's first
civil post was in Lahore and he ended his days right on the frontier
at Peshawar. The children were schooled in the foothills of the
western Himalayas and settled down to work and marriage not too
far away. Nowadays, if we think of what we in the west know of the
subcontinent it will probably be something to do with that particular area of India, the northerly third of the map, which in earlier
times had been called the Bengal Presidency. We think of Bengali
curries, perhaps, or of derring-do on the North-West Frontier, of
the Gurkhas as fighters and of Sikhs with their colourful turbans
and their business acumen. Or we will think of the Twin Towers
and the jihad wrought by the Taliban and al-Qaeda. For the Quicks
in India, from the time of Christopher's marriage to Margaret
onwards, Bengal, the Punjab, the Frontier with Afghanistan and
jihad were the background to their daily lives and because the
family's life was so intimately wrapped up in this frontier region of
the empire, I want to go back over the history of this turbulent area
a little.

The East India Company armies had gradually defeated the
Mahrattas across much of their empire in northern India, from
Calcutta back towards the Indus in the west, so that by the middle

of the nineteenth century the Company's aggressive policy of acqui-
sition led to them holding much of Hindustan, a crescent that
stretched across India south of the Himalayas as far as the Punjab.
Now they started to turn their attention to the lands to the west of
Mahratta territory, lands that were in other, equally fierce, hands.
Much of the Punjab – the 'Land of Five Rivers' – had been taken
from Afghanistan by the Sikhs. Ranjit Singh had won Kashmir in
1819 and Peshawar, the Afghan emir's summer capital, in 1823.
When Afghanistan sought to retrieve Peshawar in 1837 they had
hoped for the support of the Company in driving out the Sikhs, but
the British were beginning to realise that they needed Afghanistan
secured for their own purposes, to block Russia from advancing
into India. The Company armies attempted to take Kabul and
install a puppet emir, in the First Afghan War of 1839 to 1842. It
was the beginning of the western power's hopeless attempts to dic-
tate to this fierce and proud nation, who still claim never to have
been conquered. With the murder of the political agent, the British
had to leave; there was a notorious retreat from Kabul of more than
four thousand troops and ten thousand followers, including the
wives and children who had been encouraged to settle in the new
territory. The retreating British were massacred by Gilzai warriors at
the Gandamak pass. Apart from a few hostages, the surgeon
William Brydon was the only person known to have arrived safely
at Jalalabad ninety miles away.[1]

Meanwhile, the Company's attention turned to the Sikh kingdom
of the north Punjab. The British had already taken over Sind on the
southern boundaries of the Sikh lands, and when the Sikhs were
defeated in 1843 they had to sell off Kashmir and the northern towns
of Gilgit and Ladakh to finance their losses. The north-west was
starting to belong to the East India Company; they installed a political agent in the former Sikh capital of Lahore and two years later the
elite Corps of Guides were raised in Peshawar to patrol the frontier.[2]

In a second war the Sikhs moved on Peshawar, offering to hand
it back to the Afghans if they would help drive out the British, but
they were defeated at Gujerat and the Afghans were driven back
across the border. By 1849 the British were in a strong enough position to annexe the Punjab, making it a Province of British India
with a commissioner at Peshawar. A cantonment was soon laid out
two miles from the ancient walled city and became one of the
largest in the whole of British India. Indeed, until Quetta was established in 1877 it was the only major one along the North-West
Frontier.

Luckily for the Company, they had signed a treaty with
Afghanistan in 1856, guaranteeing that the British had no aggres-
sive intentions towards their proud neighbour; lucky, because in
May that year the Sepoy Mutiny broke out and at least while the
Company struggled to suppress it they knew they had ensured neu-
trality on their western border. Having disarmed the troops at
Peshawar as soon as they showed signs of rising, the treaty with
Afghanistan allowed a flying force under their distinguished commander General John Nicholson to march five hundred miles in a
month or so to get down to the relief of Delhi. This was the most
important tactical struggle in the Mutiny for if Delhi, the nerve
centre of the Moghul Empire for more than three hundred years,
was lost then the Company stood no chance of recovery. The Sikhs
had almost unanimously placed their implacable and resourceful
fighters at the service of the British, their new overlords, and it was
the combined efforts of these northern peoples – Punjabs and
Gurkhas as wells as Sikhs – that made it possible for the British to
field a mighty army against the sepoys. In fact, without the fierce
fighting skills of the newest recruits to the coloniser's armies Delhi
could never have been wrested back from the native troops who
held it and it would have been impossible for the Company to go on
to win back Lucknow and Gawkier.

Without them, the Sepoy Mutiny could hardly have been sup-
pressed. This ferment is significant because, although my tale is
essentially a domestic one, it is set against a militaristic, colonising
background. Jacob and James and Margaret and Christopher lived
out their lives against a constant attempt at expansion, an unending tussle by a small minority to control the hydra that made up the
peoples of the subcontinent. As soon as one area was under some
sort of control another presented a challenge; for the soldiers,
James, Jacob and Christopher, this had meant a life on the move.
For their womenfolk it had meant life as camp followers, or waiting
to greet their husbands and fathers on their return. Everyone, it
seems, had to improvise, to face violence and the possibility of loss.
Although those who came next remained geographically settled
there was still a constant undercurrent of stress, for in the north-
west border territories, where my grandfather and my father lived,
there was the rumble of jihad.

Once upon a time, jihad signified something other than its modern
meaning of a holy war against the infidel. In its essence, it means a
striving for the faith and in the writings of the prophet Muhammad
a distinction is made between the lesser jihad – the early physical
struggle to convert the peoples around him by conquering them –
and the greater jihad – the continuing, inner, spiritual and moral
struggle to lead a good life. For many in the Islamic world this
second meaning had prevailed especially after the Moghuls established their empire in Persia in the twelfth century. They were
Shias, Muslims who followed the teachings of Muhammad's descendants, and they were very different from those who, as Sunnis,
followed the interpretations of the religous leaders in the various
schools of law that grew up in the years following the Prophet's
death. The Persian flowering and expansion through its empire was
much more towards a mystical, inner spiritual path than armed

aggression, but then in the eighteenth century a more fundamentalist school of thought grew up in Arabia and was later carried deep
into India.

It was a unitarian and intolerant interpretation of the Koran
and came to be named after its first formulator, Abd-el-Wahhab.
Not only did it promote the idea of the oneness of God – so that
there was no room to venerate saints, for example – but Wahabiism
believed in absolute obedience to the religious leader. This might
include following him in armed jihad against all apostates and
unbelievers, if called upon to do so: it was seen as a moral duty to
root out any deviation from the true path, not just in the idolatrous
Nazarenes (as Christians were termed) but among any Muslims
who did not follow the same strict laws. Wahabists interpreted jihad
as an uncompromising fight against all who stood in the way of
Islamic expansion. You were promised the protection of God in
the fight, and to be killed in the course of this work was a guaran-
tee of an honoured spot in paradise, in the company of other true
believers. With this zealous focus on a dogmatic and puritan ideol-
ogy, and an implacable enmity towards all who do not agree to
follow the same, fundamentalist view of their faith, the Wahabists
were effectively sidelining some of the central tenets of Islam: charity, tolerance and mercy.

Though they were widely condemned as heretics, the Wahabist
school has survived despite many attempts to wipe them out; they
are the forerunners of the Egyptian ideologue Sayyid Qutb,[3] who
inspired Bin Laden, and of the Taliban and al-Qaeda, who impinge
so significantly on our twenty-first century western consciousness.
In my great-grandfather's time, one champion of this fundamentalist school of thought was to succeed where all else had failed in
giving a common voice to the warring tribes of the North-West
Frontier.

The Sikh conquest of the Punjab in the early nineteenth century

had already had the effect of starting to focus the eternally skirmishing Muslim border tribes on a common enemy – the Sikhs –
instead of on their traditional inter-tribal feuds. By the end of the
1820s a leader emerged who declared jihad against all *kafir* (unbelievers), whether Sikh or British. This was Syed Ahmad, who on his
return from making the haj* and a spell preaching in the mosques
of Arabia, had travelled from Bombay round to Calcutta and then
back across northern India, much of which was in British hands by
this time. He found a wide audience for his message of jihad as a
religious duty; when the Jat kingdom fell to the Company Syed
Ahmad said: 'During the last few years fate has been so kind to the
accursed Christians and the mischievous polytheists that they have
started oppressing people . . . My heart is filled with shame at this
religious degradation and my head contains but one thought, how
to organize jihad.'⁴

Ahmad regarded British India as a 'domain of enmity' and
sought to establish a 'domain of faith' from which to launch his
assault. (Incidentally, he tried to persuade the Hindu Maharajah of
Gwalior, Dualat Rao Sindhia, to ally himself with the movement on
his way. This Sindhia, father of the one so involved in the events of
the Mutiny, and in the lives of the Johnstones, declined the offer.)

There was a widely held belief amongst the Muslims of India
that the Mahdi – 'the expected one' – would arise and unite the
forces of Islam to lead them in triumph at the end of the world
(with Jesus, the lesser prophet, at his side). There had been several
who claimed the title, but since many were expecting the Mahdi
to emerge from the west, the movement needed to find a safe haven
west of the Indus in order to preach with due authority. Once in the
Pathan borderlands they found it at Sittana in the territories of
the Buner clan, who agreed to let them settle on the Mahabun

* The pilgrimage to Mecca that is one of the pillars of Islam

Mountain, a high outcrop that bulged on to the plain just to the north-west of Peshawar. This area was already known to the British as a 'hotbed of fanatics', a place that had been given in perpetuity to a Saiyyed* saint, Pir Baba.

Syed Ahmad had followers among other tribal groups such as the Yosufzai to the south of his stronghold at Sittana, and he persuaded a meeting of the Pathan elders to acknowledge him as both the imam, a title that in these Shia areas conferred a degree of infallibility on his religious pronouncements, and the Amir ul-Momineen; that is Commander of the Faithful, who would lead the war of liberation far beyond the immediate area. He thus fulfilled the requirement of mahdiism that only a person who was both spiritual and temporal leader could pronounce jihad. Soon there was a force of over six thousand fighters on the mountain, and for the first time the word mujahidin, meaning 'holy warrior', was heard.

Both Christopher Quick in his civilian life at Peshawar and several of his sons and stepsons were to spend their time dealing with the troubles along the border that developed from Syed Ahmad's zeal, for though he was routed by the Company's troops a remnant survived, scattering into the rocky terrain of the borderlands, regrouping, recruiting and renewing their belief in militant jihad as a religious duty. This is a pattern that has continued to the present day, with all attempts to eliminate the fundamentalists resulting in at best only partial success.

By the time Christopher had to deal with them, the fundamentalists had for fifty years been taking advantage of the loyal cell of supporters that had first been established by Syed Ahmad in the town of Patna. Their supporters in Patna were to continue to be the

* Saiyyed = descendent of the Prophet

supply base well into the twentieth century, providing troops, weapons, money and food through an underground network that crossed India from the north-east to the mountain in Buner, operating right under the noses of the Company but unnoticed, or at least underestimated, by them. This network did more than anything else to transform what had been a minority sect into an efficient organisation for Islamic revolution, with a supply of manpower drawn largely from the poor.[5]

A new element in the spread of fundamentalism came in the years after the Uprising when the British forced many Muslims to leave Delhi. Some of those who had been educated at the British-founded Delhi College, and had learnt there the value of proper organisation and a formal structure of management, established a mosque at Deoband, some miles north of Delhi. This mosque was to have far-reaching effects, for the system of study was new to the madrassahs in that their students – the talibs – were often from poor families and stayed at the Deoband mosque until fully trained instead of moving on to study with other masters in other mosques. At Deoband they could study in Urdu, the local tongue, although of course they learned the Koran in Arabic. Soon the Deobandis gained a reputation as authorities in shariah law and, once trained, its talibs moved on to establish other madrassahs on the same pattern. Within a very short time there were twenty or so Deobandi schools along the frontier and today there are many thousands in Pakistan alone, alongside other, more moderate, teachers and schools.

The Deobandi were more than religious teachers for their message was a political one too, and with their emphasis on the oneness of Islam they were able to transcend national boundaries and stress that Islam is a pan-nationalist faith. They were intolerant of deviation from their own interpretation of what it meant to be a good Muslim and it is worth noticing that the first graduates of the

Deoband school set up the Samaratut Tarbiyat (literally meaning 'the results of the training'), a militaristic organisation whose volunteers were the *fedayeen*, the men of sacrifice prepared to die a martyr's death for the faith.

I am emphasising this development along the North-West Frontier, for as I have learned more about it my idea of the challenges faced by my great-grandfather and grandfather has changed radically. Far from imagining their lives as remote, romantic and far removed from anything in my own twenty-first century life, I now see their experience as part of a historical continuum that to some extent defines my life too. This is not just because I am of their blood, but because those events at the end of the nineteenth and beginning of the twentieth century have coloured so much of our present reality, living as we do in a world where fundamentalist violence has been brought to our doors. I was rehearsing Shaw's play, *You Never Can Tell* in a south London rehearsal room when the bombs of 7 July 2005 went off. As I walked home across the city, from Clapham to my house in north London, along with everyone else in the metropolis, it occurred to me that indeed you never can tell.

Christopher Quick's part in all this upheaval was as a policeman. He responded to advertisements put out by the government for the 'recruitment of Europeans and East Indians of respectability and education' and became an inspector in the military (rather than civil) police in 1897, earning around a hundred rupees a week – the top man was on fifteen hundred rupees, just to put it in perspective. Inspector Quick reported directly to this Deputy Inspector General of the Western Circuit, keeping a diary of all 'duties, occurrences and information' in the area his station at Rawalpindi served. The reports were sent on to London, rather than being dealt with by the local magistrates, as civil matters were, for the western Punjab and all of the frontier was buzzing with activity yet again.

It was only four years before Christopher had enlisted in the police that the border between the British-held territories and Afghanistan had at last been defined by the Durand Line. Relations with Afghanistan had long been complicated by what the British perceived to be the threat of Russia, who had been advancing its empire to Afghanistan's northern borders, taking over first Tashkent and then Samarkand. By 1873 the Russians had agreed that Afghanistan should remain outside their sphere and the British had developed their 'Forward' policy; this meant getting there before the Russians did, either by aggressive action or by creating buffer states along the frontier. After the Second Afghan War and the subsequent murder of Cavagnari, the British envoy in Kabul, it was Christopher's Commander-in-Chief, 'Bobs' Roberts who had emerged as a hero of the frontier when he led an expeditionary force to retake the capital and later marched them 313 miles in twenty-one days to relieve Kandahar from an attack by a force of some ten thousand Afghans, earning an almost mythical reputation by these feats of quintessential border dash and pluck. The result of this last engagement was that it was finally possible for the British to attempt a firm delineation of the frontier between Afghanistan and British India. They had gradually been taking control of the lands between Afghanistan and Kashmir that lay to the north of this troublesome region in the course of the 1880s and 1890s, constructing forts and some rail links to speed communication, and in November 1893 the Durand Line was established.

One consequence of the troubles was that the frontier tribes were being radicalised in their relations with the western power on their border, and by the time Christopher was involved in policing the frontier each of the border tribes had an emerging charismatic

leader. In Kabul, Amir Abdur Rahman Khan was a formidable
ruler who succeeded where few had done before in melding his various vassal tribes into one nation; wherever he was opposed he
crushed them, whether Shia, *kafir* or simply rebels of his own
Sunni faith. The amir, who had been put on the throne by the
British and given a free hand so long as he didn't intrigue with the
Russians, had mixed feelings about the Durand Line, which now
separated his domain from that of the border Pashtuns. On the one
hand it meant that he could assert complete authority over the
peoples on his side of the line but at the same time he was happy
to foster the idea of jihad as a holy duty. In 1897 he summoned representatives of the border tribes to a theological colloquy in Kabul,
at which the envoy of the Turkish sultan was also present. The
envoy's presence encouraged all those who attended to believe
that Russia and Germany had forged a new alliance with Turkey,
and that Suez and Aden had fallen from the control of Britain; in
short, that the British Empire was crumbling and the time was
ripe for a mighty blow that would transcend national borders to be
struck for Islam. News of this assembly was carried back throughout the tribes and soon after a fanatical mullah emerged among the
Buner, who soon became known to the British as the Mad Mullah.
Mullah Sadullah was a charismatic leader who believed he had
been visited by a number of saints, including Syed Ahmad, who
had instructed him to reclaim the Swat Valley and the Vale of
Peshawar immediately to its south from the usurping British. He
gained extra credibility by having at his side an adolescent boy
who, he claimed, was the rightful heir to the throne of Delhi,
which had stood empty since the exile of the last Moghul king
when Delhi was retaken during the Sepoy Uprising. His crusade
soon attracted the remnant of Syed Ahmad's followers who had
survived, somehow, on the Mahabun Mountain. Their leader,
though in fact dead, had been mythologised in the years since his

first camp there in the 1820s, and his power kept alive by follow-ers insisting that he had not been destroyed when his troops were routed, but was only awaiting an opportunity to re-emerge and lead the jihad. Somehow the Mad Mullah was able to tap into this and other holy reputations, like that of the Akhund of Swat, a famously devout leader from the early part of the century who had more often that not condemned the fundamentalists for the extremity of their views and their actions. Somehow the scruples of his descendants were overcome and the fire ignited by the Mad Mullah spread throughout the border region. The young Winston Churchill, who had been serving as a lieutenant in India, was posted to the frontier as a reporter for the *Daily Telegraph* in London and the Indian paper, the *Pioneer*, and had this to say on the state he found there: '. . . a vast but silent agitation . . .Whispers of war, a holy war, were breathed to a race intensely passionate and fanatical.'[6]

The holy war that followed spread from Swat to Buner, then into the land of the Mohmands closer to Peshawar and eventually among the Afridis, setting a new precedent since the lands of this fierce tribe, immediately to the south of the Khyber Pass, had never before been penetrated by British forces. It took a mighty field force and months of guerrilla fighting to subdue them, but in the end they were put down – for the time being, at least.

When Christopher found himself posted from Rawalpindi to Peshawar, he was in the thick of this resistance to the British. Some seventeen years later a grown-up Bertie took his own place in the colonial force and he was to face trouble from exactly the same quarters. But I am getting ahead of myself. Even before the trouble fomented by the Mad Mullah could envelop the British forces of the frontier region, Christopher became embroiled in a domestic tragedy of his own: his wife Margaret died suddenly, only six months after she had become a civilian wife for the first time. Right at the start of a new career that should have brought him stability and a domestic life, Christopher found himself alone with two small boys to raise and an implacable enemy just across the border.

13

The School Mask

... his training had set the public school mask upon his face,
and had taught him how many were the 'things no fellow
can do'.

Rudyard Kipling, 'The Brushwood Boy'

When Margaret died in 1898 her youngest sons, Frank and
Bertie, were ten and eight years old and their father was
forty-five. Exactly six months after losing his first wife Christopher
married again, someone widowed like himself, called Connie Smith
Mellett. They were marrying when troubles were again brewing
along the length of India's western border: between 1899 and 1905
there were more than six hundred raids along the frontier. On top
of these political troubles, there were others: a severe outbreak of
plague in 1897 and two years later came the Great Famine.

In 1901 the whole area was dignified with being the newest
addition to the British Empire in India, the North-West Frontier
Province, divided off from the Punjab and with its own Chief
Commissioner who resided in Lahore. Lahore by now had the
largest cantonment of any in India, and for the next ten years

Christopher Quick moved from here to various postings in the province, including Nowshera, twenty miles east of Peshawar, and, for his last and longest posting, to Peshawar itself, right on the boundary of British rule and the Pashtun lands. Since Partition, the Pakistan government has continued to administer part of this area on the same model. It is treated as a semi-autonomous region whose day-to-day affairs are answerable to its own Pashtun mirs – councils of clan elders – rather than to central government, and policed mainly by tribal levies.

With the establishment of the new province, the police service was thoroughly overhauled. Reports had convinced the authorities in London that the old system was cumbersome and inefficient, a feeling that was no doubt triggered in part by the persistence of raiding activity along the frontier. Under the stewardship of Sir Henry Lawrence, first senior administrator of the Punjab when it was annexed by the East India Company, who firmly believed that there should be as little interference as possible in the area's day-to-day affairs, a dual system was set up. The military preventative police was mainly constituted of Sikhs disbanded from their own armies after the conquest of the Sikh kingdom; they provided guards and escorts in the gaols, and were held ready to combat any serious threats to the authority of the Company, while the civil police, answerable to the deputy commissioner and district magistrates, were 'matchlock men' recruited from the old chokidars or watchmen, and charged with the maintenance of law and order. A report of 1851 on the Punjab force had boasted that it was 'with a police force of 14,000 men, internal peace has been kept from the borders of Sindh to the foot of the Himalayas, from the banks of the Sutlej to the banks of the Indus, and this when a disbanded army of 50,000 men had mingled with the ranks of society – when countless adherents and servants of the late goverment were wandering unemployed about the country.'[1]

With the separation of the Frontier into a province in its own right, the problems of political control were a challenge. It was the inspiration of its British administrators to establish a system of districts and subdivisions, which included making the area to the south and west of Peshawar into five subdivisions, plus one to the immediate north, henceforth to be known as the Tribal Areas. Although it had attracted romantics and adventurers for many years, it was altogether too poor and too wild for most civilians. It was perceived as a primitive, barbaric, arid no man's land that was periodically threatened with incursions by Pashtuns from the west. And from now on, this would be where Christopher worked as chief clerk, side by side with his munshi* Jalal-ud-din.

If Lahore was established as the capital of the province, Peshawar was the hub of the traffic that passed through from the empire's eastern boundaries. It lay on the old trading routes that went north into China, west through the Khyber into Afghanistan and south into Sind then on into Persia. It commanded the fertile Vale of Peshawar, green and productive in stark contrast to the dusty, rocky outcrops to the west and north. And Peshawar was also a social centre where travellers and pilgrims of every sort would bring with them news of the activities in Buner and Swat, Tirah and Waziristan, the Tribal Areas – and no doubt news from farther afield, of Kashmir, Nepal and the Himalayas to the east, of the Russian states, Tajikistan, Uzbekistan and Turkmenistan to the north-west, and further still of Tibet and China, even from Arabia and the horn of Africa across the sea south of Sind. It was the gateway through which many conquerors had entered the subcontinent, and would keep Christopher occupied until his death. There was a view that 'in police service on the frontier death was always just

* Secretary

around the corner',[2] but in fact he managed to avoid turning that corner for the next twenty-six years.

When I visited the region in late 1999 I tried to find tangible evidence of Christopher's activities there. On my first day in Peshawar I went to meet the Deputy Inspector General of the Frontier Reserve Police, Mr Ahsan Mukhtar, and his secretary for home and tribal affairs, Mr Mansoor. The office was busy with people, all of whom sat patiently on chairs round the walls awaiting their turn. There seemed to be no concept of privacy. Gradually the room emptied as each person's business was completed, and still more paperwork joined the large pile on Mr Mukhtar's enormous desk. Finally there was just me left and I was lucky, for the Deputy Inspector General was very interested in the history of the North-West Frontier Province and of the police. Both men listened to the story of my great-grandfather with the utmost concentration, and though he doubted that records were held in his department's local archive as far back as the birth of the province in 1901, Mr Mukhtar immediately contacted ten regional police offices to see if they could find any trace of Christopher Quick in their records. They found nothing, though, and the same thing happened a few days later when I met the Senior Superintendant of Police, Mr Malik Saad, and his deputy Dr K. Orekse, who was whippet thin and sported spectacles and a moustache that made him look as if he was wearing a Groucho Marx mask. At thirty, Saad was already on his second tour of duty as Superintendent because he was so highly regarded, and Orekse was only thirty-three, the grandson of an Inspector of Police who had lived through many troubles and died, finally, at ninety-nine. The doctor had swapped careers from medicine to the police two years earlier because he believed that the country of Pakistan could not improve until the calibre of the police force improved.

The relative youth of these two senior policemen reminded me of how very young some of those who had won the frontier for the British and gone on to run it were, often having been sent to man an outer station of the frontier at the age of twenty-one or so. Veterans such as my fifty-year-old great-grandfather were relatively rare, since so many failed to reach that age in active service, but despite the Superintendant's tenacity, we could find no trace of him in the records here either. Five of us spent the day reading through armfuls of report books that were brought in from the outlying stations, but there was no sign of Christopher's signature on any of the reports.

I had another fruitless day with the deputy commissioner in the district court building, who spent several hours trying to explain to me the process of law as it applied to the Tribal Areas. She said many times that it 'opens the mind like anything'. I had no reason to think that she was being ironic, though the intricacies of the system were quite beyond me and as she talked to me she dealt with an unending stream of peons who brought in sheaves of papers for her to sign. I never found out what the thousands of documents were that required her signature, but she kept on saying that it 'opens the mind like anything'. Anyway, she did in the end overcome her suspicion of me for not having a proper letter of introduction from the Secretary for Tribal Affairs at the Home Office and she sent off for the record books that covered the eleven establishments of the Peshawar police force in the time of Christopher's service there.

Even though I could not track Christopher while I was there I got a good idea of what his life and duties might have included: living in accommodation above the police station, whether running the lock-up in Peshawar or another in Mardan; dealing with court orderlies; overseeing the appointment of bungalow guards for each house in the cantonment (three for most houses but nine if it was for a senior official); setting guards over sick convicts who had to be let out of jail for treatment; arranging night patrols or the pitching of tents or the carriage of official letters; keeping records of the prisoners and a tally of which native officers had been lent to the cantonments or borrowed from the city force. And somewhere, writing all this down on pieces of paper, which have been lost in the mountain of paperwork that ran the empire.

By the time his father Christopher was posted to the police service in Peshawar, Bertie was ten years old. He would have seen his father only in the coldest of the cold weather, in December and January, for he was away at school for the rest of the year, at the Lawrence Military Asylum in the foothills of the Himalayas. If Bertie and Frank, as well as their older half-siblings, the Kerr children, had been born a generation earlier there was a good chance that they wouldn't have made it to school in the hills at all, that they wouldn't even have made it to adolescence. While the children of officers were sent back to England by the age of six at the latest to keep them healthy, the children of the other ranks would have had to battle throughout the heat and the monsoon, and the diseases that inevitably followed in its wake, in the army lines wherever their parent happened to be serving. If they were lucky they would receive a very basic education in the regimental school, but it would be elementary at best, with tuition from the likes of the sergeant-major and with very little provision at all for the girl children.

The hot weather and its aftermath was the most pernicious time of year, especially for the young. In Peshawar there is a cemetery in which the surviving gravestones show a sharp increase in deaths during June, the hottest month, and another climb in October to December, at the end of the rains. Anyone who could escape the suffocating heat by going up to the hills did so: ever since the 1820s the British had taken advantage of the therapeutic coolness there, building sanatoria all along the Himalayas, first at Simla in 1819, then at Mussourie and Darjeeling, Nainital and Murree. As they were first utilised by the army they became known as stations. While the civilians of British India soon made use of the army's laying of roads and, later, railways, and colonised these hill spas, turning them into havens of British middle-class life with their malls and clubs, their picnics and bridge parties and amateur the-atricals – even moving the political capital up to Simla for the hot season, with the enormous baggage train involved in shifting every-thing halfway up a mountain for six months, only to shift back down to Delhi come October – the hill stations remained defined by that early military presence.

Until the military asylums were founded it had been out of the question for a child of the ranks to go up to the hills. In the middle of the nineteenth century Dr Julius Jeffreys went out to report on the state of the British army in India and was shocked by how vul-nerable the young were:

The mortality of barrack children is appalling, especially in the months of June, September, and October. At Cawnpore from twenty to thirty have died in one month. In short, the soldiery leave no descendants of unmixed blood. Of the half million of soldiers who have gone out to India, where are all their legiti-mate descendants of pure English blood, who by this time would have multiplied into a numerous population if born in New Zealand, Canada or Oregon, reciprocating industrial advantages with the mother country, of their parents, how much more secure and durable than the military tenure of India can ever yield? Let myriads of feeble voices from little graves, scattered through India's arid plains, supply the melancholy answer – 'here'.[3]

Dr Jeffreys' observations were partly motivated by an awareness of how precarious the colonisers' position was. There were barely twenty thousand Europeans to rule a population approaching three hundred million, and a population that, the colonisers feared, might well rise against them again. His argument was that these infant deaths were a prodigal waste of a valuable resource: with no locally raised white population the motherland had continually to ship people out from England; how much better if there had been a civilian workforce on the spot to secure the empire.

The point about 'descendants of unmixed blood' succumbing to death was that those with a share in native blood inherited a sturdier constitution and thus a sporting chance of surviving. But however loyal these 'Eurasians' or 'East-Indians' had proved during the Mutiny, however unwavering their allegiance to some idea of home inherited from the white side of their families, they were considered to be less desirable as representatives of the motherland.

Some fifteen years before Jeffreys, Major Henry Lawrence of the Artillery Regiment[4] developed a scheme to benefit barrack children. He had raised money from civil and military subscriptions to found the Lawrence Military Asylum near Kasauli, the hill of Sanawar in the Simla hills not far from the middle-sized village that would soon expand hugely as Simla became the established summer residence of the government. It was an idyllic spot, a temperate retreat where apricots and cherries grew wild, and peaky army children might thrive.

The scheme quickly took off, supported by the subscriptions, but in its early days heavily underwritten by Henry Lawrence himself. The Lawrence Military Asylum received its first intake in 1847 and there were many glowing testimonials from early visitors, who contrasted the carefree healthy life in the station with the wan existence such children had endured before in the plains,

such as in H. B. Edwardes' report on the first ten years of the
Sanawar school,

> ... a happy, healthy home where hundreds of little boys and
> girls upon a green mountain side ... run about without hats or
> bonnets [this a reference to the mandatory topee worn in the
> plains] and catch butterflies instead of deadly fevers; where they
> grow up straight and strong, to be hale, hearty useful men and
> women, instead of dying at the age of two or three, or dragging
> on a pale and sickly existence.[5]

The subjects included history, singing, drawing and Urdu, as
well as the three Rs and a liberal provision for religious instruction
for Evangelists and Catholics as well as Anglicans for, as one
Commanding Officer consulted by Lawrence had pointed out,
Roman Catholics formed the majority in every corps of the
Company's army at this time. It was also a place where East Indian
offspring would be educated beside their European contemporaries,
for as another Commanding Officer observed, this one in charge of
the artillery company at Dum Dum, two-thirds of the children in
his own regiment who might benefit from such a school were of
mixed parentage.

As they grew older more specialised preparation for the various
government departments was available: public works, land survey-
ing, merchant's accounts, printing and bookbinding, building and
carpentry. This did not apply to the girls; a few of them went on to
train as teachers, nurses and, later, doctors, but in the main they
were being prepared for the marriage market. The Lawrence School
at Sanawar was soon hugely oversubscribed and in due course
another three Lawrence schools were established, always sited in
the healthy, cooler hills.

One of them, at Murree in the hills above Rawalpindi and a

day's journey from Peshawar, developed an additional department for preparing recruits for the medical school in Calcutta. This path was followed by their much older half-brother Ernest, then Frank and finally Bertie Quick. As country-borns, this training qualified them to join the Sub-Medical Department of the Indian Army which, in a country obsessed with rank and title conformed to the general pattern. It was carefully distinguished from the pukka Army Medical Department by that soubriquet 'sub'. The teaching standards were regarded as inferior by those trained in England, even though the syllabus they followed was based on that of the English teaching hospitals. There was no question of being able to move up to an appointment in the regular army's medical department based on simple ability: once a sub, always a sub.

Bertie completed his five years' training in Calcutta and was warranted into the service in 1911. It was almost inevitable that he would look for work back on the North-West Frontier as his father and stepmother were still in Peshawar, with Christopher due to retire from the police in a year's time, and his brother Frank had already been warranted in the province. The skills of these two brothers would have been very welcome for it was proving difficult to find high-calibre recruits to the frontier service and they both progressed as rapidly as it was possible to do, up through the ranks of the Sub-Medical Department. In 1910 a 'Report of the Civil Hospitals and Dispensaries of the North-West Frontier Province' acknowledged the extra difficulties and challenges of the region:

> There is great difficulty in enlisting Assistant surgeons, Sub-assistant surgeons and compounders in this province. This must obviously be the case so long as these posts are not filled by natives of the NWFP and so far local men are not forthcoming. Men will not come from the Punjab unless we can offer them better pay.

The Quick brothers were virtually natives of the North-West Frontier Province as much of their childhood and all of their schooling had been there, until they went on to Calcutta's medical school. They were wise not to have studied at the newer establishment in Lahore, for as the report for 1909 confessed,

> . . . up to date not one of the NWFP scholars of the Lahore Medical College has succeeded in obtaining diplomas of that college. Assistant surgeonships have had to be filled by men who . . . answer to advertisements . . . inserted in the leading papers . . . The class of men has been anything but satisfactory . . . Those who answer have been the college failures who found it difficult to obtain employment anywhere.

The outbreak of war in Europe made it even more difficult. Many men were taken away from India for service on the European and Mesopotamian fronts. By 1916 – by which time Bertie found himself serving as a medical officer on the front line up in the hills of the Frontier – a Pashtu allowance was introduced for civil assistant surgeons not native to the province, in an effort to attract more and better recruits to the service. Extra allowances also came into force for sub-assistants 'in the wilder localities'. But the standard remained dubiously low: at Lahore Medical College it was difficult even to find recipients for a locally funded scholarship as still nobody had yet managed to pass the exams. There was also the recurring problem throughout the subcontinent of a certain scepticism about the value of honesty; even down to the thirties, when my Uncle Basil was training in Lahore, he thought it likely that he and his friend Whiskey were the only two candidates who did not bribe someone to crib their exam papers.

*

I don't know how good a doctor my grandfather was, or whether his training in Calcutta was indeed inferior to that in the British teaching hospitals. But it is clear that, from the beginning, the Lawrence schools aimed high for their pupils. The academic model was the English public school and the school motto was – and still is – 'Never Give In'. Bertie would have sat Cambridge external papers at both elementary and higher level, and the school's militaristic ethos would have instilled its own discipline.

It was supervised by the Military Department of the Government of India, and was run on military lines. The boys wore a scaled-down version of the artillery uniform in homage to their founder's regiment: 'a blue coatee with red facings, grey trousers and a leathern helmet. The girls wore a jacket of drab edged with scarlet . . . and white bonnets and tippets.' The children were organised into companies and divisions, which were run by boy NCOs and girl orderlies. They paraded to the sound of bugles and were expected to conduct themselves with military precision. There were over fifty rules governing school behaviour. Here is the song of the Murree school:

> *To set the cause above renown.*
> *To love the game beyond the prize.*
> *To honour, while you strike him down;*
> *The foe that comes with fearless eyes.*
> *To count the life of battle good.*
> *And dear the land that gave you birth.*
> *And dearer yet the brother-hood;*
> *That binds the brave of all the earth.*
> *To-day and here the fight's begun.*
> *Of the great fellowship you're free.*
> *Hence forth the school and you are one.*
> *And what you are, the race shall be.*

The Ghora Gali Lawrence School at Murree had been founded three years after the Sepoy Mutiny and perhaps this colours the idea of 'the cause' in the song's first line: the cause was what, exactly? British civilisation? Christianity in its evangelical, Victorian mood? And the idea of 'the game' that is to be valued above winning the prize is of course founded on the idea of being a 'good sport' but has also echoes of the 'great game', the constant challenge on the Frontier of keeping would-be interlopers at bay, earlier the Russians, but now, again, in Bertie's time, the jihadists of the Frontier clans. These were surely 'the foe that comes with fearless eyes', and who, as the British had already discovered as they engaged with the peoples of the north-west, whether Punjabi, Sikh or Pashtun, were worthy opponents who deserved to be honoured. Every time they sung the school song, then, the pupils were reminded that the 'fight's begun' already, and urged to 'count the life of battle good', to regard themselves as part of the brotherhood of the brave, part of the 'great fellowship' – and, of course, to love India, 'the land that gave you birth'. But they are also reminded in the last lines that they and the school 'are one'; it is as if they are being taught to regard their destiny as inextricably connected to the school and, given that they were all to spend all but three weeks at Christmas, a weekend at Easter and a week in June there every year until they were seventeen, it is almost as if the school was more of a parent than the parent. Certainly when H. B. Edwardes was praising the first Lawrence Asylum he had stressed that the children were going to be in a place 'above all where they should be well-educated; where they should see no drunkenness and hear no oaths, and where all the impressions of their childhood should be those of religion and not those of vice.'[6] For Bertie and his brother Frank it may have been a particular blessing to be away from home, for Christopher was not averse to a drink himself.

*

While the motto of the Lawrence schools was 'Never Give In', at the Sanawar school, written up on the wall of what is now the school gym, but was once Gaskell Hall, is a quotation from Rudyard Kipling's *Kim*: 'Send him to Sanawar and make a man of him.' Any graduate of the Lawrence schools would have been outraged at the suggestion that they were in some way lax; they were country-born, inescapably, but absolutely separate and different from the natives.

It was a view not necessarily shared by those who came out from Britain. Sir Olaf Caroe, last governor of the North-West Frontier Province, had this to say about the ill-fated actions of General Reginald Dyer, who was in charge when as many as a thousand demonstrating natives were herded into a square and shot at by British troops in the notorious Amritsar massacre of 1919:

> Now, General Dyer was what we called a country-bred man . . . that means . . . he had been brought up and educated in India, and had never been home to England. And I think that these people were much more . . . they would react much more like Indians in this sort of situation than we did . . . And he took a much too ruthless action . . . I mean objectively . . . quite unnecessary ruthless action.[7]

This prejudice against people who were country-bred – and therefore almost certainly of mixed race, even if diluted through several generations – came not only from people out from Britain. Those who were themselves country-born at times shared these prejudices, as here, in the thoughts of the son of an Anglo-Indian railway family looking back in the 1980s:

> . . . in the last fifty years many Anglo-Indians were the result of sometimes pretty trashy Europeans and undoubtedly trashy Indians, prostitutes and women of the bazaar and so on. So that

while there was a category of Anglo-Indian that was of high
quality, there were a very large number who were pretty wishy-
washy. They had no strength of personality, they were
accustomed to being underdogs and they had that hangdog 'chip
on the shoulder' attitude to life. Some of them on the railways
did first class jobs, and some of them as individuals were delightful. But not many companies were prepared to regard them as
high management quality . . . There was a very strong colour
bar . . . Conditions in those days strongly resembled present conditions in South Africa, with this difference: that while in South
Africa it is imposed by government, in India it was accepted by
a mutual arrangement and by tacit consensus.[8]

This sort of attitude must have made Dr Bertie Quick, Sub-
Assistant Surgeon, feel he was marked out by the accident of his
birth. At the same time, he had been educated at schools modelled
on the English public school, a system that admired the ideal of the
English gentleman and officer, with all its notions of obedience,
duty, sportsmanship, discipline and fair play. In his wish for an
exemplary life Bertie must have felt a tension between these two
opposed circumstances and it perhaps created in him the wish,
above all, to belong: not to be balancing on the edge of what was
acceptable but to be instead at the heart of the society he found
himself living in.

He was an angry man, a frustrated man, and this feeling was to
inform all his actions and influence for ever the lives of his children. When, finally, I met him in England he was still angry and
frustrated, and it was that, without any acknowledgment from the
adults around me, which I picked up on.

14

Bertie

'The life of a frontiersman is hard and he treads it daily on the brink of eternity.'

Lord Ronaldshay[1]

I am thinking of Albert Norman Quick, assistant surgeon, fourth grade, in the Indian Medical Department, and attached to the First Peshawar Division.

I am thinking of him in August 1915. He knew what he was doing when he had volunteered to be posted back to the Frontier. There had been turbulence there for as long as he could remember; when his father Christopher was posted out west back in the 1890s there had been talk of the Pathan Revolt, and then the Malakand Campaign when Chitral, Malakand, Swatis, Mohmands and Bunerwals all united against the British. That had run on for years, until 1900, and then just as things seemed to be quietening down the unrest had started again, rumbling on to 1910 in what was called the Holy War and leading to very serious efforts by Britain to retain power in the region. The kick-start had come from a new leader of the Deobandi movement, Mahmood ul-Hasan, who had

David Bailey

hot by David Bailey for the October 1969 issue of *Vogue*, just after I had moved to
ondon.

As Princess Lilamani in Edward Bond's *Phaedra Britannica* at the National Theatre.

My Red Ladder days.

Above left: With John Shrapnel in *Nicholas and Alexandra*. He and I were the token peasants. I have just been crushed on Bloody Sunday when, led by an agent provocateur, the workers attempted to storm the Winter Palace.

Above right: As the Mother in *The Screens* by Jean Genet, in a version by Howard Brenton, Bristol Old Vic, 1973.

Photographed by
Cecil Beaton, 1979,
for French *Vogue*.

With Laurence Olivier in *Brideshead Revisited*.

Above: With Julia Malewski, who played the young Eva in *Kindertransport*.

Left: We deliberately tried to make this playbill look like a 1950s photograph. Thanks to David Knopov and Christine Allsop.

Below: In *After Mrs Rochester* with, from left, Madeleine Potter as Young Jean and Sarah Ball as the Madwoman.

obert Cops-Fawcett for Theatre Royal Presentations (Bath) PLC by arrangement with One World Arts (UK) Ltd presents

DIANA QUICK

The Woman Destroyed

by SIMONE de BEAUVOIR
translated and performed
by DIANA QUICK

The language of this play may be
offensive to some people

rected by
ANESSA FIELDING

graphs by CHRISTINE ALLSOP
work by DAVID KNOPOV

designed by MICHAEL VALE
music devised by BRIAN CONNOR
lighting by NILS DAHL

Nigel Norrington, Camera Press, London

The caravanserai near Jhor, where the fugitives from Gwalior sheltered on their way to Agra, and the first Mary and I visited outside Dholpur.

Ganesha at Hampi, Karnataika – widely revered as the Remover of Obstacles, and Lord of Obstactles, patron of arts and sciences and the deva of intellect and wisdom. He is honoured at the start of rituals and ceremonies, and invoked as Patron of Letters during writing sessions. I have included my drawing of him here for good fortune.

Ganesha

The shower at Dholpur

The shower at the Raj Niwas Palace, as recorded by Mary.

Raj Niwas Palace, Dholpur.

ary in the bay at Alyha Fort, Maheshwar, 2007.

With Bill and Mary
Nighy in Dominica
during the filming of
The Orchid House.

The Khyber Pass. Photograph by kind permission of Maurice Broomfield.

emerged in 1905 from the mosques run on strict puritan principles that had been proliferating along the western fringe of India since the Sepoy Mutiny. By the spring of 1914 ul-Hasan was encouraging small bands of volunteers to make their way to the borderlands and link up with the remnant of what the British called the Fanatics; he himself went to Jeddah on the Red Sea coast of Arabia, and then sent back one of his team with a mandate from the Turkish government at Mecca, urging the clans along the frontier to invade the Punjab. In Mohmand, two mullahs, impressed by the involvement of the great Islamic power in Turkey, rallied their people and prepared for war.

None of this could get to Bertie, who had been married for less than a year to eighteen-year-old Mildred (Millie) Rumbold, who was, like him, a child of the army ranks. They were modest people, him the son of a bombardier in the Royal Artillery, her the daughter of a sergeant-overseer in the Commissariat. Was he near her in the late-August heat, with temperatures soaring ten degrees above normal, as they awaited the birth of their first-born, due any day? Assistant surgeon Quick had been back in the thick of it for five years, dealing with injuries brought in from all over the Tribal Areas. Back in January 1915 there had been the wounded of the North Waziristan militia; true, they had won against great odds, but they had done a long march before the engagement and it was only their dash and spirit that had got them through. There had been as many dead bodies as casualties and Bertie had still been getting used to the sheer volume of work he was expected to deal with when the border clans rose. And as if that wasn't enough, there had been trouble to the north of Peshawar at the same time. Since before Christmas there had been talk of anti-British preaching by certain Mullahs all along the Mohmand–Swat–Buner boundary: nothing serious, they said, except for one raid in January on the Fort at Shabkudur, but everyone had been warned of the need for 'constant

watchfulness'. As a result, the Khyber Moveable Column was
brought down to the fort in case. Just as well, as it turned out, for by
mid-April they were called out to deal with a lashkar of nearly two-
and-a-half thousand tribesmen at Hafiz Kor. And just when they
had dealt with that, there was more trouble in Swat – not a raid, but
disturbing rumours of quarrelling among the tribes. It seemed to
Bertie that that young lieutenant Winston Churchill had got it
right when he had described the clans as living in 'a state of warlike
leisure'.[2]

Then, in June, Brigadier-General Young had nearly come a crop-
per defending the crucial road north to Chitral, the silk road that
led on to China. These skirmishes never seemed to involve more
than two or three thousand tribesmen at a time, and the First
Peshawar Division had enjoyed most of the engagements almost as
if it was sport. Young and their other commanding officer,
Bloomfield, were as keen as mustard and the troops, however hard-
pressed, were always ready to cheer the enemy's spirit and dash, as
much as that of their own side. For Bertie that had been his first
glimpse of the lashkar in action close up. They had all felt that it
was a challenge, but a challenge in which the two sides were evenly
matched, equally strong and playing by the same rules.

That June engagement, however, was far more serious. Thankfully
George Roos-Keppel held overall command: he was the Chief
Commissioner of the North-West Frontier Province and the only
man who really understood what the mullahs could inspire in their
Hindustani Fanatics. If the 91st hadn't done that forced march and
come to their rescue, Bertie and the nurses would still be patching up
the bodies. Then there had been a bit of a lull during Ramadan: the
combination of fasting all day and temperatures a good ten degrees
above normal had kept things quiet among the Swatis.

No one in the hills felt like wasting what little energy they had
on fighting. So Bertie had managed to get home and give Millie a

kiss on the forehead and a rub on her bulging belly, and reassure her that everything would feel more comfortable once the baby came. He loved his funny little wife and was ambitious for their life together. It was clear to him that, since both of them were country-born, the army was never going to look kindly on his promotion through the ranks, so he was already plotting his escape. Bertie knew that if he stayed in the Sub-Medical Department he would be wearing a warrant officer's badge for the next twenty-five years with no chance of a full commission. His career would be a slow, dreary climb: in five years he'd be a sub-assistant third grade, then in ten a second grade. Maybe if he stuck it out he'd finally achieve the pinnacle as a sub-assistant, first grade, under some boy just out from Britain who knew next to nothing about tropical medicine and even less of the complex mix that made up life on the Frontier. If he was very fortunate he would be invited to the club as a guest, but never admitted as a member.

He didn't intend to stay a 'sub' in any job for long, to watch juniors from home swanning into the officers' mess while he and his colleagues would never be accepted there; and Mildred's lilting voice and deep gold skin would never appease those for whom home was a real place, and not just the stuff of stories handed down through several generations. He'd taught her not to stick out her hand and say 'pleased to meet you' but just to bow and say 'how d'you do' when he introduced her but she couldn't get out of the habit of saying 'cheerio' or 'chin chin' when he brought her her evening peg. This was a dead giveaway, nearly as plain as Miss Castries's 'little opal-tinted onyx at the base of her finger-nails' she'd read aloud to him, with a giggle, from the Kipling story[3] in her old copy of the *Gazette*, and which doomed the hero of the tale who married her to 'a millstone round his neck at the outset of his career'. Millie had thought it was a hoot, pointing gleefully at her own dainty hands, but he took it more grimly. He heard talk in the mess of a woman visiting the club who had been obliged to bare her gums in order to prove no taint of blueish-black in her gums or her bloodline. He'd managed to keep that one from Millie's ears, though no doubt she would have heard it from someone in the lines. There were no secrets in the cantonment – none that is, except his own passionate wish to get out. And if his wife could laugh at the pretensions of the English then he would at least try to shrug them off.

One day it wouldn't matter. He had little else to complain of: he adored Millie and she him, and she was ambitious for him and went along with all the little sacrifices his aspirations made necessary. When he proposed he had warned her that they would be living on short rations for a while: only one frock for her and the rest of their money squirrelled away to speculate on the currency markets. When Bertie had made enough he'd buy his way out of the department and set up in private practice, and then they'd show the world. Linen and silks for Mildred, servants and a house up in the hills for the hot weather, and a car . . .

Meanwhile, there was going to be a baby to provide for. That would mean an ayah. Perhaps they would be able to find a Pashtun girl, not an unmarried one, of course, since they were kept at home, as carefully guarded as the Koran itself, but perhaps his orderly would know of a young widow who might prefer life in the cantonment to a life of purdah in the hills. He knew that Mildred's mother would not be around: since her divorce she had kept away, moving into the Portuguese circle that was her new husband's world. In any case, there was a whiff of scandal about a divorced woman and Bertie wanted an exemplary life for him and his family.

But now there was talk of jihad. There was always talk of jihad and jihadis, had been right through his boyhood, from stories of his mother's flight from the fierce cavalrymen of Gwalior when she was a small girl, then from his father when he came out of the artillery to police the Frontier and for the last five years, since he'd been warranted, wherever he went there were tales of the men in their blue tunics and black waistcoats, with green turbans and waistbands. But now was as bad as he could ever remember it; trouble always seemed to come thickest at the end of the hot weather. It inflamed everyone; it brought with it fevers and feuds. Even the pi-dogs* were affected. Instead of their usual sheepish skulk they could snarl and give a filthy nip. Bertie had had to deal with many consequences of that in the divisional hospice: there was a certain nobility in falling to an Afridi or – especially – a Yosufzai foe, for they were noble fighters, hardly ever defeated in battle, but a flea-bitten, rib-sticking pi-dog . . . It was one of those terrible levellers that had made him start to wonder, with a thin curling whisper of discomfort, if the subsidiary medical service was really the place for him.

Everything had started calmly enough. When he'd come back to the Frontier fresh from the medical school, his half-brother, twenty years older, was already a senior assistant surgeon and it was Ernest's example that had encouraged Bertie to follow him. Now Captain Kerr was doing highly secret work on troop movements through the Frontier and on into Iraq and the Mesopotamian theatre of war, having left the blood and mess of the field hospital behind.

Their mother Margaret had, of course, trained for nursing as a girl at the hill school and had made good use of it to keep her first family from destitution: for five years after Sergeant Kerr's death she had used her skills to pay for the family until she met Christopher and married him. And then there was his big brother, Frank, who had preceded Bertie by two years. Frank, the steady one, working away in the X-ray laboratory. It was a great introduction to the service to be sent to the same posting as Frank and for that post to

* Stray dogs that survived by scavenging

be back in the beautiful Murree hills. This place had been home to Bertie and Frank for as long as they could remember. They had lived there in the Lawrence School for eleven months out of every twelve since they were tots, and in fact it was a delight actually to be allowed to spend all winter up here, with the jackals and the bears and the odd Pashtun travelling through. As boys they always had to leave for the police lines in the cantonment down on the plains just as the first snows draped the deodars, oaks and olives, transforming cottonwood and acacia into the Christmas they knew from cards that came from the other home, far across the mountains, beyond the Kush and the land of the Turks, beyond the furthest reach even of Alexander's ancient Empire, beyond those other mighty mountains, the Alps, that he and Frank used to dream of crossing on an elephant, like Hannibal, when they were boys, beyond the battlefields of Napoleon and Wellington to the landfall where Drake had bowled on Plymouth Sound and his father's kin had crawled down narrow shafts on the edge of Dartmoor to reach the seams of tin and copper and arsenic. He'd never been there; the only one who had was his father, and even for him it was a distant memory, a place thankfully left behind some thirty-five years before. Bertie had no idea if there was even anyone left in England who might know the family for all he had heard from his father was that everyone – his father and all of his brothers and sisters – had gone off to North America when the work dried up in the mines.

And all of his mother's family – his mother, his five grown-up siblings, his mother's parents – all were born in India. Between them they'd come to know the subcontinent well, his grandparents in Bengal near where he'd trained at the Calcutta medical college, and then in the Princely states at the centre of the subcontinent, and his father serving north, south, east and west during the twenty-two years he'd spent in the artillery. Bertie couldn't imagine serving in the army so long himself, but it was hard to know what else he would do with his life. They were all army folk, whether from Britain or from India, and this bit of the north-west had always been home for him. That now meant a bungalow down in the lines at Cherat, on the plain below Peshawar, and his moors were the dusty peaks and narrow passes of the western Himalayas.

In many ways he was lucky to be posted up here. For the other ranks down on the plains there was no possibility of a cooling mountain breeze, nor the shade of the tall jungle trees. Under these circumstances it was no wonder that they welcomed the chance of a skirmish in the hills. It was like sport for them: in fact, on the long forced marches in single file to get the troops up into this remote and inaccessible area it soon became standard practice to send a herald ahead to the next village to issue a challenge to the locals for a sporting contest. Any sport would do: shooting, swimming, hockey, tobidi tag. It was a welcome diversion, even after a twenty-mile march in the sweltering heat.

Of course it was different for them here in the medical department: they worked long hospital hours and there was always pressure on them at their field hospitals on the North-West Frontier because there were no amenities for the civilians. Bertie's first posting had been to the Bannu field hospital in 1911, and of the eighty-two hospitals and dispensaries established in the province Bannu was the shining beacon, thanks more than anything else to Dr Pennell and his wife, who were in charge there. Bertie had learnt more in his three years there than he would have thought possible. Whenever there was a lull in hostilities the subs found themselves dealing with cholera or plague or famine or syphilis, for there was no civil surgeon in Bannu, and all that kind of work among the local people fell to his department too. In Bertie's first year there had been 1700 interned patients and a whopping 23,636 outpatients at Bannu. The chief was keen to keep up their pioneering work attending to the cataracts in the eyes of the tribespeople too: it was good for relations with the locals, he said. The workload was far too much for Pennell and his two English doctors to cope with alone, so the subs found themselves performing a lot of the operations. In his first year there, Bertie and the other mission doctors managed 405 cataract operations between skirmishes, and that alone had won them more hearts and minds than anything else. Indeed, the demand for eye treatments had accelerated almost faster than they could manage, and in his last year at Bannu they treated the eyes of more than five thousand locals.

The other urgent need was for dental work and over that first year they had done more than seventeen thousand extractions, as well as performing around four hundred other dental operations. There had been no possibility of leave for Bertie while he was at Bannu, for there were no civil surgeons within reach. They were always on call and the demands of the work set the sub-assistants apart from the regular soldiers; that, and speaking the local languages – Urdu and Pashtu – which hardly any of the regulars could do. There was thus little chance of him being roped into the sporting activities and in any case Bertie had never been one for team games. He had always preferred shooting and fishing, sports that allowed him to be quiet in the landscape and to feel part of it, a connection to the animals for whom it was home.

Since his time in Bannu he had been in Nowshera, in the plains near Peshawar, and how glad he was to have escaped service in the main Peshawar hospital at Egerton, situated as it was between the main town sewer and a row of butchers' shops. There were so many flies swarming around in the spring and autumn that half the community refused to come in for treatment, however great their need for attention: they feared infection from the flies more than their existing ailments. There were worse things, of course: Bertie had heard from a colleague that during the troubles up in the Khost

Valley* the civil hospital at Parachinar had been inundated with men who arrived with their wounds wrapped up in decomposing goat skins. As his colleague had wryly told him, there were many interesting cases and much good work had been done.

After Bannu, Bertie found himself posted to the Dir, Swat and Chitral district board, and he prayed fervently that the movable columns at Malakand would keep things in hand for a couple of weeks until the baby came. They had been short-staffed for the last year, what with the transfer of so many medical officers to the war in Europe. In one way Bertie saw it as an opportunity, for it might make promotion a more attainable possibility for him, but it also meant he was more hard-pressed than ever.

There was constant skirmishing throughout the region and no one knew where trouble was going to break out next. Since the quarrels had moved to the Adinzai tract in June 1915, threatening the post at Chakdarh, and the road north to Chitral, everyone was on tenterhooks. If the Malakand Moveable Column hadn't moved up to Chakdara, with the 91st marching up to help them, many more would have fallen. Bertie had seen the grim consequence of falling to the Mussulmen. More often than not, prisoners were handed over to the Pashtun women and whenever the women took over there was little that the surgeons could do even if they could get to the poor prisoner. The victim would be begging for death to end the agony of a gut torn out by vultures, of a bleeding mess where the genitals should be, of the humiliation of bleeding slowly to death with your privates rammed in your mouth.

Between skirmishes and their civilian work, life for Bertie had been full and interesting. He had met the young heir to the Akhund of Swat when he was sent up country to Saidu Sharif. Sharif means 'holy' and the place had been named for Abdul Gaffar,

* In Afghanistan, on the extreme western border of the Kurrum Agency

a Sufi Pathan and revered religious teacher from Upper Swat who was buried there. This man had assisted the Afghan rulers of Peshawar in their battles with the encroaching Sikhs, but when they were defeated he moved north-east to Saidu, married a Yousafzai woman and had two sons. This was unusual because he was an outsider, and it was hence a sign of great respect that he was allowed to marry into the Yousafzai. He was called 'Akhund', meaning teacher, by his followers.

It was one of the Akhund's descendants who was now emerging as a leader of the Swatis, and a person Bertie was especially struck by. Though he did not know it yet, only two years later this new acquaintance would be appointed to lead the new-formed kingdom of Swat;[4] the Wali of Swat would remember the young assistant surgeon's skills, too, and from time to time would invite him back to his capital to treat his court over the next thirty-five years.

That adventure lay in the future for Bertie. Meanwhile the Americans had set up a field hospital and the best part of it, as far as he was concerned, was that they had a dedicated dental department that was far superior to anything his own department had to offer. He was certain that such a department didn't exist in the whole of the British army. If someone came to him with toothache the best he could offer would be a peg of whisky and a quick yank with the dental pliers, but he'd heard the Americans talking proudly of drilling out the bad bit of a tooth and filling it with metal. When the Fanatics had been subdued he planned to seek out the Americans and ask if they would be willing to instruct him: if he could master these new techniques, he might be the first in the field in the whole of the north-west. Dr Quick, dental surgeon . . .

Of course Bertie would not actually have been the first in the field: that title was claimed by people who had lived not far from where he now found himself stationed, but separated from him by a chasm of centuries. In the sixth century BC – more than 2400 years before Bertie's time – people had come from far and wide to study at the world's first dental school, which was founded by Atrey at the ancient Buddhist university in Taxila. They came from Arabia, Greece, Syria and China, as well as from the Indian subcontinent, as many as five hundred at a time, to follow a course of medicine and dentistry that lasted for seven years – longer than Bertie's own training had been. He wondered if it had been more thorough, if they had perhaps understood things which in his own time were now forgotten. One of the requirements for studying at Taxila had been 'a contented frame of mind, politeness in speech, and pleasing manners . . . He who did not possess these was considered unfit for studying medicine.'[5] Bertie hoped that he would have met these qualifications for he felt himself to be happier than he had ever been, and the school in the hills had drummed good manners and courtesy in to him.

Even before Taxila had become the world's first great centre of learning, ancients of the pre-Buddhist age understood much. They knew how to preserve the natural teeth in a healthy state: before the Greeks, before even the Egyptians, dentistry had been an integral part of Ayurveda, and its practices were recorded in the literature of the Vedic age some three thousand years before Christ. Not just dentistry, either, as birth by Caesarean section, trepanning of the skull and amputations using anaesthetic were all part of the surgical repertoire.

Bertie also knew about Sushruta, who had practised at Benares. He had heard a native apothecary speak of him as the 'father of surgery'. Around six hundred years BC, Sushruta had been dissecting human bodies and had been able to describe the bones of the jaw with astonishing accuracy. He and his contemporaries had understood that to be healthy you must be clean, and there were recipes for toothpastes made from powdered tobacco, salt, burnt betel nut, pepper, dry ginger or long pepper, as well as for gargles and liniments. He gave instructions on the best order in which to eat, as this was conducive to the health of the mouth cavity as well as of the body: 'take soft viands first, hard butteracious food in the middle and liquids at the end of the meal. Sweets first, then acid things and the bitter and pungent things the last if all.'[6] Sushruta warned not to hurry food, to chew well and to clean the mouth inside and out after every meal; his advice about using toothpicks was something that had amused Bertie, for he rarely went without one. Sushruta had also named sixty-five diseases affecting the mouth and gums, including scurvy, boils, abscess, pyorrhoea, gingivitis and tartar. And, most useful of all, he had collated all earlier surgical knowledge that had accumulated at the universities at Taxila and Nalanda and described operations not so different from ones Bertie had seen the Americans performing: extractions of live teeth, lancing boils, removal of tartar, fillings, ligatures and even inserting artificial teeth carved from 'sea horse' – perhaps meaning walrus tusk – or ivory. Indeed, he had described these operations with such clarity that Bertie, for one, believed that a present-day surgeon like himself could look up to them with respect, and maybe learn from them. They even had about 125 different surgical instruments made of the best steel which were very similar to modern instruments.

Ayurvedic medicine had however lost its authority once the Muslims came to the country in the tenth century and, though it had enjoyed a brief revival under the Peshawars from 1715 to 1818, once the English gained a real foothold in India their rule 'had brought about the death of that once famous & perfect medical science, because the English came with the notion that Indian medicine was a quackery.'[7]

Compared to this sophisticated ancient eastern knowledge, the practice of dentistry in the west in the early twentieth century was still primitive. People had been experimenting with false teeth for a long time and had tried many different materials, from animal tusks to battleground teeth. Bertie had seen an advertisement copied from an English newspaper of a hundred years earlier offering 'Waterloo teeth': perfect specimens extracted from the young dead on the battlefield at Waterloo and now available as false teeth to be fixed, somehow, in the mouths of those lucky enough not to have been involved in the fighting. Bertie wondered if he might be up to doing something similar with their own dead up on the Frontier, but it was only a grisly fantasy and in any case beyond his competence at the time. Dentistry had only been recognised as a subject within the general training for medicine at the Calcutta medical school in 1820 but now, with this new inspiration from the Americans – and, perhaps, intuition about the ancient wisdom that had once flourished in this very area – Bertie developed a plan for whenever he could escape from the confines of the Sub-Medical Department. Blow being for ever a subordinate anything: he would learn all he could about teeth from the Americans, and as soon as he could find a way to get out he would set up a practice as the first dentist in Rawalpindi.

Bertie did perhaps get leave to visit his wife in the plains in June 1915 but by late July the Hindustani Fanatics were leading the raids along the Buner border, and the Royal Field Artillery were called in to defend the Ambala Pass. By 20 August things were reaching a dangerous climax in his own territory; the Mullah of Sandaki led a force of between fifteen and twenty thousand down from the Upper Swat Valley to invade Lower Swat. The Malakand Moveable Column repositioned itself on the Landakai Ridge, on the left bank of the Swat River, and everyone knew it was going to be serious. On 28 August attacks were made on the outposts and there were heavy losses in driving the fanatics off. The next day the column moved out and destroyed a fort and several villages, and with that the tribesmen started to disperse. But this success did nothing to quiet the talk of jihad along the Mohmand border and there were large tribal gatherings in the area under various fanatical mullahs. Two brigades and a mounted column were on semi-alert and the mobile column was ready to move out from Mardan at the first sign of real trouble. Reinforcements were standing by. By early September the British force could plainly see that large groups of tribesmen were moving through the foothills and sangars – encirclements – were being prepared near Hafiz Kor. Within two days the assembled native force had grown to ten thousand strong and the big engagement everyone had been expecting finally happened on 5 September. The enemy resisted stoutly and displayed great bravery, tenacious of their newly constructed sangars. In the end they were driven back by a successful cavalry charge and sustained heavy losses. It was only a brief respite for by October nine thousand men had once more assembled near Hafiz Kor. They attacked these tribesmen from Shabkadar, and although the tribesmen were able to put up strong resistance a detachment of the Khyber Rifles from Fort Michni soon sent them flying. This engagement was the first time that armoured cars had been deployed in India, and though they were little more than saloon cars covered in metal plate, they were an inspiration to the senior command that they would, eventually, be able to subdue the Frontier. Once the Mohmand country was calm and the bodies were repaired Bertie was free to go and inspect his first child – my father – who had been born in the middle of the fighting, on 1 September 1915. But Bertie did not have long to enjoy this freedom; he was soon involved in mending the casualties of another campaign, when three thousand Bajauris came down from the hills intending to take over the fort at Chakdara by arousing the tribes of Swat and Dir. Before that could happen the Malakand Moveable Column moved out and attacked them on 27 October. The Bajauris were routed, severely handled and lost a standard.

In all these jihad-driven attacks, Bertie was to distinguish himself, earning praise in the dispatches published in the *Gazette* for the 'fine spirit and great cheerfulness' he displayed daily. Major-General Campbell said that he could not 'speak too highly of the endurance and conduct of the troops, British and Indian. The temperature, always very trying in the Peshawar valley in hot weather, was 10 degrees above normal, but the troops . . . were eager and ready at all times to march and fight.' The despatch went on to acknowledge the help of the police officers of the entire region, too, so it may have been that Bertie even found himself involved in a campaign alongside his father Christopher. Bertie's name was singled out for particular notice and praised for his 'gallantry and good service'.

Perhaps he had been feeling especially inspired to do well by the birth of his son Leonard Albert Groves Quick. There is no doubt that he loved him very much and much later in life he was to say that when he died he wanted to take Lenny with him. He cannot have known that he was going to lose his wife Mildred at the age of twenty-four to colonic cancer and find himself a widower with two small children, Lenny and Esmerelda, who was born two years after her brother. It was a repeat of what had happened to his own father, except that Bertie's children were even younger and he and his wife had had very little time to enjoy their married life together, and none at all to experience the rosy future Bertie had been saving everything for.

15

Leonard

'. . . it is a corrupting thing to live one's real life in secret. One should live with the stream of life, not against it . . . You've got to be a pukka sahib or die, in this country.'

George Orwell, *Burmese Days*

The emerging theme, as I write, is that denial seems so frequently the best option for survival. Perhaps it is our most basic response to the fear of dying; ignore the fact that death will come to us and ours, bury the feelings of panic, loss and futility that fact calls up, the terrible need to be cherished, the anger that the waste of a life arouses. In India this process of facing death happened so frequently and often with little time to prepare for it that it was no wonder there were so many ways of moving on: find a new partner, bury yourself in work, do not cave in to desolation. But for a child it must have been hard to move on and for my father death was only too present at a cruelly early age. His mother died when he was four, his sister two.

Very little had changed for wives between the time when his grandmother Margaret had taken a significant step up the social ladder by marrying first her English sergeant Charles and then her English bombardier Christopher, and the time when his mother Mildred was raising him and Esmerelda on the North-West Frontier. There was still no proper provision for wives in the ranks, and in any case his father had decided that they would live frugally so that all spare cash could go into the escape fund – the money to make good their escape from the frustration of limited opportunity. If they were careful now they could look forward to a free life in the future, for them and their children, away from the army. But for Bertie's young wife that day never arrived. At twenty-four she was carried off by peritonitis, a consequence of her colonic cancer, leaving a stunned husband to care for Leonard and Esmerelda.

Mildred is buried in a walled cemetery on the road that leads to the Khyber Pass, shaded by lofty trees. The gravestone is inscribed:

> *All tears are vain, we cannot now recall thee,*
> *Gone as thy loving voice, thy kindly face,*
> *Gone from the home where we so dearly loved thee,*
> *Where none again can ever fill thy place*

I know this because, when I went to Peshawar in 1999, I visited the cemetery and found my grandmother's grave at once with the help of a book produced by the British Association for Cemeteries in South Asia – BACSA – a charity dedicated to recording such relics of the era of British settlement. The grave was a little neglected, the cross broken, the grave itself covered in weeds, but the chowkidar promised to repair the cross and clean the grave in return for double his monthly salary. This particular cemetery had been researched by Susan Farrington – 'Cemetery Sue' – who had done her work so thoroughly that her handbook even provided a map showing the site of the grave and a record of the inscription.

As we cleared the debris from the grave two further lines revealed themselves:

> *Deeply mourned and sadly missed by her sorrowing*
> *Husband, children and relations.*

It must have been a period of heightened emotion for Bertie, with the pressure of jihad erupting in places along the Frontier and his own intimate involvement in the action at its most intense, when some sixteen thousand Afridi Pashtuns descended along the Swat Valley. As one of the team of medics he found himself dealing with the results of what was termed in the dispatches an engagement 'with loss'. In the aftermath he was probably settling into his long-term plan of learning all he could about dentistry from the Americans posted nearby, enjoying the infancy of his little girl, whom they had called Rayonette Esmerelda. We who came much later knew her only as Esme, but I speculated aloud in Peshawar as to where her odd first name had come from and was delighted to learn that there is a Pashtun word that means 'little ray of sunshine'.* Rayonette was clearly an attempt to translate that into tolerable English. Realising this, I warmed to Grandfather: he must have adored his little girl. For a moment my frozen memory of the formidable patriarch from an alien country melted into a loving young husband and father and I started to sense the domestic tragedy common to so many in the Empire and on that frontier in particular, the routine banality of death and bereavement.

The little ray of sunshine was too small to remember her mother but her brother Leonard remembered his own early childhood only too well and later wrote about it in a short story he composed for a

---

* 'Pashwala'

newspaper competition, writing about himself in the third person as if it was too painful to do otherwise:

How would it all end? As far back as he could remember he had had no will of his own. Even as a kid he was made to do this and that: to utter not a word of protest. Yes he had once, but God, never again; even now he could remember the look on his father's face, as he had made his childish excuse for running away from school, that big dreary convent in the little station on the North-West Frontier of India, to enjoy for a few hours being a stationmaster in Charlie King's house amongst his marvellous trains . . .They might have shown some mercy to the little chap of six; but no, his father's ungovernable temper had got the better of him, with disastrous results. Wasn't he laid up for over a week, unable to sit down in comfort, with a burning fever which nearly removed him from the living world?

If only his dear mother, whom he could still remember faintly, though she had passed away when he was four, had been there; she always could manage Dad and his temper. How clearly he remembered her, as she lay in that big white room in the station hospital, when he used to run across the road from the house opposite, to take her a glass of that awful egg drink. She was so sweet, and he had loved her. And then they told him she had gone to Heaven and he wouldn't ever see her again. He had missed her terribly then.

'She could always manage Dad and his temper.' So Bertie had a temper even back then. Was it from being an army child, sent away to the Lawrence Asylum as a small boy to be brought up under the school motto Never Give In?

Was it connected to his own father's drunkenness, which had been getting worse since he'd retired? Bertie was regularly summoned to pull Christopher out of ditches around Peshawar. Was it the sheer frustration of a clever man who knew he could never rise within the establishment because of prejudice, snobbery and chauvinism of the most narrow and spiteful sort?

There were no women close enough for Bertie and the children to turn to. His own mother had died when he was eight, leaving only himself and his brother; now his wife had followed the same pattern and his mother-in-law Florence had moved away from them following her divorce and re-marriage.

Perhaps it would have cost him too much simply to have acknowledged his loss, but within six months of becoming a widower Bertie was invalided out of the Sub-Medical Department. He got his wish to be shot of the army, but not at all in the way he had dreamed of. Before he could leave, though, fate took a hand in his future. Among the soldiers he had been tending on the Frontier was one who knew that he wasn't going to recover. He begged Assistant Surgeon Quick (now third grade, after eight years' service) to take charge of his personal effects and to do his best to return them to his fiancée down south in Bangalore. As it happened, Bertie was soon posted thousands of miles south to Madras, where one of his last actions as a sub-assistant surgeon was a detour on this mercy mission. The dead soldier's fiancée was called Nora Eldridge, and Bertie was not to know that the bereaved young woman to whom he brought these last effects would, in course of time, fall in love with him. There was tremendous opposition from her family, who were Roman Catholics, and a certain resistance from Bertie, who by the time Nora fell for him, two years into his widowerhood, had started courting someone else. But Nora overcame all resistance and married him. Bertie could not have known that she would turn out to be controlling, and jealous of her stepchildren. She converted him to the Catholic faith and made him abandon freemasonry, which was widespread in the medical profession in India. She introduced herself to Lenny and Esme as 'Mother', packed the two of them off to boarding schools and got on with establishing a social life up at the club.

Nora also seems to have deliberately wiped out any trace of her predecessor. No photographs or mementoes of Mildred were to be tolerated. She was to be the only wife, the only mother. She was jealous of everyone; in order to eliminate the obstacle of the woman Bertie had begun to court as a widower, Nora started to send her poison pen letters.

Esme grew up believing that Nora was actually her mother. It was only much later, when she was twenty years old, that this was put straight, in the middle of a cataclysmic family row. To her amazement she found it out from a family friend who took pity on her unhappiness and whispered the truth – that this woman was not, in fact, her mother. This woman, who had sent her away to school in England in her teens, where she knew no one, and who was now making her life a misery, forbidding her any contact with the man she hoped to marry and was sending anonymous, spiteful letters to her colleagues at work. Esme had come to hate her and felt only relief that the woman did not have a legitimate claim on her love by birth.

All of that was to happen years later, at a time when her brother had left India behind and was making a new life – against his will – in the other place called home. Meanwhile, Leonard needed an education. He didn't follow his father and uncle to the Lawrence Academy. Instead, he was sent to St Joseph's College, a school at Nainital, near the British summer capital of Simla, which was known as the Seminary, or simply the Sem: his stepmother insisted that the children were raised in her own Catholic faith. There were no army echoes at the Seminary, but morning swims across the beautiful lake fed from the glacier above, and a lot of mass and a lot of sport – cricket and hockey.[1]

A lot of crying too. He missed his family, but then all the children at all the schools in the hills (and there were many of them) had travelled huge distances. For some it was two or three days' journey:

Other children came from Kabul, Kathmandu, Calcutta, Kashmir. For nearly everyone the journey meant getting to Lucknow, usually by train, then on by overnight train to the railhead at Kathgodam, then a crazy bus ride on a switch-back mountain road with the mountain face on one side with a sheer drop of several thousand feet on the other. Survivors of this bus-ride got to lake level at Nainital.[2]

Once there, at the beginning of the school year, there would be no return for nine or ten months. My father wrote this about his life at the Seminary:

Lord he did have some good times . . . amongst the youngsters of his own age; learning the team spirit of fighting to keep the school supreme in sport and work. What was the motto? – 'Fight the good fight'. Yes, he had learnt to do that all right. What a surly young-ster he had been when he first went to College but they had knocked it out of him, yes, especially that big French bloke, André. But what great pals they had become, during the next eight years; they had stuck together in everything; mugged together, played in the 2nd and 1st XIs together . . . And then Sports Day. Jove, he had given André a close run for the Victor Ludorum.

He had had to fight hard to keep the tears back, as he left the college; yes, he had learnt to love old St Joseph's during those eight years.

My feeling, though, is that there was little family life to look forward to in those brief weeks at home at the end of each year. The family didn't visit the school and, once home, his father was at work and his 'mother' was out socialising.

I didn't like Grandmother. I didn't take to her, without knowing why, when I was that little girl being mildly humiliated in her kitchen. As I've learnt more of the social milieu that was the lot of the Englishwoman in India, I've come to like her even less. There are many accounts of the emptiness of life for most women: relieved of all traditional household duties by their array of servants, the children cared for by ayahs and then schoolteachers, one might expect that they would make the most of their opportunity to get to know the country and its people – certainly a modern woman with such enviable freedom would. But did these women take the opportunity to learn about the local culture or the language? To look at the Mohgul art and architecture around them? To explore the highly evolved Gandhara culture close by in the Vale of Peshawar? Or even just to pass on what they knew, such as their own language or rudimentary hygiene?

No, such opportunities were ignored by the majority. The European women were to some extent imprisoned by the rules of purdah that prevailed in the native community around them; it was not easy to move around in a society that cloistered its own women away from the public gaze, and of course this also meant that there was no relaxed way of meeting their menfolk either, who were used to socialising mainly with men, or the women of their own family. In any case the British had come to India to exploit the country and its resources, and if there had once been a honeymoon period when its history and traditions had been revered and studied by the so-called orientalists of the eighteenth century, that was now largely forgotten. Evangelicalism defined the native religions as pagan and backward, its followers as benighted and cast out from grace. How then could friendships be cultivated on an equal basis, even without the diffi-culties of purdah? Since soon after the Uprising Britain saw its role as an imperial power and not as the bringer of democracy; by its very nature the administration and its servants remained aloof and a cer-tain distance between the peoples was an inevitable consequence.

There was the additional complication of caste. At the beginning of the twentieth century this had become a rigid code for the British too, with absolutely everybody who was anybody's status codified and quantified and established beyond negotiation in the Warrant of Precedence. This was published and updated at regular intervals between its first appearance in the early 1800s and the end of the Raj in 1947, and ranked everyone from the Viceroy at the top down to the lowest rung on the social ladder, which included assistant direc-tors of public health and senior tax inspectors. Sub-assistant surgeons were not considered to be anybody, they were below ranking, but the obsession with status would doubtless have percolated down, and in fact snobbery at this level was even more entrenched than further up the social scale. There are many testimonials to this obsession with position, such as this recollection of a disastrous dinner party where precedence had not been observed:

> The senior lady must always sit on the right hand side of the host, and the next on the left and all the way down the line. [There was] a row because the Engineer's wife sat right, the cane-manager's wife left – she walked in, slapped the host's face and walked out.
>
> The women bothered about this far more than the men. Men had far more important things – and the women had very little to bother about. So they seized on anything like this.[3]

In a society obsessed with the minutiae of protocol, women eked out a life, not like J. Alfred Prufrock with coffee spoons, but with tennis rackets and bridge and gossip and tots of whisky.

Grandfather had found a very promising niche for himself. He was known as Dr Quick, but specialised more and more in dental surgery. There was little competition: the British Military Hospital would have dealt with all army dentistry, but for the civilians the only other choice was to go to one of the 'bazaar chaps who had no idea about sterility: they were quacks'4 and Bertie soon established a thriving practice in Rawalpindi, where he had settled with Nora. He was appointed the school dentist for the Lawrence school at Ghora Gali as well and, talking not so long ago with some of his former patients, who had not seen him for at least fifty-five years, they still remember him as a man with a certain panache and an enviable lifestyle. He had finally escaped from the terrible limitations of life as an assistant surgeon; he continued to develop the private practice he had begun while still in the sub medical department and acquired a spacious house in Pindi. With his appointment as the school dentist he was soon in a position to acquire a second one up in the foothills of the Himalayas at Murree, a charming wood and brick bungalow in the middle of a deodar forest, with sweeping views across the Himalayas to Kashmir on one side and to the Vale of Rawalpindi on the other, that he called Ashburnham Cottage. Bertie's only professional rival, for the five months that he was in Murree each year, was known as the Butcher because of his tendency to stand outside his rooms wearing a bloody apron. Patients flocked away from him to Dr Quick, with his modern skills learnt from the Americans. He acquired a rather grand car, although it often broke down on the long haul up the mountain from Pindi to Murree, and he used his earnings to speculate on the currency markets, and did well. Bertie and Nora were welcomed at the civilian club, although the son of a fellow country-born doctor has told me, with a great deal of bitterness, that 'The English who went up there [to Murree] hardly knew of our existence . . . we were not accepted in their circle; our fathers were not accepted in their clubs, although they would sometimes come "slumming" to ours. We had happy times, and good jobs, though not the best.'[5]

This was the source of much of the tension in the family; for all his skill and success, Bertie was country-born. His father might be a superintendent of police answerable directly to the Foreign Office in London, but his mother had been country-born too. Both Margaret and and her children had been educated in India, and both were further marked out by their 'chi-chi' accent, the sing-song voice that characterised those who had not had the benefit of an education in Britain. Both – whisper it – had a touch of the tar brush; both then must be unreliable, emotional, not one of us.

Leonard and Esmerelda were taken to visit Nora's family down in Bangalore but their father was never invited. Nora's relations with her parents were not easy in any case: she always felt that her sister Gertie was the favourite. She took Leonard to Bangalore for a last visit in the early months of 1932, just before he was to leave India for ever. In the photos he is a solemn-faced, gangly seventeen-year-old, standing awkwardly behind Mrs Eldridge, a grim and skinny Victorian matriarch, her black skirt reaching to her ankles, a starched cap and apron imprisoning her far back in time. I have been struck over and over again by this sense of a time warp, of a society isolated not only by its physical distance from the western twentieth century but by its customs and attitudes. Their ways and social habits were at least twenty years behind the times. Leonard had an Edwardian, if not a positively Victorian, childhood: people knew their place and on the whole kept to it; children were seen and not heard, expected to do as they were told, and above all keep their distance. In the autograph album he was given for Christmas 1926 his father wrote:

> *The boy that is tidy, as tidy can be,*
> *Oh, he is the boy that will just suit me;*

And if he's a 'sport' and has rather nice ways
I shall hope to be his Daddy now and always.

There is no doubt that Bertie adored his children and so my conclusion is that it must have been Nora, behaving as stepmothers are expected and feared to do, whose actions put a distance between the children of that first marriage and their father. First by sending them away to school in the hills, and later by sending them to England to continue their education alone. No doubt it would be better for their health to be out of the hot weather and better for their self esteem to be away from the prejudice against country-born folk but, above all, if they could be given an English education then they would be able to rise above the taint of their birth. In 1932 they were brought over and left in England where they knew no one: Esme in a convent school, Leonard at Guy's Hospital studying dentistry, which did not even particularly interest him – he had hoped to go to Cambridge to read either classics or maths. Three years later, in the middle of the almighty row that developed once Leonard did know what he wanted and started to fight for it, he wrote bitterly: 'Why am I not independent, instead of what I am. I would write and tell Dad everything, did I not know what he'd do. Oh! Why wasn't he more human and understanding with me when I was young, and been a pal to me, instead of a feared monster as he is now.'

What could have turned Bertie from that loving, optimistic young husband and father into this 'feared monster'? His son yearned for a father who could have been his 'pal' when he was young, and he was only twenty or so when he wrote that letter of regret, so for him 'young' must have meant about eight or nine, the age at which he was sent away from Rawalpindi to the Roman Catholic Seminary at Nainital. The school became the defining influence in his young life, inspiring him to read widely in world literature, to do well in his lower and higher Cambridge exams and to become an avid sportsman. It also turned him into a devout Catholic. Later, in England when he was struggling through the bitter long-distance fight with his father back in India, he concluded his diary entry with: 'Oh! Jesus, God of love, guide me as you think best, not as I will, but as thou wilt.' He was not quite twenty-one, and had just fallen in love with the woman who was to change his life for ever.

16

A Good Clean Friendship

Why, when Bertie professed so much love for his son, was he unable to express it or spend time with him? Or make him feel loved and valued? It is clear that Nora was the dominating partner in the marriage, setting the agenda of religion and schooling, and I presumed that the withholding of love was because Leonard was a stepchild to Nora, but later her own son, born eleven years after Leonard, told me that his mother was nearly always absent when he, in turn, came home for the school holidays, leaving him to the care of the ayah and Esme. Leonard had probably been handed over in much the same way.

Leonard was the eldest child and his father's pride and joy, but Bertie had a fierce temper and was often frightening to his son. Bertie himself had grown up with an artilleryman for a father, a career soldier turned policeman with twenty-three years' military service and as much again policing the most lawless sector of India. A man who was known for his drinking, who had done time for a serious offence under the relatively tolerant military code. Bertie was often forced to rescue his father from various drunken mishaps, as he got older and in retirement had time on his hands in which to indulge himself.

All this seems to suggest that Christopher was an alcoholic. Perhaps at one time he was a happy drinker along with his fellow soldiers, but alcoholism is a progressive illness in which, sooner or later, the consumption becomes unmanageable and the drinker's personality is changed, always for the worse. If Christopher was a bully in his cups then his son would have been affected by the experience of growing up with the effects of alcoholism. It is common for the child of a drinker to feel a need to be perfect, to control as much as possible, and this drive to manage the world outside oneself is driven by the need to cover up a deep sense of shame and low self-esteem – many children of alcoholics seem to feel that somehow everything is their fault. The child in an alcoholic family may also come to be out of touch with their own feelings. It is hard for such a child to grow into a parent who is good at reciprocal feelings and to offer the unconditional love that their own child, in turn, needs. That is not to say that love is absent, but the distorting prism of an alcoholic parent means that, possibly, the adult child cannot but react as a supposed adult in the ways he has learned in dealing with his drinking parent. He may go to great lengths to keep the peace; he may hand over control to a more dominating partner for long periods; but finally, if crossed, he may explode into disproportionate anger. It is a scenario of emotional violence and it occurs to me, after some years of puzzling over the clues assembled about their life in India, that Bertie and his children in turn suffered the consequences of Christopher Quick's love of alcohol.

My father Leonard was clever and a good all-rounder. Sent off at nine to the Sem in Nainital, too far away to be visited easily, he was soon immersed in the life of the school and that became the place where he belonged. There was a glowing reference for him, tucked in the front of his autograph book, carefully copied out in his father's handwriting:

Leonard Albert Quick has been a student in St Joseph's College for the past eight years. He has been a boarder all the time. He won a scholarship and took Honours in the Preliminary and Junior Cambridge and will appear this coming December for the Senior. He is a thoroughly well conducted boy, regular in his habits, honest and reliable. I have been here nearly forty years and in this large College a great many boys and young men have passed through my hands. I don't remember many I would trust more than Leonard Quick.

J. B. Connolly, Principal

Leonard does seem to fit into the portrait I have painted of a child from a family in reaction to alcohol; though there is no sign that Bertie himself was a drinking man, his very high standards and, perhaps, his need to cover up his 'questionable' mixed-race background, plus the sense of guilt to which he would have been introduced in his intimacy with a devout and practising Roman Catholic may well have passed on to his eldest child a sense that he must excel, that he must always be worthy of trust. It is some accolade for your headmaster to recommend you as 'thoroughly well conducted' and among the most trustworthy to pass through the school in forty years.

Leonard would have liked an extra year at St Joseph's, having done so well in the higher certificate in order to prepare for Cambridge University entrance. But money was very important to Bertie, and status too: he had made something of himself in India despite the unfortunate fact of being born and educated there, and having made an early marriage to someone similarly disadvantaged, but he had overcome that. With the encouragement of an ambitious second wife he had found a route to professional respect outside the Sub-Medical Department: two thriving practices, the 'best house in Rawalpindi' and a snazzy car to take him up to his other house in the hills. He wanted his son to do the same, if not better. Bertie's plan was that Leonard would train in England, so as to be a pukka member of the establishment when he came back out – no tarnish of the country-bred for him – and he would then join his father as a partner.

He had pushed aside Leonard's own interests: dentistry was the coming thing, especially in India, and dentists, in his experience, made more money than doctors. I don't think Bertie could have had any idea of the rift with his son that was about to occur. Few in India could have anticipated that the end of the Raj was so near, a mere fifteen years in the future: they expected greater self-determination, certainly, but not a total collapse of empire. But, just as paternalism brought about the struggle to break free in the empire, so it did in the Quick family. Bertie's desire to control his son's life was the very thing that led to their estrangement. Later, when the row was at its most painful and no one knew how to patch things up, Leonard, alone in England, confided to his diary: 'You have a mind and a will of your own and yet it isn't your own, but is governed by one which is bending yours to do just as this big will wants it to do (and has from childhood) . . . I am not so weak but suffer terrible agonies when I have to do just as I am told.'

I would love to understand what it was that had turned Bertie Quick into a 'feared monster' instead of the 'pal' his son had craved, but find myself frustrated by the distance of time and geography, and the silence of a family not given to discussing their feelings and certainly not to recording them on paper. Frustrated, too, by the stiff-upper-lipness of it all. They were practical people on both sides, and of a class and a convention that said you just got on with it. No one spoke of these things. And yet I picked up hints. There was a strong sense of a domestic tragedy narrowly averted, a family drama that was never resolved and a distance, a distance of silence and disappointment and denial between us and the other Quicks over in India. There was only one side to the family, my mother's side. Nobody would talk about these things. Then, when I was well into the research for this book, deep in genealogy and following up strange leads, suddenly I was handed a treasure trove.

My mother, who had always resisted my questions, was by now quite frail with Parkinson's disease and preoccupied with tidying up her own affairs as her long life slowly declined. She passed me a big blue chocolate box one day, saying, 'You may find these helpful.' It contained papers of my father's that I had no idea existed: the five-year diary he had begun in 1932 just as he was quitting school to come to England; the autograph book with its encouragement to be 'as tidy as tidy can be'; a short story; and nearly a hundred love letters from Leonard to his 'Freckles' and a handful of hers in reply. Suddenly I could get behind the evasions and read for myself what had been going on in the years leading up to the Second World War, the loss of the Raj and the loss of father and son to each other.

It was Nora who brought the children to England. She had not been well and perhaps the trip gave her a chance to visit a specialist in Britain. She placed Esme in the convent in Eastbourne where she was to spend the next three years. She saw Leonard, now aged seventeen and a half, settled into his digs and ready to start the pre-medical course at Guy's and then she and seven-year-old Basil returned to Rawalpindi. It was 1933.

Leonard spent the next two years in digs in South Croydon, slogging through chemistry, physics and biology to get him up to speed for dental surgery. It was an uneventful life, commuting daily to the hospital in south-east London, playing hockey on Saturdays, attending church twice – early mass and evensong – on Sundays, and whiling away the afternoon between with long walks on Streatham Common, where he became familiar with the 'converters',* a convict, and the Blackshirts† he heard on their soapboxes every weekend. Some years later, when he had taken to biking holidays, he found himself sharing a youth hostel in the West Country with forty members of the Hitler Youth. When he could afford it, he took music lessons in the accordion and the drums, but found them very expensive, at 1/6d a time. Otherwise he read: Shakespeare and Boccaccio, Dante and Goethe. Money was very tight, with ten shillings a week to cover everything.

He studied hard and passed all his tests; his fellow students often didn't do as well, sometimes failing and resitting the exams several times. The strong work ethic and high Victorian values that had been instilled in him at St Joseph's had formed his character and although his letters show how deeply lonely he was at this time, and terribly isolated by his lack of funds, he made his father very proud. He was doing exactly what he had been told to do.

Then, after eighteen months, his social life changed: he was introduced to Joan, the daughter of family friends in India. Soon he was taking her to the pictures three or four times a week. His diary records that they saw *From Hell to Heaven* ('very nice'), *Song of Songs*, Ronald Colman in *Clive of India* ('quite good') and Gracie Fields in *Look up and Laugh* ('quite good' too). He was nearly twenty, and liked girls a lot; as well as his steady girl, there were others he met on holiday or just 'larking about in classroom 3'. He was fascinated by the female of the species and often recorded when he had been 'weak' with a girl, or 'behaved badly'. One day, while doing practical work at the hospital, to which he has just graduated after the tedious slog of the pre-medical course, he watched an operation for appendicitis on 'the prettiest girl I've ever seen. 19, blonde, fine complexion, but married 9 months.'

---

* I presume he means preachers.
† Members of the British Union of Fascists

He was desperately lonely for his first years in England, having no friends at all except the other students – and then the girl from India. A year later, looking back, he described himself as 'a green-horn', but, no doubt thanks to the girlfriend, 'the green youngster became more of a man in spite of many attempts to crush my search for something I badly wanted – human companionship to cheer me up'. It seems that the family were trying to put pressure on him: 'many attempts to crush my search for . . . companionship' is strong language. Leonard was not only lonely but depressed. He describes the 'slough of despondency of hum-drum hospital life' and 'that awful gloom which only a stranger can feel in the extreme loneliness of a big city'.[1] On top of that – or perhaps because of it – he failed an anatomy exam. It was his first setback and the family reacted by moving him back into their sphere of influence. So far he had been living alone in Croydon but now, with the rumours about a girlfriend and this failure in what had so far been a golden career, a letter came from India telling him he was to go and live with his 'Auntie', Mrs Delia Case, the sister of his stepmother Nora.

The official reason was that Esme was about to leave school and so the two of them would be able to live together at the aunt's. Esme later told me that she had aspired to follow her brother to medical school – it was, after all, a family tradition by now – but it was not considered an appropriate career for her and so she was to go as an apprentice to a hairdressing salon in the Kent town of Dartford, where Mrs Case lived. Moving Leonard from his independent life would also save money on the rent, for at about this time the letters from home started to talk about money being very tight. He still loved going to the 'flicks' but he realised that he would have to economise somehow. He would still have to commute to the hospital every day, so he had to cover his fares, but now there would be a cooked meal on his return and a place to study as his training became more demanding. It also meant that there would be someone to keep an eye on him. His 'Auntie' was very devout and he found himself spending a lot of time discussing serious topics with her late into the night (and clearly enjoying this). Perhaps following her example he redoubled his own attendance at church, often going on Saturdays as well as twice on Sundays.

It was a huge relief for him to pass the anatomy exam when he re-sat it in October, as he confided to his diary:

Friday October 4 1935
Results came out at 4.30. Was pleased to hear I had passed.
Could have leapt sky-high. Past few weeks seems like a
nightmare. Was I relieved or was I?

Now he felt he could afford to relax and started to look around for a new hobby, one that was not going to cost him money – 'Must think of some nice hobby to cultivate. Wish I could write.' At around the same time, the affair with the girl from home came to an end: was that the result of 'the many attempts to crush' his search for companionship, orchestrated by Mrs Case on a mandate to keep him on the straight and narrow that came from her sister in India? However it came about, the decks were cleared and at last Leonard found the new hobby he'd been seeking. A friend took him to a meeting of the local amateur operatic and dramatic society, where he auditioned and was accepted to play in the chorus of *The Pirates of Penzance*. That same evening he practised Act I in his room; he was very keen though formal rehearsals didn't start for another week. Until they really got going he spent his free time attending church, going to the cinema with his sister and reading novels.

November came and work started in earnest two nights a week on the songs for *The Pirates of Penzance*. Leonard didn't know it quite on sight, but singing away in the chorus near him was Esme's boss at the hairdresser where she was an apprentice. Joan Brise was a year or two older than him, the eldest of a happy family of four children, with the benefit of having trained in Paris, two hairdressing shops of her own, and a nippy little sports car. She was far beyond Leonard's league, but friendly and good fun.

I had always known that my parents met in the chorus, but reading my father's account of their early encounters moved me sometimes to tears. In a letter to Joan from this time, he wrote: 'Perhaps one of these days, I might endeavour to write a little story of what your friendship and love have done to me, but . . . I don't think I'll show it to you till many, many years have passed, because you might think me to be too much of a sentimentalist and much too serious.' Since he never did quite get round to telling the story of their relationship, I will do it for him here.

In December they started to rehearse on stage and Leonard thought himself quite good, though rather clumsy, and wished he could land a leading role. Christmas came and went. There was no more news from India after stern warnings that money would be tight, with cuts to come. It left Leonard in a jam, but it also worked in his favour, for Joan Brise, seeing he had no spare cash for his bus fare, offered him a lift home from rehearsals in her car, and this soon became a habit. The annual dance for the operatic society was in late December and Leonard took his sister Esme. 'Most enjoyable', thought Leonard, especially as 'Joan Brise gave Es and self a lift home'.

His life continued in the same pattern of working each day at the hospital, evenings and weekends at home reading detective stories and going to church with his aunt and sister. The bright spot in the week was the rehearsals for the show, which he thought were 'going very well'.

Late in January 1936 the King became weak and Leonard reported his decline and eventual death with artless loyalty and concern:

King's state serious. Latest bulletin 11:30 p.m. 'The King is passing peacefully away' I do hope and pray he will be spared us this
time. Oh Lord spare His Majesty to us for a little longer if it be
Thy Will.

He is so beloved by his own people and the peoples of many
other countries whom he has cemented together in friendship.
So please Jesus spare him if you think it will be better that way.

Poor George – the strain of this – his Jubilee year – and the
loss of his sister Princess Victoria have left him with little
strength to fight this the greatest battle of his life.

'Lord Jesus spare him, not our will but Thine be done.'

Tuesday January 21
His Majesty King George V passed away last night at 11:55 pm.
'May the Lord have mercy on his soul.' The Prince of Wales is
thus today King Edward VIII. The whole country is in mourning
and the court for 9 months.

His concern for the monarchy seems to be a sign of the deep loyalty he felt as a young man from the colonies, now at home for the
first time in his life. Leonard is perhaps more of a patriot than
anyone who had been born and raised in England and it is clear that
the habit of church-going, prayer and trust in God's will was also
deeply ingrained in him. These were aspects of his character that I
as his child born eleven years later was utterly unaware of until I was
handed his diary some seventy years after he had written it.

Leonard had another exam to pass before he could relax and enjoy
the run-up to the show, which was due to open in a month's time.
It was in practical dental mechanics, and, despite a good start, he
forgot to anneal a gold bar and when it broke he was certain he
would find himself re-sitting the exam. After 'a week's mental agony

with nothing to do, I went up to see the results of the exam. Can't say how pleased I was to hear I had passed. And so goodbye to mechanics. Very glad I managed to get dental anatomy last time.'

With the last obstacle out the way, he could relax and enjoy show business:

Monday: Dress rehearsal this evening. Walked home with Joan Brise and her pater gave me a lift home. Jolly decent of him.

Tuesday: Dress rehearsal. Had our photograph taken for papers. Must buy *Daily Mirror* on Thursday.

Wednesday: First night. House wasn't too good, but seemed to enjoy the show. Joan Brise took me to her house tonight. Super place.

Thursday: Show was awful tonight. Very bad audience. Hope it's better tomorrow. Went to Joan's place. She gave me a lift home.

Friday: Show was simply super tonight. Went on to Joan's place and had a very jolly time.

Saturday February 29
'The big night' and what a success. Everyone surpassed themselves. Bouquets afterwards. Joan took me to her house and we danced and had an egg-flip cocktail each and enjoyed ourselves immensely. Then at about 12:30 Joan gave me a lift home. Her people enjoyed our show.

Sunday March 1
Mass at 11. Our Dramatic Society made enough money to ensure their existence next year.

Tuesday March 3
Esme came home today saying Joan spoke to her quite nicely
today. I wonder if Joan thinks of me at all or is just amusing herself.

It is plain from these diary entries that in the week from the first
dress rehearsal to Esme's report that her boss had been quite nice to
her, Leonard had fallen in love. He was captivated and impressed by
Joan's life. The fact that she lived in the security of a large and easy-
going family – two boys and two girls, all of whom were encouraged
to bring their friends home – in a large white house with a green
tiled roof on the edge of a heathland, with commanding views out
through a stand of elms and a large garden with greenhouses, an
orchard, tennis courts and a billiard room. It was everything that he
and his family in India would have dreamed of when they imagined
a cosy life in England.

Joan's father was a self-made builder who had started out as a
cabinet maker and had bought a plot of land soon after the First
World War on which he built a pair of semi-detached houses. They
sold well, and he was able to build a few more. So his building
enterprise expanded and he moved the family from a modest terrace
to larger premises, and by the time Leonard met his eldest daughter,
he had achieved the comfort of the five-bedroomed detached house
in its own grounds, made over and embellished to his own design.
He employed a fairly large workforce and was designing and building whole estates across south London's suburbs that would
transform the look of the southern Home Counties and the expec-
tations of the upwardly mobile lower middle class who flocked to
live in them. I have seen the brochures for some of his early efforts:
in 1926 you could become the proud owner of a vaguely art-deco
three-bedroomed semi with a through lounge, integral garage and
front and back garden for about £260 all in.

He was known universally as 'the Guv'nor', and was much loved by his workers. He was enjoying his success and his family. He had married a country girl from Suffolk, Annie Maude Bailey, who had lost her mother when she was a scrap of a child, just as Leonard had. Perhaps that made a special bond between them, for from the minute he met her, my father adored the woman who was to become his mother-in-law, and would often confide in her. She brought her country ways to the big house on the heath, transforming the garden into a kitchen garden, and keeping chickens, a goat and a pig or two.

The four Brise children were good friends, it seems, and all learned to play an instrument. Weekend evenings would often be spent making music: nothing too highbrow – they would get the sheet music for the popular band tunes of the day, and though Joan and her sister would sometimes play the violin and piano together they were more likely to be led in a merry dance by their father on the banjo. All in all, it was a family set up that could not fail to captivate the lonely twenty-year-old, whose experience of family life thus far had been formal, critical, at times violent and terribly self-conscious. Leonard's experience of girls had also been with a more risqué sort, with a certain free and easy social manner. He seems to have been a little in awe of Joan's composure and self-restraint:

Saturday March 7
Had a whole holiday. Took Joan to Dramatic Dinner and Dance. Had a good time. She is an awfully nice girl, and is a good clean pal so different from my usual type. I feel so differently towards her; a sort of clean friendship. I do hope it continues.

Sunday March 8
Mass at 11 again at 6:30. Have resolved to give up smoking till I can afford it. I seem so different from what I was a fortnight

ago. I seem to be stronger mentally – in willpower – could it be that Joan Brise influences me so, and yet she says not a word on anything that could possibly have a bearing on it. I think perhaps it is our clean wholesome friendship – which I must keep as a friendship, though God knows how hard it is for me to tell her that I care. Nevertheless it would be no good as I have nothing to offer her yet or am likely to for another two or three years, and as they say 'Tempus Fugit'. Last night she was very sweet, and it was so difficult for me not to tell her just how much I cared and how she has changed me. I can't understand it, but I couldn't feel towards her as I have to girls previously. There is no thought of the flesh at all 'as in all cases before' but just an infinite pleasure in her society (and still three years to go). I know everything will be all right, because God is good and merciful.

Thursday March 26

Went with Joan to a dance given by the Council with two of Joan's pals in the MG.2 Jack Jackson's band played exceedingly well and I had all but two dances with Joan. She and I are jolly good friends, and I shall have to keep it at that – although it is going to be hard. Why are my people so against me having a girl, especially a girl like Joan? She is so sweet and sensible and so full of life, and not the kind who is weak and likely to get into trouble.

Unfortunately Mrs Case did not share Leonard's confidence that Joan was not the kind to get into – or to cause – trouble. As the friendship deepened, she had started sending negative reports about the situation back to his anxious parents in Rawalpindi. Meanwhile Leonard, unaware of the storms that were brewing on several fronts, both domestic and Far Eastern, saw Joan as much as he possibly could – no mention of hockey or the flicks now, nor any of his work at the hospital either:

Saturday March 28
Can't understand myself lately. Reading serious books in the accumulation of knowledge, and being more optimistic than I have ever been. Looking for Joan everywhere – on every bus or car, and finding an infinite pleasure in her company. So different from all previous experiences.

Monday March 30
Mr Brise took [us] to the Ideal Home Exhibition. Joan and I wandered around and saw the homes of the film stars – from the showy glassy bathroom of Claudette Colbert, to the quiet restful library of Ronald Colman and Shirley Temple's bedroom. Joan had her hands manicured free.

Later we had supper at a neighbouring restaurant, and so home to bed. Joan was very sweet today but as usual she knew just where our friendship should stop. She seems awfully strong and I admire her for it.

A week later their 'clean friendship' threatened to become something else, for Leonard at least. Joan's mother had invited him to accompany her to the first annual dinner and dance of the Ratepayers' Association. He thought it was a much better dinner than they had enjoyed at the Dramatic Society do – probably his only other experience of the high life so far – and he appreciated the glass of port they were given for the toasts, though he was vehement in his criticism of the speakers – to his diary, that is: 'The many speech makers – who are a kind of vermin that ought to be exterminated, each pouring out flattery as much as they can and saying how good each is and what he has done, etc. they make me sick with their lack of sincerity.'

When Joan was able to join them later, things brightened up:

Mrs Brise stood us a gin and soda each.

About an hour later the dancing begun. Had all with Joan except the Paul Jones. Went to her place about 1:15 – both feeling dead beat. Joan slumped down on an armchair, I made some coffee. After we had finished our coffee we sat down on the armchair talking trivialities, when somehow I don't know how I had her in my arms. I suppose I was very tired, anyhow I felt I couldn't go on without letting her know that she was more to me than a friend. She nearly returned my affection but was very strong and pulled herself together and I cruelly compelled her to tell me why. She said there was a 'somebody else' and I had spoilt everything. At this I broke down and wept like a child (this showed how weak I was). She comforted me and asked me not to. After a few minutes of silence, I managed to pull myself together and got up. We then had a cocktail to the beginning of a beautiful friendship, and so home, feeling as though something had broken. How very true was the man who said 'Sorrow was the schoolmaster'. I can't describe how I feel. It feels as though it were only a dream, but no, as I look at my red eyes in the mirror I know it is all horribly true. I seem to have lost something infinitely valuable. I know there is God who watches over us and he would not want us to suffer unwittingly so I leave everything to him, to do as he wills, and I know he will make everything all right.

He did not leave everything to God; of course he didn't. He was only twenty and in love for the first time. The next day he sent off a letter, full of good intentions and jealousy:

April 8th:

Dear Joan,

I daresay you will be very surprised to receive a letter from me, but I had to write to give myself some peace of mind.

Believe me, Joan, when I say how sorry I am for the way I imposed on our friendship last night, and made such a fool of myself. The only excuse I can make – and a paltry one at that – is that I must have been exceptionally tired or extraordinarily weak.

I had heard some time ago that there was a 'somebody else', but I refused to believe it. Please do tell me what you meant when you said I must be blind.

You also said that 'curiosity wouldn't kill the cat on my behalf', and that 'I took a lot for granted'. I would like to ask you two questions to satisfy my curiosity, but don't answer them if you don't want to.

1) Who is the 'somebody else'?

2) Do you really care for him? (A most presumptuous question, which I shirked asking last night.)

After all this, don't you think we could consider the subject closed, and never to be mentioned again?

You said you were willing to resume our friendship as it was before yesterday, and I sincerely hope you still feel the same way. I promise you that there will never be a repetition of last night's display and you simply must believe me, Joan.

I feel that all this is boring you, but I could tell you so much better in person, only it is a delicate subject, and one we did agree to consider closed, didn't we.

Please, please don't reproach or blame yourself in any way for last night's climax which was entirely my fault.

You would take an immense load off my mind if you could find it possible to forgive.

Yours sincerely,
Len

P.S. I have got a form for you from the library and will bring it
along on Friday at about 3:30.

That Friday meeting, officially about a library form and the
resumption of their good, clean friendship, was to change the direction of his life.

Yours to a Fag Butt Always

When Leonard turned up at the Brise house on that Friday, he got a rather cool reception from Joan. They went off and played golf for a while – probably just putting balls into the hole – and then, to his relief, Joan was 'as she used to be' – friendly and relaxed. She told him that she was going off next day with her partner in the salon, Miss Fisher, to spend Easter in Paris. She wanted him to come along too – I daresay she would have enjoyed showing off the Paris she had got to know as a student to the greenhorn from the colonies – but poor Leonard had to confess that he was 'unable to get necessary cash'. Then Joan suggested he might at least like to come down to Newhaven with them in her father's Railton car to see her off, and Leonard said he should love to:

Saturday April 11 1936
And so to Saturday night and the journey to Newhaven. It was the happiest night I could ever remember. I told Joan I meant everything in my letter, and she said I never said much so how could she understand my feelings towards her.

Anyway she returned my affection and we were both so

happy. It all seemed like a dream, but oh! how different from Tuesday's. How I love her . . . Why am I not independent, instead of what I am?

I would write and tell Dad everything, did I not know what he'd do. Oh! Why wasn't he more human and understanding with me when I was young, and a pal to me, instead of a feared monster as he is now?

Anyway I love, love, love Joan with all my heart, and am sure she feels the same.

I feel, though, that it is all too good to last. Oh! Jesus, God of Love, guide me as you think best, not as I will, but as thou wilt.

They wrote to each other while they were apart, but Leonard still found it hard to believe that she could really care for him: 'You've no idea how I wish I could have gone with you, but I don't suppose you'd have got much of a kick out of it, would you?'

His letters are full of apology for his 'weakness', his 'morbid, gloomy moods', his frustration at his lack of independent money and his obligation to do as his parents wanted. All his life he has been obedient and a good student; suddenly, though, he has a new teacher, and one he is delighted to learn from.

I did so promise myself that I'd be always cheerful like the good advice in the cutting you gave me. Why can't I be like you, Freckle-face? You are always so cheerful, and face everything with a smile, and do so cheer me up and sympathize with me . . .

Oh! There's such a lot I could tell you, but – soon, maybe not tomorrow, but soon, if you can call two long years soon. Anyhow I shall be patient like 'Patience, sitting on a monument, Smiling at grief'.

Cheerio, Freckle-face.

I suppose that the two long years he had spent alone and broke in Croydon would have made any young man feel unconfident, and he had recently met his first public failure with the anatomy exam that went wrong, and then the family's insistence that he give up his independent life, lonely though it had often been, to live under the supervision of Mrs Case; but on the other hand he had passed the re-sit of the anatomy exam – indeed the new hobby of theatre was his little reward to himself for getting back on track. And now he was in love and assured of being loved in return, so why was he filled with the superstitious dread that it was 'all too good to last'?

I believe that the villain who was undermining him was his hostess and 'aunt', Mrs Case. She was very religious, attending church several times at the weekend. Esme was also in her care, fresh from the Eastbourne convent and education by nuns in India before that. Leonard noted in his diary the summer Esme left school and joined him in Dartford that she was 'very keen on being a nun'. The prevailing atmosphere in the Case house was thus very devout, and I suspect that Leonard taking up the Stage as a new hobby was not popular. Mrs Case would have been charged with reporting back to the Quicks in India if there was any cause for concern; others in the family have said since that she was very difficult and very demanding, and could be 'a bit of a bully'. She probably thought that Leonard was getting too frivolous when he should have been happy to continue in his old habits of work, detective stories, hockey matches on Saturday afternoons and lots of church-going. It does not seem to me to be a coincidence that he started rehearsing in late October, and that by early December a letter had arrived from his father telling Leonard how broke they were – this from a man who now owned three houses: his own, 'best house in Rawalpindi', Ashburnham Cottage in the Murree hills, and a third house in Pindi that was let to close family friends – and who had his two dental practices still, which were both thriving. There was just time between Leonard excitedly announcing that he had passed his audition and was going to be in the show and his father's letter announcing that the family was broke and economies would have to be made, for a letter to have been fired off by Mrs Case. The response that was dashed off was the beginning of an elaborate manipulation to make Leonard toe the line in deference to the sacrifices the family had had to make in order to afford to send him to England.

Sure enough, when January came, with the start of the new term, there was no sign of the usual letter with a money order that would enable Leonard to pay for his new season ticket. He bought day returns and spent his free time at weekends staying in bed reading because he could not afford to go anywhere or do anything. When the letter finally came from India, two weeks late, he was docked all the money for his lunches and told he would have to make do with a homemade sandwich at lunchtime and his hockey money was reduced as well. 'How I am fed up of sandwiches . . . anyhow must bear it,' he wrote in his diary, but he did not economise by giving up the show, for which the rehearsals were becoming more intense all through January and February, or by giving up smoking, which he had been trying to do for two years now. He had become more friendly with Joan and was spending less and less time with the Case family. In his innocence he would come home and speak enthusiastically about the Brises' big house – 'super place' he wrote in his diary the first time he went to Heathside – and the free and easy 'open house' atmosphere there, where the four children were encouraged to invite their friends over on Sundays so long as they did the cooking and the clearing up. Of course, if he was beginning to be tempted to spend Sundays at Heathside it would be taking him away from some of his church attendance. It was all a bit too bohemian for Mrs Case, and her reports to India

and the letters that came to him in response were doing their
utmost to control Leonard by emotional blackmail. The result was
that he fluctuated between wondrous elation at his new-found
happiness, and depression and despair that he was not after all
worthy of love, for his family was not showing him any. But above
all it made him implacable in his determination to stick with Joan:
'I shall make you mine, in spite of the tremendous oppositions
which is [*sic*] trying to keep us apart.' A week later he was citing
Shakespeare to confirm his determination:

> . . . but I'm not going to lose you, instead I shall do as the poet
> says:
>> 'The friends thou hast and their adoption tried
>> Bind to your heart with hooks of steel.'[1]

The letters kept coming from India throughout April and May,
and the more emotionally secure Joan suggested that they spend a
month not seeing each other in order to calm his family's fears. This
threw Leonard into a worse panic; he reacted angrily to the suggestion and then had to apologise when he saw the wisdom of
discretion. I imagine Joan was being pragmatic about not fanning
the fires of a family row, though she might well have started to
wonder what she had embarked on, such was the intensity of
Leonard's adoration of her in a few short months. Matters had,
however, gone too far. Both Mrs Case and the family in India were
on his trail; the letters from home were threatening to cut his
money off completely if he didn't concentrate on his work properly.
In July the older and wiser Joan turned twenty-two, and Leonard
celebrated her birthday by sending her a poem by Petrarch:

> *I find no peace, and all my war is done;*
> *I fear, I hope, I burn and freeze likewise;*

[. . .]
I wish to perish, yet I ask for health;
I love another, and yet I hate myself;
[. . .]
And my delight is causer of my grief.[2]

It was not, perhaps, the most generous of gifts, to be told that you are the 'causer of grief', even if you are also someone's 'delight'. By October Joan suggested that the only thing to do was for them to cool off for two years until such time as Leonard had finished his training at Guy's. If they were to meet it would have to be secretly, and there was no question of any official commitment to each other. Leonard had little choice but to agree even though he had turned twenty-one that September, since he was utterly dependent on support from his family, but the prospect filled him with gloom. For Joan it was going to be much easier: she lived at home in the bosom of her loving family and she had her own career and a wide circle of friends. Also, her character was less romantic and more practical – she told me later that she chose to marry Leonard because he was such a decent fellow, but that she did not really come to fall in love with him until after they were married – so for her the prospect of two years' casual friendship was never going to be so hard as it would be for him. That was another thing that made Leonard feel bad:

Two years of secret meetings, away from local public gaze, is going to be very tough on you, my dear, and is going to cost you terribly. Just think of all that you are missing by choosing to meet me; I am sure you know lots of young men who could offer you much, much more than I could; they could take you out to everything locally, treat you to whatever you like, but what can I do? I have to meet you secretly; I can't treat you to anything; I can't take you anywhere locally. Oh, Joan, can't you see what you have let yourself in for? Think deeply on what I have written & if you think that you would rather have the life and freedom you had before; then it is not too late; but if you decide to carry on as at present, then darlingest Freckles, I promise that you won't regret your choice in later years.

Yours till hell freezes,
Freck

Sometimes it was just too much for him, he could no longer afford even the price of a stamp for his daily missives and their snatched ten-minute meetings at the station before he got on the train to London and she went off to her salon could barely keep him going:

October 1936. Monday:
The day after a very lonely weekend.
You know, Freckles, sometimes I wonder whether it is worth it – I mean my working at the hospital, getting no thanks for any exams I may pass, & threatened with the direst punishment should I fail in one. Unable to choose my own companions & to enjoy the pleasures I would like to. Oh! Freckles if only I could tell you how hard everything has been & is. Everything I do I must write home about & give a detailed account of it, & then generally get as a reply a strict censorship of my actions upheld by weak and childish arguments. I sometimes feel like running away from it all to fend for myself, but I know I should never do this, for it would mean losing you and I certainly don't intend that to happen. I don't know why I am writing all this to you, making mountains out of what are probably mole-hills, but I simply had to get it all off my chest.

How marvellous it would be to be able to take my petty troubles to you at any time, & know that you would sympathize &
not laugh at me as others would.

I have had as my tutor in the last few months a real philoso-
pher, who has taught me so much that is good and beautiful in
this world.

I wonder if you have met this person – the most wonderful
person – who goes about in a funny little car, freckled and always
smiling.

He felt that she had transformed his life and turned him inside
out:

Really, Freckles, knowing you and finally loving you as I do at
this moment has been a liberal education, and I thank God time
& time again for being privileged to enjoy your friendship.

Thank you for your delightful letter, containing your good
advice about anger and sulking. Thanks a million for forgiving
the show of anger I gave the other night, & I promise it will
never happen again.

Of course it did: quite a lot, for he was under constant pressure
and no doubt full of Catholic guilt to boot. Reading through these
exchanges it seems that he was putting Joan under heavy pressure
too – most girls would surely have run a mile. In his more cheerful
moments Leonard entered into the cloak-and-dagger spirit of it all:

I was hoping to see you at the library tonight, but didn't go after
all. Auntie & Betty were going to the pictures, & as Auntie
wasn't keen on going, she said she'd stand me if I went, so after
all the tales I have told about yesterday, I thought it would ease
my conscience if I went, and incidentally put her off the track.

He was charming, and ardent and steadfast – the more pressure he felt, the more determined he was to stick it out and deserve Joan's faith in him. After one Wednesday 'without my darling' he tried to get her to come to a shorthand class he had started attending, to meet him briefly either before or after the session; he urged her 'now don't forget, Freckle-face, darling, dearest, sweetest, most adorable sweetheart, big brown eyes, my baby girl, at 15–10–5 mins to 7 or 9 p.m. at the gate.'

I hope she went to meet him for the pressure was on him still, and despite all his good intentions and his extreme poverty he still could not manage to give up smoking, though his diary frequently exclaims how much he needs to, and he signs this particular note to his beloved 'Yours to a fag butt always'. I would have found it hard to resist such droll ardour myself. He enjoyed teasing her a lot, especially when they contrived to meet so she could teach him to drive her sporty little coupé they had christened Leaping Lena:

You didn't tell me whether you had dreamed the night before, so conclude you didn't, but I did, & it was a most marvellous one too; all about a fat little girl, with skinny legs & big feet, & lots of freckles on her face trying to teach a big – a great big – man to drive a tiny little car. It took this clever little girl two years to teach this big man, & then he became her chauffeur, & they settled down in a cottage in the country & lived happily for ever after.

Leonard still wrote to her almost daily to make up for all the time they were not together, dropping his notes off by hand, and they were often full of fantasies of escape from doing the responsible thing that Joan had counselled. She encouraged him to go off to Devon without her on holiday with friends from the hospital, and his reaction was: 'let's run away in Lena tonight for a week, or a month, or a century, or forever, away from criticism, convention, disagreeable relatives & all that makes life so unpleasant'.

She was the responsible one who took the long view; he the ardent, dependent one who was often angry and panicked at the prospect of separation from the comfort and tenderness he had so recently found:

Tuesday December 1st 1936

I had to write to you, my dearest, to apologize for being so obstinate and unreasonable tonight. I knew that what you proposed was the best solution, little darling, but I thrust it away from me, refusing to accept it, because I am very selfish about you, knowing how hard it would be to see you for perhaps only a couple of hours a week if I accepted your proposal . . .

Not to see you in the mornings, evenings, on Wednesdays & Sundays, not to go to class with you, not to drive you home on Saturdays & thousands of other little things & now that we have decided to be strong & do as you have suggested I feel as if my whole world has become a blank, & I feel positively weak, so much so that I almost feel sorry that I promised you that I'd be strong. But I'd never break my promise to you, Freckles, so will be strong and eagerly look forward to the bright tomorrows when our long cherished dreams will materialize, & we can always be together 'till death do us part'.

It had been just about a year that the two had known each other, but their discretion was not to be rewarded yet. By late January 1937 the situation with Leonard's family got even worse. Perhaps Mrs Case saw through the charade of a cooling period for the young lovers and certainly Leonard was a different creature from the biddable, devout boy she had welcomed into her home only eighteen months earlier. He felt keenly the contrast between the welcoming support of the Brises and the coldness from his own family:

> To think there are 2 solid years ahead before I can be free to live my own life, instead of going about in public with a sort of super-ficial veneer, & kowtowing to those who know they have the whip-hand of me, & use it too in a vain endeavour to rob me of that which I hold most dear.
>
> At the present moment I feel like one hypnotized (compelled by a mind controlling mine to do as it wishes), and those two years seem much too long to ask you to wait in patience, to give up so many of your pleasures for the moody – and I am sure at times, positively revolting – companionship of a mere student.
>
> Oh forgive me, Freckles, for writing all this rubbish, but I happen to be in the blues, and the future seems so terribly gloomy.
>
> Maybe it's just another air mail letter I received from home in which my father's distrust of me hurts me terribly . . . perhaps you may be able to find some little good in me whatever others may think.

It has always been very difficult to get anyone in the family – those who are old enough to remember these times, that is – to open up about what was actually said. My mother always said she wanted to remember only the good times, and it was a big, and late, concession for her to give me the box of Leonard's papers. Her younger sister, and Leonard's younger sister Esme, were kept in ignorance of what was happening. They were too young, or perhaps it was just not considered seemly for young women to be involved in such matters. Everyone else who was around in Dartford at the time and might have remembered what actually happened was no longer living; there was just a strange legacy that hinted at cruelty and bad feeling. As a last resort I tried to find out from Nora's only child what he knew of these events which were happening in England while he was a boy of ten in India, and on top of that away at St Joseph's for most of the year. Uncle Basil was not best placed to know what was being said at the time, but he too came to England after the war and remained in close touch with Leonard and his family. Could he shed any light on all these whispered unhappinesses, I wondered?

He certainly agreed that Bertie had a temper – 'A very, very severe temper, unfortunately'. He remembered how he 'got a good walloping' when Kaloo taught him to fly a traditional Afghani fighting kite with the glass-coated string designed to cut through the strings of other competitors, and it cut through the wireless aerial at his parents' house. He also remembered a row his father had with Nora in which he threw all her clothes out of her wardrobe and set fire to them. He was very strict, very Victorian and he was married to a woman who was herself 'very controlling, very demanding: very Irish and very Catholic'. Basil felt that she was also 'a very loving person really, though she tended to get hot under the collar' and that she 'just existed for the children'. But she had lost one child at the time of Basil's birth, for he was a twin and the other child, Derek, was a blue baby who did not survive, and after the twins she suffered three miscarriages. By 1936 she had been married to Bertie for sixteen years; all of the children were away and it did not look as if she would be having more. And now stories were coming back from Mrs Case, her sister in England, about Leonard's irresponsible behaviour.

On top of all this, Nora was ill and Bertie wanted to take her to Switzerland for a gastric jejunostomy.* Perhaps money really was as

---

* A procedure in which a feeding tube is inserted into the small intestine, in cases where there is a need to bypass normal feeding routes

tight as Bertie had said in his letters, for it can't have been cheap to travel all the way to Europe from India and to pay for private surgery. If that coincided with the news of Leonard's 'waywardness' in failing exams, smoking too much, going out to the flicks and spending most of his evenings attending either a rehearsal or a performance and then being driven home in a racy little sports car by an 'older woman' it is not so surprising that the family pleaded poverty, resenting his ingratitude for the sacrifices they had made to send him over to England to study.

Mrs Case's reports back to India only fanned the flames, or perhaps it was that his parents' attempts to order him into submission had finally made Leonard answer back. In any case there was an almighty row. And there was something else. When I really pressed Basil he finally told me something quite vile in its racism, which made me understand at last why no one in the family would ever discuss what was said. The Quicks apparently believed that Joan's family were Romany Gypsies. Mr Brise was thought to own the whole of Dartford, and to have lots of visits from Romanys: he was the 'head of the gang sort of situation and the others came to him for advice and help'. Later Basil said he was 'thought to be of a Jewish distinction', to have 'come from Eastern Europe somewhere'. And how could they have got this impression? There was only one way – Mrs Case had been telling them this.

Did it have any basis in truth? That is a more difficult question. There was no doubt that Pop Brise, as we grandchildren later called him, was very unlike the people around him in Dartford: he was olive-skinned and black-eyed with thick black hair which, by the time I knew him, had turned snowy white. He also had a magnificent conk of a nose, which had been inherited by his four children in varying degrees. Later, when I would ask my mother where her father had come from, she would say Armenia or Syria via Switzerland. It was known that his mother had been a French-speaking Swiss woman but that was about it. When I would ask for more detail she couldn't supply any. All that she knew was based on how he looked and how she and her siblings looked, none of whom had inherited the fair hair and blue eyes of their Suffolk-born mother. Certainly they were very strong genes, for in my generation too there is at least one if not two in each family of my cousins who have that same look. It was, after all, this family appearance that had started me off wondering as a child whether we might have come from somewhere east of Vienna. But when Mrs Case spoke of them as being Romany or 'of a Jewish distinction' it was as if she had called them the devil's spawn: she was an ardent Catholic and nothing but her church was acceptable in those she expected to associate with.

On top of that, Pop was a successful entrepreneur in the small town where they lived and his company was expanding fast, employing more and more apprentices, among whom were both McAlpine and Wates, I was told, both of whom went on to found enormous building concerns of their own. Pop was a paternalistic employer known as the Guv'nor or, as I was told by a former apprentice, 'Darky Brise': when I asked why he had been given this nickname I was told it was 'because he was so blimming dark, of course'. This particular employee said he was very well liked by his staff and popular with everyone in the area except the Case and Quick families. Pop had in fact built the street of houses in which Mrs Case was living; she may even have been his tenant, since he retained title to many of them, and perhaps she felt exploited. He had no interests or hobbies outside the business and his family, and he enjoyed doing things with them, whether it was making music on his banjo or accordion, or playing ping pong or billiards. He was good with his hands and I remember him teaching me to mitre corners so that I could make picture frames for Christmas presents when I was about eleven – he was always available to help the children. Perhaps these are Jewish or Romany qualities: the love of family, the artisanal skills, the head for business, the paternalistic concern for his workers. To us, then and now, they were simply the qualities of a very humane man and who cared where his family had hailed from? The irony is that this hostility was coming at him from those whose need to belong in the English fold was so great because they were themselves outsiders, Irish Catholics and Anglo-Indian colonialists who had barely lived in Britain.

All attempts to placate them were doomed to fail and by early 1937 Leonard found himself utterly cast off by the family and still with a long way to go before he could make any money. His life looked as if it would be a 'hell of loneliness with a few short moments of Paradise to give me strength'. He had to work out how he would survive with no means of support and another seventeen months until his finals: bereft of a family and dangerously dependent on Joan's love and good opinion to keep him going at all, he was absolutely desperate.

January 1937
Oh, Freckles, if only I had a job or some money of my own to enable me to be independent, and be always with the one person I love above everything else in the whole world, and I do so love you, Freckle-face, that with you to back me & encourage me, I feel I could do anything. You don't know how many times I have been tempted to borrow a few hundred pounds to enable me to finish this last lap of my studies in independence. And then I think what a handicap to start off in life in debt for 3 or 4 hundred pounds. If only I had a rich uncle or somebody who would die and leave me the necessary amount, I never stop praying for him. But alas! I have no such wealthy relation.

Anyway the next 17 months will pass very quickly, won't they, and then, oh, darling, the very thought of it sends me dotty.

He applied for a small bursary from Guy's, which enabled him to move into hospital accommodation while he sat the next round of exams, but that was only enough to keep him for a few weeks. He was beset by anxieties:

Friday 19th March, Guy's
Darling Sweetheart,
    I am so downhearted about this exam, as I don't feel as though I'd done too well. Sweetheart, I feel so terribly lonely & miserable . . . you have come to mean so much to me, mentally, physically, morally: I simply couldn't exist without you, perhaps I could for a short time bodily, but something would be dead inside me.

When the bursary ran out he scraped around, borrowing tiny sums from everyone he could think of. It simply wasn't enough, though, and the hospital routine was now so demanding that it was impossible for him to think of earning any money on the side. In the end Joan's parents came up with a solution. Mrs Brise gave him twenty-five pounds towards the forty he needed to pay his fees up to the next exam in four months' time and she told him they would allow him to use a room in one of the houses Mr Brise had built until such time as he was qualified. He could spend his weekends with the family at Heathside and if all went well he would pass his finals the following year and would at last be in a position of independence.
    Leonard had moved well beyond Mrs Case's sphere, and he was much, much happier but, reading through these letters now, I feel

moved but also fearful for him as his happiness seems to depend so
much on Joan. The star-crossed lovers were about to face another
test. They had been brought closer by the threatened wrath of
Leonard's distant parents in India, but now a more immediate
proposition, delightful for one, dreaded by the other, came up.
Joan's father was to take a four-month cruise to the Caribbean and
South America. His wife was not a keen traveller and so it was
decided that Joan should take her place. She was twenty-three, a
successful owner of two businesses with an ardent boyfriend who in
any case was going to have to keep his head down for the final push
to qualify and be free of parental restraints for ever. The paper in
general surgery and pathology was looming. It must have seemed
like perfect timing to her, removing herself so that he could work
undistracted. And Leonard, encouraged to find his love returned,
and welcomed into Joan's family, put his best face on their imminent separation:

Lonely Thursday
I thought when we went down to Newhaven to see you off to
Paris, when first I kissed you, that I loved you as much as
humanly possible, but . . . my love for you now is more than the
whole world. Besides filling my whole being, spiritual, temporal,
physical, mental, moral, in fact you are now my life, my being,
my existence.

Darling, we must never, never part from each other, & when
we feel our mortal span is over, let's seek happiness & eternity
together.

True to her nature, Joan had a whale of a time, throwing herself
into all the on-board activities, making good friends in Trinidad and
Brazil and Argentina, and responding to her lover's ardent, yearning missives in a lighthearted tone. The plan was that by the time

she got back in April her Freck, as she had nicknamed Leonard, would have triumphantly passed his final exams, put student life behind him and be ready to join her in making his way as a professional. But he missed her too much; he couldn't concentrate without the encouragement she'd been giving him in the flesh, even if only for a few snatched minutes each week. He was desperately in need of confirmation that he was loved. He must have felt jealous, although he never quite comes out with that in the daily bulletins he fired off across the Atlantic, and he was 'terribly worried' about how he had done with his answers on the symptoms and treatment of tetanus, of secondary haemorrhage and on the value and uses of antiseptics: 'These exams are a real nerve-racking experience and I do so want my soother here to steady my nerves. I keep saying to myself, What will my Freckles say if I don't pass?' He wrote this the night before the oral and by the evening of the next day he knew he hadn't made it:

What can I say? I've let you down, Freckle-face; this evening I got the biggest shock of my life when I was told I came down in part 1 in the oral. Please believe me when I say I tried hard, and swotted hard. I was certain I knew my stuff backwards, and yet in the oral the examiners just tied me up in knots. I can't write much more, Darling, the disappointment is so great and I am so disgusted with myself and so unworthy of you that I don't know what to do. I am sending this by ordinary mail because I don't want to send you this kind of news too soon in case it should spoil your holiday. I feel an absolute failure; but am determined never, never to let you down again. Please say you still believe in me, or else I just couldn't go on. I could explain so much better to you the whole thing and just what I mean. There's so much that wants to come out, but I'm afraid if I put it on paper it wouldn't make sense, so excuse me.

It was a very downcast Freck who was waiting at the quayside in April. Would she still care for him, and how was he going to keep himself going through another slog up to finals? Until Joan's return Leonard had swung between despair and ebullient hope. He was oppressed by his troubles: there was, first and foremost, his conspicuous failure to pass the exams and then the continuing estrangement from his family and, on top of that, his lack of money. He had been surviving with loans from various friends but it would be many months before he could re-sit the exams. He went to the Dental Board, cap in hand, and they told him that the odds were about a hundred to one against him being granted anything on top of the money he had already borrowed:

All I seem to do is ask for money, money, money for this & some more for that and so it goes on.

And I had hoped that I would meet you at Southampton an LDS,* and that soon I would have you to myself for always.

My love it's agony, hell without you, and yet I'm glad I wasn't selfish enough to stop you, though I wanted to, how much I couldn't tell & at times I feel quite a hero.

I want to make myself somebody in the world, someone you would be proud of. See how much you have made me love you . . . but please understand darling Freckles, it's how I feel – not only at the present moment – but always since that day two years ago when we first told our love . . . Since then I am a changed being from the quiet, pessimistic, helpless youth who was me when first we met.

* Licentiate in Dental Surgery, the qualification needed to practise as a dentist

He tried so hard not to feel bad, and not to feel threatened by her gadding about the globe:

> Thank you for the photographs darling; you certainly seem to be enjoying yourself. Please look after yourself, & see that you come back fatter. I wish I was with you, but what's the use of wishing. You seem to be having a very nice time in Grenada, shooting, riding, fishing etc, but don't grow too fond of these places abroad, darling, remember there's no place like home.

In fact, my mother told me in later years that she did have a romance while away, with an Argentinean gaucho, the owner of a vast ranch who had pressed her to stay and become his wife. She was wise enough not to mention this when she returned to England on schedule, tanned, confident and in magnanimous mood. Soon she was able to comfort him, by her sheer physical presence, of course, but also with her innate common sense. His failure in the exams was just a blip; he could study and re-sit them with the confidence to know that she had returned to his side and that their relationship had survived her four-month adventure.

Her family welcomed him into their circle, just as they did with all of their children's friends, and the more so since it was clear by now that Leonard was more than a passing romance. He spent much of his time with Joan's family at their large white house with the green tiled roof, riding out with her brothers, making music in the family band (his drumming had improved over the past two years), learning to play golf or driving Joan about in her little car, while he slogged his way back to finals. It was everything he had wanted from family life and finally, now that his Freckles had come home, he was able to say 'at last I am living again'.

Pop Brise consulted his wife, and they came up with a solution to Leonard's practical difficulties. Since he was absolutely without funds they would advance him a modest loan to see him through the last year of his studies, which he would pay back once he was qualified and earning. The dream of happiness he had seen when he first fell for Joan was now all set to come true: all he had to do was work hard, pass the exams and everything else would follow. He cheered up and set to, and recovered his sense of humour – for me always one of his great qualities – so that when by chance he bumped into the cause of much of his misery, Mrs Case, he was able to share a joke or two about it with Joan:

21–3–38

Who do you think I met today? Quite right, my aunt; & she talked & talked & talked. She said she'd heard from my father that since you'd 'gone away', I'd soon found consolation by marrying a girl called 'LENA'.

You should have seen her face when she asked me if it were true, & then when I told her that Lena was a car you had (I wish you had been there).

Sweetheart the way that woman hears about things amazes me. She had heard that you & I were thinking of joining the tennis club this year, and that it would cost me 14 guineas for the next 3 months at the hospital. I don't know how she gets these things, my love, because I've told no-one apart from our family (is it very presumptuous of me to say our instead of your family just yet?) I'm sure she must make enquiries at the hospital or something.

She asked after you, and also what my plans were, which I didn't tell her, and of course the usual scandal of Dartford, which doesn't bear repeating. You don't know how thankful I am at having finished with her. It's you, sweetheart, I have to thank, because you gave me strength & courage to leave her & her gossip.

How different his tone is from the diffident boy of before:
'. . . last year I thought I couldn't possibly love you more. How
pessimistic my letters were then . . . you have changed me completely from the morbid youth of a year ago', but now his letters
inevitably start to tail off because communication became so
much easier. He could see Joan whenever he was free of the hospital, with the blessing of her family, and there was no looking
back. He sailed through finals and took his first posting as a
locum, far away, for one who had come to depend on being close
to Joan, in St Helen's, Lancashire. Leonard complained that 'the
weekends here are awful, absolutely nothing to do'. His next
postings were nearer home, in Brighton and then Southend,
with steady increases in pay. He went back to his old habit of
writing to Joan daily, and confided: 'It feels as though I've gone
up so many rungs of the ladder for my sweetheart . . . the time
does not seem so far-off when the dreams we've dreamed will
gradually reach maturity to repay some of the bad dreams we've
lived through.'

The next year Joan and Leonard married, and it was a Roman
Catholic ceremony in deference to his strong faith. It was June
1940 and Leonard enlisted in the Dental Corps as a Major. My
older brother and sister were born during the war, and I was born
nine months and four days after his return to civilian life in
1946.

I understand that part of the commitment of marrying into a
Roman Catholic family is to promise to raise the children in the
faith. However, it seems that while my older brother and sister
were at least baptised, by the time I was born there was no
attempt to enrol me. I have a vague recollection of sitting in a
perfumed church while my siblings went to confession but I
must have been tiny and never really grasped the significance of

it all. When I asked my mother about it all, the requiem, Daddy's faith, our 'Godless' childhood, in the aftermath of my father's funeral, all she would say – stiffly for her, the most relaxed of women – was that she did not want to raise her children in a religion that, while professing universal love, could be so apparently unloving and so specifically cruel. Perhaps the war had weakened my father's faith too, and it is no wonder that in the letters he was writing to Joan in the year and a half after his financial support was cut off by his family, he made absolutely no reference to the Quicks back in India. It is as if by denying their very existence he could deny their power to hurt him. And that was what he continued to do, more or less, for the rest of his life.

It was a way to survive and he made a pretty good fist of it. He was happy with Joan, but I know that we were all somehow affected by that omission at the heart of our life. Daddy never raised his voice; he simply wouldn't fight. In any case I only ever wanted to please him, but if he was disappointed he would simply go and get on with something. It seems comic to me at this distance, the way that my mother would be exasperated by something one of us four had done, send us to our father to be punished and the offender would emerge after a 'talk'. But my brothers have a different version: they were treated with a real coldness, an absence of love and interest, even a violent passion of disapproval and censure, that made them feel forlorn their whole lives. Somehow girls were different: you gave them a talking-to, then hugged them, then sat down together to make something – it could be anything, a ring with a semi-precious stone, or chicken cacciatore, or a prop for the next show at the amateur theatre – and the punishment was forgotten. The boys were treated with a severity that was a clear repeat of how my father had been treated by Bertie, his father, leaving scars that have healed but are still visible. I didn't see it at the time; it was only in the liberal seventies, when we grown-up children would talk about growing up, free of the unspoken family habit not to indulge one's feelings, that this became clear.

18

Trailing Ghosts

As a child I was driven mad by the refusal of adults to let out how they felt: no one would say they were sad, or frightened or didn't know what to do. Most of the time life was pleasant and fairly low key, and so one was haunted all the more by the demons of unnamed fears. I don't think it can be a coincidence that many of the parts I have played as an actress have been about that same response of denial, where it was simply impossible for the person to acknowledge anything negative because it would cost too much to admit it. Everything is instead swept into a locked cupboard in an attempt to keep it from hurting or inhibiting you. It can make for great drama when the lock on the cupboard no longer holds, and the longer things have been held at bay, the more dramatic it is when eventually they come pouring out. I want to look at some of these parts with hindsight, with a new sense of what made me, the person, the one who was attracted to playing certain characters. There have been a whole slew of them, but before I go there, what about the family in India?

The great crisis for Leonard and Bertie was in 1938, and their personal war was set against the mounting tension in international relations in Europe. Having lost Leonard in their very

attempt to keep him close to them, Bertie and Nora summoned
Esme back to India, fearful of leaving her in Europe during the
war which was now inevitable. She was twenty now, had forgotten her aspirations to the convent and was hoping to leave
hairdressing behind to follow Leonard to Guy's and a career in
medicine, but that wish, thwarted by her controlling parents and
imminent war, was never going to happen. Once back in Pindi
her skills meant that she found a job easily, but her presence did
not make things harmonious at home.

In due course she met and fell in love with an architect who, at
the time Esme met him, held the rank of Major in the army. When
it was discovered that he in fact had German roots, he was interned
in India for a year as an enemy alien, since war had engulfed Europe
by then. His grandfather Christian Louis Melosch had moved from
Bremen to become a successful rice trader in Moulmein, Burma.
There his son, also called Christian, had met and married Kitty
Grasemann, the child of the English-born George Grasemann and
Mah Tsee, a full Burmese girl. So Esme's beloved, whose real name
was the same as his father and grandfather, was half German and a
quarter Burmese, neither bloodline likely to endear him to the
Quicks and Nora and Bertie refused to accept him as a son-in-law.
The family's assets in Burma were lost during the First World War
and the senior Melosch returned to a life in Hamburg. It was in
order to secure his release from jail that Esme's beloved changed his
name to Victor Cristian Hughes – 'Victor' perhaps being a sign of
how determined he was to reinvent himself and win the right to
marry Esme.

'Mr Hughes' was much older that her – twenty-six years older –
and had been married before, to Olga Klein in 1917, the year that
Esme was born. The marriage produced two children, Victor and
Kitty, only a year or two younger than Esme, and since Olga lived
on until 1984, Victor must have divorced her in order to be free to

marry again. So it seems that Bertie and Nora could object to Esme marrying him on many grounds. Nora started sending out poison pen letters to blacken his name – Esme told me, 'She was great at writing anonymous letters to everyone . . . to make mischief.' She also said that Nora had 'a terrible temper, and would yell and tell lies to my father'.

Esme immediately left home and if Bertie, who loved his daughter, wanted to see her he had to pretend her was just taking the Pekinese dogs out for a long constitutional in the park. When Esme married her Victor in October 1943 she did so, like her brother, without her parents' consent or their attendance at her wedding. She moved to Lahore where there was plenty of work for her, and relations between them were never easy after that. When Esme did visit them some years later, bringing her first two daughters with her, Nora tried to insist that Esme leave one of the girls behind with her; she must have been desperate for another child to raise. Esme took her daughters and fled, and didn't return.

With the war's end, and the imminent approach of independence for the Indian subcontinent, Muhammad Ali Jinnah's Muslim League had been successfully agitating for a Muslim state separate from Hindu India. With the great migrations across the border, of Hindus eastwards into what was to become independent India and the incoming Muslims from everywhere else in the subcontinent into the new country of Pakistan[1] there was a great wave of violence that affected Pindi just as everywhere else. Around two million people were on the move, and in the clashes that erupted more than a hundred thousand died.

One day two Pashtuns, father and son, arrived at Bertie's compound saying that they had been sent by the Wali of Swat to protect the family, in return for the kindnesses done to their clan by Bertie. He had regularly returned there ever since serving in the Swat Valley while in the Sub-Medical Department. As long as the vio-

lence of partition raged outside, with personal scores being settled
and massacres and trains between Lahore and Delhi being waylaid
so that everyone on board could be slaughtered – all but the driver,
that is, who would then be ordered to continue to the destination
with a cargo of dead Hindus in one direction or dead Muslims in the
other – as long as this violence was being vented the two Swati warriors slept in Bertie's compound, monitoring all who came and went
and by their sheer presence there kept the family safe.

Nora and Bertie's remaining son Basil, who had by now qualified
as a dental surgeon at Lahore, decided he must leave as soon as he
could. He got out with the help of Hindu friends who vouched for
him and virtually smuggled him out of the country. Now Nora and
Bertie were alone, and soon Nora wanted to leave too. Many of
their circle had left at Partition, for Britain or South Africa or
Australia, but Bertie refused to go. He felt a loyalty to his household
staff, and in particular his former batman, now his laboratory assistant, who had been working with him for more than twenty years.
He was ill with TB and Bertie wanted to keep an eye on him and
his family. When the man eventually died Bertie made sure that his
widow was well provided for. Nora, meanwhile, decided to go to
England alone. She had family there: her son Basil (as well as her
estranged stepson Leonard), her sister Delia Case and also aunts and
nieces. In due course Esme left for Australia with her family, fearing
for the safety of her three young daughters in a country that was still
far from settled, but it was some considerable time before Bertie
made up his mind to give up his life in India and came over to join
Nora in England with their Pekinese dogs. This separation, to me,
explains the frostiness I felt as a small child on the one occasion I
met Nora and Bertie together. They were simply not on good terms
and this uneasy truce must have continued through their remaining
years in England. When Bertie became ill and was in hospital (the
second and only other time I met him) Nora announced that she

could not possibly look after Bertie when eventually he was released from hospital, and so Basil's young wife, who had just given birth to twins, took on the long-term care of the convalescent Bertie too.

Nora was now effectively alone. She had managed to isolate herself first from her stepchildren and then increasingly from Bertie. She is clearly the villain in this tale of domestic estrangement, a real wicked stepmother. I thought of her often when I came to play Murielle in my own translation of *The Woman Destroyed* by Simone de Beauvoir because I already felt that Nora and Murielle might have a lot in common. Some years later, when I came to revive the play for a production in New York, I had already been busy researching the family's life in India and Nora was even more at the forefront of my mind as I set about making Murielle mine once more.

The play is a monologue for a twice-divorced wife who finds herself alone at home on New Year's Eve while the world is out revelling. Even her best friend doesn't call: 'She's out dancing and having fun, and does she think of me? Does she fuck!' She is dreading the obligatory holiday visit of her second husband, Tristan, and longing for it too. They have been separated for some time and he has custody of their thirteen-year-old son. She knows she will screw it up but is desperate to prove to him that she can be good, that her impossible behaviour is a thing of the past and that she is now worthy of his love and capable of looking after her son. In her fantasy she is going to win him back and become normal, instead of the freak she feels herself to be. By doing this she will confound everyone who has ever dared criticise her – her mother, her brother and sister-in-law, her first husband, her friends, even, eventually, her daughter Sylvie, who has made her feel the ultimate failure as a mother by killing herself when still a child. As the night wears on and no one comes to call, Murielle lets out more and more of her demons and does her level best to blame *anyone* she can think of for her predicament. She gradually peels off the layers of self-justification until she is left with the painful events around her daughter's suicide, and for the first time she allows herself to feel the absolute anguish of that loss. On her way through this dark night of the soul she goes from righteous anger to deep sorrow, and I had her gradually strip away the veneer of glamour as she goes from a monied woman dressed up to dazzle to a forlorn, dishevelled lost soul, scrubbed of make-up, with a face pack and cucumber slices on her eyes, crying into the telephone to her family, who hang up on her.

What made me think of Nora more than the specifics of her situation, for clearly none of her children had committed suicide, was the way in which both women were trapped in a world of their own creation, with few resources of their own and therefore dependent on the good opinion of others and at the same time rejecting it. Both blame others and drive them away. In real life Nora's isolation was compounded by the tragedies that struck Basil's family: some years on from the birth of their twins, after several miscarriages, Basil and his wife had a third child who happened to be a Down's baby, and as a young girl developed leukaemia, which she did not survive. One of their twins, Stephen, also died young, after a fall from a cliff-top on the Isle of Wight where he was at school. A post-mortem revealed that he had had a tumour in his brain, which may have been the cause of his fall. The family's grief was made even more painful by the arrival of a series of poison pen letters that jeered at their inability to produce healthy children who could survive into adulthood. These caused so much distress that the police were alerted and their investigations traced the letters back to Nora – the grandmother of the two children who had died, the mother of the grieving father. All this information was new to me, confided by Basil's wife as I began to research the family. I found it very sobering and the similarities between her and the fictional

Murielle leapt out at me as I revised and re-rehearsed *The Woman Destroyed*. Murielle is a creature who has for a long time got by on denying any responsibility for her own fate. She is out of touch with any reality, living in a world of her own construction in which she has always been right and everyone else is torturing her. But we meet her on the night she finally owns up and, having at last allowed herself to feel all that she has been avoiding, she is able to move on and to find some bleak consolation in the idea of revenge. The play closes with her belly-laughing at the idea that in the next world she will be reunited with her children. She will 'stroll along the paths of paradise with my little boy and my darling girl' and watch all the others, exes, mother, brother and friends, 'writhing in the flames of envy. I'll see them all roasting and wailing. And I'll laugh. I'll laugh and laugh and the children will laugh with me.'

I don't know whether Nora, with her strong Catholic faith, took any consolation from the idea of reconciliation and revenge in the afterlife. In a way I hope she did, for she was to meet a lonely end some time after Bertie's death. She was found dead on her kitchen floor. No one had known of her demise for perhaps three days.

I do not wish to criticise Nora any more than I do Murielle, for I believe that both women were victims of their circumstances, a theme reflected in the afterword I wrote for the published text of *The Woman Destroyed*:

> . . . a common theme: marriage and motherhood as a trap in which women of a certain age are cruelly and helplessly ensnared. Brought up with the expectation that love, marriage and babies are her destiny, Murielle finds herself at the age of 43 bereft of all three. She has no other resources; no skills, no confidence (just a blind narcissistic arrogance), no sense that she might transcend her present lot through her own actions. As she says herself, she is stewing away in her own juice. There are many women like

Murielle – and they are not, alas, all of an age where they can claim ignorance of what feminism teaches. Think of the average women's magazine, with its regular fodder of how to be attractive, sexy, a better home-maker, a more understanding mother or lover – not that I think these are bad goals in themselves. It's just that the emphasis continues to be on making oneself more desirable to someone else. The majority of women are still like Murielle: they seek to authenticate themselves by their value to someone else, rather than through their own action in the world.

I believe de Beauvoir wrote this piece as a morality tale; she claimed it came in response to the hundreds of letters she had received from her readers describing the confusions of their own lives. Whilst working on it, however, I came to believe that the violence of feeling in it could not have been created at second hand: rather that, as in all her writings, de Beauvoir had put herself into it. Thus my view of de Beauvoir has been profoundly changed by the piece. I no longer accept the rational, controlled person she presents in the autobiographical writings as the whole story. I am more and more convinced that the relationship with Sartre, which she called the crowning achievement of her life, was won at the cost of enormous denial on her part – denial of the very needs which Murielle trumpets so loud – to be nurtured, to be found sexually desirable, to be a successful mother, to not be lonely, to be allowed to be foolishly needy and to be loved despite it; to be saved from suicide.[2]

What do I feel about Nora in the light of this? With the fictional Murielle and the powerful personality of the real-life de Beauvoir in mind it became easier to understand why Nora did what she did. She was a victim of her circumstances, denying responsibility, concealing the truth, longing for revenge and blaming others. In fact these were characteristics shared by many of the roles I've played, and when I came to Mrs Alving in Ibsen's *Ghosts*, the parallels were very obvious.

Mrs Alving, a widow for ten years, has just welcomed her son home. After a lifetime in exile from family life, first at school and then as a bohemian in Paris, Oswald has come back at last to see the unveiling of a memorial to his long-dead father, the Captain Alving Orphanage. She is looking forward to an idyllic life where she and Oswald will enjoy the mother–son relationship they have never had, for her only child was sent away so that he wouldn't discover the truth about his father. This is the big secret she has been living with, that, far from being a pillar of the community who is to be honoured in the orphanage named after him, her husband was a drunk and a womaniser. In the course of the next day Helen Alving's life unravels as events reveal the house of cards on which her hopes have been built.

One consequence of her husband's secret life is that he had an illegitimate daughter with a housemaid. Mrs Alving was involved in the cover-up from the start: two decades earlier she had paid off the maid, Johanna, who had then contrived a hasty marriage, and for many years Regine, the child born of this secret liaison, has been living with Mrs Alving, not as a member of the family but as a companion. Now when her friend and mentor Pastor Manders suggests that the girl should return home to look after the man she believes to be her father as he grows old, Mrs Alving will only say 'No, no, she is not going back to him, not if I can help it,' and when the pastor notices her agitation 'almost as though you were frightened', Mrs Alving replies: 'Sh sh! Enough dear Pastor, don't say any more.' Her silence is not only to protect herself from scandal, but to protect her son who falls for Regine. Rather than reveal the truth to the young people – that they are half-brother and sister – she even considers sanctioning their incestuous marriage.

Mrs Alving is ruled by fear and is in deep conflict. This is the

1880s, the very beginning of higher education for women, and she
has been reading foreign books on the Woman Question. She
believes in free love, but has never dared say so out loud, and now
hopes that her son, who is used to a bohemian life in Paris, will be
there to speak for her. She longs to break out and be free but her
actions imprison her and bring about her own tragedy.

There are many ironies in her situation and it is in the unfolding of
these ironies that I saw the echoes of Nora Quick. For the memorial
that will preserve her son from the taint of his father's depravity, Mrs
Alving chose an orphanage but she has already made her son a de
facto orphan by sending him away so young and Nora sending the
children away to the hills and then to England made them feel like
orphans. Also, she pretended that she was their real mother, when
they were both old enough to have some memory of their biological
mummy, surely producing another, albeit unconscious, layer of anxiety.

Mrs Alving believed that in sending Oswald away as a child she
was saving him from being spoiled by too much parental attention;
but the play reveals just how much his life has been ruined: he feels
no love for his mother and tells her bitterly, 'I shouldn't think it
much mattered to you whether I was alive or dead.' I am quite sure
that there were times when Leonard and Esme must have felt that
way too.

In building the orphanage in her husband's name she had hoped
'to kill off the rumours and remove any doubts', and what's more
she thinks that if she uses up all of Captain Alving's money for
the orphanage she will 'decontaminate' Oswald's inheritance:
'Everything Oswald will inherit comes from me,' she tells the pastor.
As the play unfolds we see just how impossible it is for Oswald to
escape from his father's ghost. Mrs Alving sees her life as a 'long
hateful farce' and believes that once the orphanage is functioning
the nightmare will finally be over. All her hopes are confounded
when she overhears her son with Regine in the next room, like a

ghostly re-enactment of her husband's infidelity with the maid – the maid who was mother to this very girl. Once again she retreats into denial – the closing words of the act are 'Not a word!' – and Nora too went to extreme lengths to keep the family pure, jeopardising Leonard's career by cutting off his funds and summoning Esme back home to India where she could control her, but all her efforts were to end with both children marrying the very people she considered unsuitable and being lost to her family for ever.

By Act Two it is clear to Mrs Alving that the web of lies she has spun for so many years must be done away with; she wants to 'work her way out to freedom'. Looking back, she can see she has always been a coward and now wants there to be no more lies. She can suddenly see that everything around her has been based on 'old dead ideas', that everyone is 'just stuck there and we can't get rid of them'. She resolves to tell the truth at last and is about to spell it all out for Oswald when catastrophe strikes: the orphanage burns down. And when Nora thought to come home at last to England, perhaps to be reconciled to Leonard, she found herself instead estranged from everyone. For her there was to be no reconciliation with her stepson and Esme had by now moved to the other side of the world.

With the fire out but the orphanage destroyed, the pragmatic Mrs Alving believes she has made a clean break with the past. All the fear she has lived with for so many years, the fear of being found out, is burned away by the fire and she looks forward to an honest life at last with her son beside her. But this is not to be. The pastor leaves, probably never to return, and Regine leaves too, scornfully rejecting Mrs Alving's offers of help and the chance, however slim, of a kind of happiness with Oswald, no longer her lover but still her brother. And by the end of the play Oswald has left his mother too, in spirit if not in the flesh. He makes her under-stand that her dream is all a fantasy; her fond hope that he will feel love for his dead father or even for her is only a superstition she is clinging to: it has no basis in reality. At last Mrs Alving understands that her wish for an idyllic life with the son she has never been close to or spent time with is a hackneyed sentiment on her part – a mere ghost.

Nora died all alone, having lost all contact with her stepson and daughter and their families, losing her grandson and granddaughter to untimely early deaths. She had tried to get rid of those she didn't want by spreading calumnies about them – Joan in England, and Esme's fiancé in India – and when that didn't work, she cut herself and Bertie off from the children. How painful must that have been for Bertie, who loved them.

Nora went further and did the same thing with her own flesh and blood, too. There were the letters she wrote to her son and daughter-in-law after her grandson Stephen's death, and the ones mocking his little sister who had Down's syndrome. And there was her refusal to nurse Bertie when he was gravely sick. Bertie was to die before her by several years but there had been no rapprochement with her husband either. She was to die alone, so estranged from all of them that she had even disinherited her own son Basil and her granddaughter in favour of her sister Gertie back in India, a sister whom she had always envied, thinking her better favoured in looks and very much the favourite with their parents, more loved than she had ever been. Basil was generously silent on the subject of his mother's actions towards her children and husband when I quizzed him about it, saying only: 'Nora came to the UK before Bertie, who wouldn't leave his batman. She thought she would be better off here.'

To return to *Ghosts* for a moment, Mrs Alving also comes to understand that for her son there is a further ghost of his father's debauchery: he has inherited his father's syphilis. To her horror he starts to lose his mind and sink into a mental torpor, a helpless invalid crying for the light. What was to have been her glorious day ends with the ruined hope of her son's living death and I can only imagine the horror and confusion that Nora Quick must have felt that made her write poison pen letters when she was trying to deal with the fact of her grandchildren's illnesses.

In the play, perhaps the most chilling ghost of all is the way in which Oswald becomes virtually the ghost of his father, not only by forming a relationship with the maid but in the development of his relationship with his mother too. In Act Three he becomes flirtatiously mocking and ambiguous, careless almost, as if the fact of his inescapable descent into madness has liberated him from his earlier dutifulness. Mrs Alving finds herself constantly wrong-footed and starts to treat her son almost as if he were her husband. She is trapped in a deathly deceit where she no longer knows if it is the son or the father who is lying there helpless, yearning for the warmth and illumination of the sun he can no longer enjoy. It is too late for her to escape the prison in which she has lived ever since she married. As wife, as widow and now as nurse to her helpless child she is trapped by the ghost of the past and by her own conventional and frightened behaviour. There is never going to be an escape for her. After a lifetime of hiding the truth about her husband from the world, Mrs Alving is so disabled by the prospect of losing her son to a syphilitic death that she retreats into a hysterical fantasy of their life together.

For Nora, Leonard's marriage to a Protestant 'gypsy' of 'impure blood' and Esme's marriage to a part-Burmese are ghost echoes of what her own parents had feared and disliked in her marriage to Bertie Quick, a man who was not only a non-Catholic but whose family were tarnished by a touch of the tar brush, however much they might have tried to overcome it. Even though Bertie had become a respected member of Rawalpindi's professional community; even though his brother Frank had trained in England and returned to India to become a distinguished doctor himself; their mother and their other siblings, and Frank's wife Myrtle, all bore the unmistakable look of someone with mixed blood. On top of that, Esme's husband was not only German, which was, under the circumstances of the war, an equally unacceptable choice, but also divorced and therefore ineligible for marriage in Catholic eyes. Nora and Bertie, estranged in life and by geography, had many ghosts of their own to contend with.

There is one more family ghost that is a consequence of all this. My father Leonard's relationship with his two sons had echoes of the way his own father had treated him. Remote, undemonstrative, disengaged from their day-to-day activities, quick to anger if they failed to achieve the highest standards, he more or less obliged his own first-born to follow him into a career in dentistry, even though it would never have been his own first choice. In fact my brother soon rebelled, leaving home early in his training after bitter rows with our father, and I was the one deputed to deliver the letter to our parents twenty-four hours after he had made his escape. Clive did complete his studies in dentistry at Guy's, just as our father had, but as soon as he had qualified he re-enlisted to train in medicine, later becoming a surgeon.

My sister Julie and I had found Leonard tender, tactile, and interested in what we were doing. The resentment that Clive and Richard felt towards their stern father was a complete surprise to us. How could this be the same man? I can only think that our father was unable to transcend the pattern that was set in his own early childhood, where his only loving relationship was with his little sister, his mother's tenderness a distant memory snatched away when he was an infant. For him, it seems, the idea of love was confined to the female of the species and his fathering echoed his own father, a person remote and disapproving, even though that remoteness had made him so deeply unhappy and left him feeling that he had never been loved or understood, just as his own sons feel now.

And yet I am certain that Leonard's own father had loved him very much, unable though he was to show it. I was unbearably moved when I learned Bertie had told his youngest child, Basil, that when he died he 'hoped he could take Leonard with him'. There he was, near the end of his life in cold, unfamiliar England, and in the midst of so much estrangement and loss: his grandchildren Stephen and Kim had already died, and he was not close to any of his other kin, neither Leonard nor Esme, nor their spouses nor any of his seven other grandchildren. I will never know exactly what he meant by that but it betokens a desire for closeness and a regret of how much he had lost by cutting off his beloved son so many years before. Perhaps it also reveals his faith, or maybe just a desperate wish that there was to be an afterlife for them where Bertie could heal the wounds he had inflicted so many years before.

There are other echoes of all that had happened before in my own generation. The brother who left home so early married very young, a woman two years older than himself, and my other two siblings both married devout Catholics. As for me, there are all the parts I have played that have that same combination of defiant denial and fear of discovery. There was Evelyn in *Kindertransport*, Madam in *The Orchid House*, Murielle in *The Woman Destroyed*, Mrs Alving in *Ghosts* and Jean Rhys in *After Mrs Rochester*, but what I have learnt in trailing my father's history back to its Indian roots has, with hindsight, informed the playing of other women: Sophia in *The Discovery of Heaven*, Deeny in Mamet's *The Old Neighborhood* and Frances in *Mother Teresa is Dead*; and Julia Flyte, for it was in playing her that this exploration started.

19

Waiting for Dr Quick

I don't think I would have been able to play, or even have been interested in taking on, some parts had I not been aware of the thread of 'covering up' one's real self that has emerged as I found out about my father's early life.

In *The Discovery of Heaven*, a film based on a popular Dutch novel by Harry Mulisch, the human characters are unwitting puppets in a plan devised by the powers that be in heaven: they wish to retrieve the Ark of the Covenant given to mankind in the time of Moses because humanity has failed to keep their side of the deal. I played Sophia Brons, whose daughter has been selected to become the mother of an angelic creature whose purpose will be to discover the Ark and take it back to heaven. Sophia is first seen through the eyes of two young men who both fall in love with her daughter Ada. What they see is a woman with 'a straight disciplined back – black hair . . . handsome, buxom . . . something severe about her'. They think she would make a perfect abbess.[1] Later, when Sophia's husband dies suddenly, the three young people set out to console her when they get caught in a storm. A tree falls on their car and leaves the now pregnant Ada in a coma. The husband must accompany his wife to the hospital and so their friend

Max goes on alone to Sophia's house to offer his double condolences, for her husband's death and now her child's and grandchild's grave accident. Sophia is a stoic: Max finds that in her grief 'still she remains beautiful and invulnerable'.

They decide that, as it is far too late to travel back, he had better stay the night. Sophia, moved by the way Max reminds her of her dead husband when she had first met him many years before, climbs into his bed and sobs. Suddenly they are entangled in a furious embrace and make passionate love, and before he has a chance to recover, before he even realises what has happened, 'she's gone, without having uttered a sound'. This first, startling sexual encounter sets the pattern for their relationship: Sophia will never discuss what is happening and shows no emotion whatsoever, either about her daughter or towards Max. But he keeps coming back to her and each time the same thing happens.

When Ada, still unconscious, gives birth to a son by Caesarean section, Max has a brainwave. It is clear that her husband cannot cope with a child. What if he, possibly the real father of 'their' baby, were to offer to raise the child with its grandmother's help? At a stroke he has also provided a cover for his liaison with Sophia. Thus begins a fifteen-year idyll while they raise the boy and the true nature of their relationship is kept secret. It is only when Quentin is grown and ready to leave home that Max takes a new lover and Sophia accepts it, merely commenting that she had noticed the smell of a new soap recently.

So, a woman of deep passion who acts on it but never acknowledges it – not even to her lover. The only time she cracks is when her teenage grandson leaves home to look for his 'real' father, for she is afraid that something terrible will happen if he goes.

It does, of course. They are all being manipulated by heaven and when they have served their purpose they will be disposed of. Max is killed by a thunderbolt. Quentin sets off on a quest that will lead him to the Ark and he will ultimately disappear to the angelic zone that created him. Sophia discreetly kills her own child, Ada. For me, this action of the mother killing her child was a metaphor for Nora destroying her own relationships with her child and her stepchildren and grandchildren, but at least Sophia was motivated by compassion, not wanting her child to continue in a state of living death. Furthermore, she had the backing, albeit unconscious, of heaven. It is only when Ada is dead that Sophia allows herself, at last, to really cry.

I do not know if Nora Quick ever felt remorse for her part in cutting off the children, and there is now no way of finding out if she was ever able to express sadness for her loss of the family. For Sophia there was no real catharsis either. She never shows her grief for her husband, she is incapable of a spontaneous expression of joy in the ecstasy of sex, and gives no outward sign of conflict in the double life she has led for so long with Max. Even years later, when she hears news of Quentin and finally understands that this child she raised as her own has gone from her life for ever, she controls herself before emotion can overcome her. It must be the most bitter thing in the world, to survive your child – as Sophia survives Ada, and as my grandfather survived my father – and how much more terrible, to go one generation on and find you have outlived your grandchild, as Sophia does Quentin and Nora and Bertie did two of Basil's children, Stephen and Kim.

Playing Sophia, thinking about my Indian grandparents, I started to feel compassion and perhaps a glimmer of understanding about what it must have been like for them. Perhaps they had suffered too. For Sophia was not invulnerable, as Max had thought at first; certainly severe, but also capable of deep feeling and a passionate exchange with a fellow creature. Perhaps it is no accident that she reminds the young men of an abbess for in *The Discovery of Heaven* the audience understand from the beginning that everything happens in the story because heaven has willed it and it may be that Sophia, for all her sensuality, and for all her silence, is the agent of that heavenly purpose. I am sure that Nora would have liked to be able to justify her own actions with that thought too.

Once again I was drawn back into the Roman Catholic world. It was a marvellous part to play, not least because I felt an instinctive understanding of how to do it (no acting required) and then, of course, it was wonderful, as an older woman, for my character to be allowed a passionate sexual life, when the prevailing wisdom in much of show business had been that women over forty were really only useful to play mothers, or in this case grannies. I called this part the first of the 'bonking grannies', and I have played a few of them since. The Duchess in Alex Cox's film of the Jacobean *Revenger's Tragedy*, who has incestuous relations with the youngest of her five sons as well as a vociferous life in bed with her Duke was one. On television I was a spurned lover who seeks revenge through murder when her young protégé goes elsewhere, and I have twice played the older woman with a young lover, in the comedies *Catwalk Dogs* and *Sensitive Skin*, all of them passionate creatures trying to live in a secret world and all of them surviving but at a price.

I was another woman full of pain but pretending that life was fine in David Mamet's *The Old Neighborhood*. On a visit to his hometown, Chicago, Bob encounters an old friend, then his sister and finally Deeny, his girlfriend from way back, who now works at the cosmetics counter of a big store. I was Deeny, who refuses to say that life is bad or to even look at the possibility of feeling regret that her life has not turned out differently.

She was difficult to play because she was so oblique in the way she expresses herself: poetic, and also brief – a mere twenty minutes of an encounter with the man who was her lover many years before he left the old neighbourhood. But I loved Deeny. David Mamet had written her for his new wife to play, which she did in New York, and he has given her a tenderness and humanity that makes her very poignant. Deeny is dignified and without complaint; she is interested in the idea of joy and looks at it sideways, but underneath she is full of a sense of loss and a sense too of what it costs to become a grown-up. She made me think of my father:

> . . . and all the revenge we foreswore, and that we could not have. Always, and turning, don't we? Toward death – Do you think? Do you think so? [Pause] And, you know, and the things we'd given up. When you elect it's consolation to grow up. And it is consolation. But so what?

I always felt that she was a wise soul and for all that she can barely articulate her ideas she is at terms with her world. Thinking about her now I am full of regret that her life on the stage was so brief. A whole world, a whole life, contracted to a twenty-minute play. And I always felt that she was a grown-up: as she says herself, it is a consolation for life's disappointments to grow up, and that consolation was something that I am sure eluded Nora Quick. Deeny and Sophia have been the most mature of these characters who have lived a life in denial. Her attitude might have been to shrug off her achievement with a 'But so what?', but I loved Deeny – and I loved her most of all for the things she does not allow herself to express. It is Mamet's genius that you understand her life from the things she refuses, for whatever reason, to put into words. In her, denial can be seen as heroism.

I came back to the Royal Court a couple of years after Deeny to explore another melancholy loser in the love stakes, Frances in *Mother Teresa is Dead* by Helen Edmundson, a painter who has lived much of her life in India. She is a person whose life has been defined by love, or the absence of it.

A young Englishwoman has been found wondering around Mumbai railway station in a traumatised state and Frances has been looking after her in her studio on the outskirts of the city. Frances says as little as possible about herself. Polite and self-deprecating, she is the very model of a Hampstead arty type and there is comedy in her being thrown up against the bluff, working-class husband who has come out to India to rescue his wife, Jane. When the young Indian who was the one to rescue the woman and bring her to Frances arrives, the husband suspects he is after his wife and it is Frances, practical and authoritative, who calms him down.

The relationship between the middle-aged Frances and the young Indian Vas is more than mere friendship, but it is complicated by the growing attraction Vas feels for the young wife in her care. Frances cannot act on her feelings and can only express herself in irony, never revealing her fear: another kind of denial.

The action of the play is the painful jerky movement of these four people towards some sort of an understanding of each other. Frances's main strategy in a relationship had always been to be receptive. Vas, her young lover, thinks that she is needy but it had been different once. Vas tells his fondest memory of her, when as a boy she had got him to put his feet in two pots of paint and then danced him round her studio, leaving footprints all over the canvas on the floor. She had been the confident one then, but now she knows all the reasons why it can't last: he's young enough to be her son and from an alien culture, albeit one she knows well, and even if he doesn't leave now with Jane, it is going to happen sometime soon with someone else.

One of the great pleasures of playing Frances was the sense of her coming out of her shell as she develops a relationship with the younger woman. She realises that if she is going to lose her lover anyway, because of all the imbalances in their relationship, she might as well go for truth over irony. She does learn to let go in the end, to give up Vas gracefully, and manages to work through this deeply disturbed disequilibrium, coming out at the end a wiser, kinder, more honest and more humorous creature. When the young English couple are about to leave to return to England it is Frances who suggests they should all four sit down for two minutes, thinking quietly about where they are each going. Slowly, in that brief calm, they begin to reach their hands out to each other, the hand of conciliation, of recognising a connection whatever their differences.

If only Nora and my grandfather had been able to offer that gesture to their children and stepchildren. So much unhappiness could have been prevented, or if not avoided at least healed. But perhaps that is too easy to say now, after I have spent so many years and two trips to India and Pakistan trying to understand just what had made the family explode as it did.

The part more than any other that made me begin to think about this rift in my own family was Julia Flyte in *Brideshead Revisited*, who tried for many years to defy the conventions of the society into which she had been born, but who comes at last to accede to the code in which she has been raised and sacrifice her personal happiness. Her unlocking moment comes when she is seemingly at her happiest. She is engaged to Charles, her brother Sebastian's friend from university days, whom she had barely noticed then – though Charles describes the 'thin bat's squeak of sexuality' he had felt in his first encounter with Julia when she asks him to light her cigarette and he places it directly into her mouth as she drives him from the station to Brideshead. Now it is some twelve years later, they have both been through unhappy marriages and are more or less living together, anticipating divorce from their first spouses and remarriage to each other in due course.

They have the run of Julia's family home, which they are able to

enjoy because Julia's older brother Bridey has long been a confirmed bachelor with little use for the facilities of the big house,
when he announces that he will shortly be getting married to the
widow of an admiral he had come to know through a shared passion
for collecting matchboxes. Julia is more than a little patronising in
her amusement at what seems to her an inappropriate match but
delighted for her brother and keen to get the admiral's widow down
to Brideshead so she can inspect her, when Bridey drops his bomb-
shell: 'It is a matter of indifference whether you choose to live in sin
with Rex or Charles or both . . . [but] . . . Beryl is a woman of strict
Catholic principle fortified by the prejudices of the middle class. I
couldn't possibly bring her here.'

Bridey has put into words the thing that Julia has been denying
all through her relationship: that in the eyes of her faith, she is
living in sin with Charles. Julia leaves the room and later Charles
discovers her outside by the fountain and can only listen as she lets
out a great anguished vision of what she feels, shut out from God's
mercy by her wilful denial of the religion in which she was raised:

> They know all about it, Bridey and his widow; they bought it for
> a penny at the church door. All in one word, too, one little, flat,
> deadly word that covers a lifetime . . . Living in sin, with sin, by
> sin, for sin, every hour, every day. Always the same, like an idiot
> child carefully nursed, guarded from the world.

We were all scared of filming this part of the story – me, Charles
who was directing, Derek who was producing and John Mortimer,
whose original script for this episode had pared down Waugh's
threnody. From time to time in the preceding months, Charles
and I had met to discuss the scene in minute detail, but we all had
a matter-of-fact certainty that it would prove unusable: fifteen or
twenty minutes of a lapsed Catholic's nightmare vision of how she

is shut out from God's grace didn't feel as if it could be lifted from the page to the screen and make good drama. We ended up filming virtually the whole of it as Waugh had written it and somehow it worked.

How to play it? We had already done most of the scenes of Lord Marchmain's return to the fold with, for me, the powerful echoes that Lord Olivier invoked of my father and grandfather. So I thought about these men in my own family, both converts to Catholicism and especially of my father who had spent thirty years not going to mass, but who must have shared Julia's childhood imprint of what grace is, and therefore of the hell that ensues when you feel yourself shut out from that grace. Charles Ryder is lost when confronted by the tumult of emotions that well up in his usually self-contained lover and tries to dismiss that conditioning as 'the nonsense you were taught in the nursery'. Of course he becomes a convert to the Catholic Church, but that is later and he has not yet come to understand the torment and the hope of salvation that his lover is going through, for if my study of Catholicism had shown me anything it was that grace is the Church's great gift to its followers.

Filming it was horrible. We were in Yorkshire in late September, out of doors at night. We had very temperamental lights to contend with, which kept going wrong and delayed us for hours. I was wearing a backless scrap of gold tissue and was furious that, despite careful negotiation by me and my agent, I was nevertheless having to do this impossible sequence in freezing weather when in my view it could just as easily have been scheduled for a summer night. And none of us had a shred of optimism about it working.

In the end, though, acting is about knowing the lines and saying them as if you mean them. You make them your own by whatever means you can, and with this it felt as if I was about to dive from a very high board not knowing if there was any water in the pool.

Acting does take courage at moments like that. We shot the whole sequence, uninterrupted, in one take. We did that each night for several nights. Charles now gave me very little in the way of notes. Jeremy Irons, with whom I had now been acting for the best part of eighteen months, could contribute little more than the most attentive listening. We had often given each other comments on earlier scenes, but with this one I felt very much alone. I could only allow that feeling I, the actor, had to feed into Julia's profound sense of isolation, her identification with the Christ figure of being an 'outcast in the desolate spaces where the hyenas roam at night. No way back . . . thrown away, scrapped, rotting down.' Waugh makes Julia extraordinarily vivid in her sense of loss; my feeling as I played it was that it was almost like poetry – not that it required a consciously 'poetic' delivery, rather that the language swept me along and did most of the work for me.

Waugh was a passionate convert to the Catholic faith, at one time even upbraiding his friend John Betjeman for shilly-shallying around with the Anglican high church instead of going all the way into the arms of Rome. It is part of his exquisite gift as a writer that he gives to Julia, whom we first met as a shallow society creature, this 'mysterious tumult of sorrow'. He is very good on her quality of 'magical sadness' that is what had drawn Charles back to her when they re-met by chance on a transatlantic liner: 'the thwarted look that had seemed to say, "Surely I was made for some other purpose than this?"' Thwarted: it's a word he uses again once Julia has recovered, almost instantly, it seems to poor Charles who is left feeling 'all at sea', for Julia apologises to him with a formal politeness that effectively denies the cataclysmic depths of what he has just seen her go through. 'I'm sorry for that appalling scene, Charles,' she says. 'I can't explain.' Can't? Or won't? We never know, and the lovers are left discussing the subject of 'thwarted passions'.

After five days of these night shoots I returned to London for a break while other scenes were filmed. I went to bed, slept deeply and woke the next day to find my neck had locked. I couldn't lift my head from the pillow. I was more or less carried to an osteopath, who took a quick look and cried, 'My God! You must've been very unhappy to get yourself in this mess.' I said I wasn't, but described what I had just been filming – what Waugh calls 'the death of her God', which leaves Julia at the end of the night feeling 'tired and crazy and good for nothing'. That would do it, he said, and it took several hours to gently unlock me.

The huge relief, even euphoria, of completing this sequence in a way that seemed to satisfy all the people who mattered – director, producer, television company – unlocked the end of the story for me too. It had been many months since we had filmed Lord Marchmain's return and eventual death. Julia had a momentous responsibility in these events, aware that she is the one who will have to deal with the crisis of faith that her father's deathbed presents. Should she let him die without repenting of his life of sin? I had been to talk to priests at Farm Street Church, where we were to film, and at the Brompton Oratory, a step away from where I was then living in Brompton Square, but the thing that really illuminated the situation for me had been borrowing the books my nephews and nieces brought home from Sunday School to prepare them for catechism. It was a hair-raising moment when I read in one of these little tracts that Mary, the mother of God, sat in heaven weeping tears of blood for your sin. If you are given an idea like that at seven, as these children had – as Julia no doubt had – then how could you hope to shake it off in later life? That was what did for her, the idea of sin: 'A word from so long ago, from Nanny stitching by the hearth and the nightlight burning before the Sacred Heart. Cordelia and me with the catechism, in Mummy's room.'

By the time we came to film the end of Julia's story, where, in order to expiate her conscience and her God, she renounces marriage to Charles, 'this one thing I want so much', I had been immersed in the emotional and spiritual life of the character for twenty-one months. I had invoked my father frequently, had tried to imagine what his reactions would be, but when the time came it was a question of just letting go. Again we filmed the scene in one long take and by now it really was a case of No Acting Required. Looking back on that time I can see that it was a unique opportunity I had been handed as an actor. Never since have I had the opportunity to play so faithfully to an author's script, nor been surrounded by others with the same counsel of perfection. Usually constraints of money and time mean that a book is filleted, and even if the narrative survives, characterisation, which so often exists in the small moments where nothing very significant is happening in plot terms, goes out the window. But with *Brideshead* I was encouraged to just exist in scenes, and being together with the rest of the cast for so long helped us all to feel that we really did inhabit those skins and those relationships.

Then followed all those other troubled women I have inhabited as an actress – Madam, Murielle, Evelyn, Deeny, Sophia, Frances, Mrs Alving and Jean, to put them in the order in which I played them. Perhaps it is no accident that these are the characters I have played in my maturity. Perhaps one does become more entwined with one's past as one gets older, or perhaps it is simply that one starts to look backwards and become aware of where one has come from and be consciously part of a self-fulfilling prophecy. I have of course played all sorts of other parts too, some exotic and some frightfully English, but those I have described, all to a greater or lesser extent women leading secret lives cut off from a big part of what makes them what they truly are, have been some of the most intriguing and challenging I have taken on.

I do not believe I would have come to play them if it weren't for the accident of what had happened in my parents' and grandparents' lives. It is easy with hindsight to be wise. And easy for those who come after the event to feel compassion. When I made my first research trip to Pakistan in late 1999 I knew almost nothing about the family and next to nothing about the history of the country they had lived in. The last decade or so has seen a sea change in the way we regard the past: everyone is busy exploring their ancestry and celebrating the mixtures that make us unique and yet curiously alike. We have come to see that we are nearly all mongrels, that my grandfather's desire for 'pure blood' is no longer an option, if indeed it ever was.

The other big thing is that soon after I had been to Pakistan, where I had such a serendipitous time – finding the two houses in which the family had lived, meeting the descendants of the Wali of Swat for whom my grandfather worked, making friends among the Pashtun who all urged me to come back as soon as possible, and wandering around the hill station of Murree just in time to witness the huge transformations that unregulated development was bringing as the old was swept away, wiping out the traces of the colonial station my family had known – within a year of this happy, exciting time, when I was full of anticipation of coming back, planning further visits to the far north between Kashmir and Afghanistan and up into the Khyber hills to stay with my new friends, came September 11th. Like the rest of the world I watched in horror and disbelief, and with perhaps a little extra insight into what that was going to mean for my own personal plans.

When my family's old friend Whiskey had returned to Pakistan in the mid-nineties after an absence of forty-five years he had gone up to Murree to revisit his own family home. Like Grandfather, his father had been a surgeon in the Sub-Medical Department. Like him, he had suffered the limitations imposed on his career by the fact of being country born and trained. And like him too he had always loved the country in which he had been born. On this return visit Whiskey went on from his own family home to look at Ashburnham Lodge, my grandfather's house. Indeed, it was his account of this visit that made me determined to go out and find it for myself, for Whiskey believed that it still belonged to my family. When I in turn got there the house had been sitting empty for years, more or less since grandfather had come to England in the fifties, and it seemed that I was there just in time to see it as it had always been, for it was in the process of restoration. I had had a fantasy of claiming possession of this house and of finally owning that part of my family's heritage but alas it belonged to a Parsi,[2] Yazdiar Kaikobad, who had around forty other houses in boom-town Murree. It had originally been a wooden chalet, later faced with stone, and was now being properly restored with hand-cut stone by five or six workmen, including one Muhammed Nazeer, now white-bearded, but who once as a boy had worked in grandfather's clinic for eighteen paisas (three annas) a day. The house was very well situated, as I had expected, for many Old Galleans* had told me before I left England that it was 'a very nice house', high above and behind the other houses of the town, and still surrounded by gigantic deodars – the Himalayan cedar – and chestnuts. I was very moved to be there, especially because it had been standing empty since Grandfather and Nora had left. Mr Kaikobad no doubt had big plans for letting it, perhaps as three separate units with a large room onto the veranda and three or so cubicles behind. The workmen thought it would be at least another six months before it was ready to occupy, but in any case it was clear that I would not be able to stake a claim.

On the way back down from the hill station I asked my host, Colonel Jaffir Khan of the Corps of Guides, if he thought that there

---

* Alumni of the Lawrence School at Ghora Gali, where Grandfather had been employed

was any lasting legacy of the years of British occupation. He mentioned the irrigation system of Mr Lyle of Faisalabad, which extended from the Jelum right through the Punjab, turning it into a fertile and productive region year round, but beyond that, and his own living embodiment of military and public school values, he felt it was all negative. No spread of education; no attempt to industrialise; over-hasty independence; and bribery, which is endemic. Many had told me that it was impossible to find incorruptible judges and on the subject Jaffir said, 'The man who bribes is worse than the man who accepts the bribe.'

I am looking back at that conversation nearly ten years later. Benazir Bhutto was assassinated only a few months after her optimistic, if foolhardy, return to her homeland. She had been at my Oxford college a few years after me, and I had been hoping that I would meet her some time soon, not least because of the anomalous situation of so prominent a female public figure in a society where women are never encouraged to be on display and where the literacy rate amongst females runs at not much above 10 per cent of the population. At the time of writing the idea of a free and democratic election seems as fragile as when I first visited the country. The federation itself, perhaps the most significant consequence of the British occupancy, is in danger of disintegrating: the south with its incoming population from India in favour of democracy, the Punjab as the stronghold of the military, and the North-West Frontier beyond the reach of central government and strongly connected to Afghanistan and Iran on its western borders, and more particularly with the Sunni and Shia fundamentalist tendencies within those neighbouring lands.

At the same time as these tremendous forces are making the country of my father's family a symbolic frontier between our western society and the world of Islam, I am haunted by one of the things told to me by Whiskey in that first conversation, which set me on course for this ten-year journey of exploration and discovery. When he had been at my grandfather's house all those years after his own departure he had bumped into the same Muhammed Nazeer that I was to meet five years later. Whiskey had introduced himself as an old friend of the family. Mr Nazeer remembered him from his childhood there and the two soon fell into conversation. Who lives in this house now? asked the visitor, for the house with its shutters closed looked as if it was just waiting to be opened up to welcome its occupants. 'Oh, no one lives here now,' said Mr Nazeer. 'We are still waiting for Dr Quick to come back.'

Notes

CHAPTER 1

1   Hermione Lee read English at St Hilda's College, and went on to be the first female Goldsmiths' professor of English Literature at Oxford, as well as the first female professorial fellow of New College. A writer and critic, she is also the president of Wolfson College, Oxford.

CHAPTER 3

1   Simone de Beauvoir (trans. H. M. Parshley), *The Second Sex* (New York, 1989), p. xxxv.

CHAPTER 4

1   The Statutory Regulations Act 1835, Chapter 62. The full passage, as quoted in the Queen's Regulations for 1892, runs:

> The name in which a soldier enlists and is attested cannot be erased from his documents. Should, however, a soldier require his true name to be added as an *alias* to regimental records and other documents, he must, at his own expense, make a statutory declaration before a magistrate as follows:

> I, ——, do solemnly and sincerely declare that I was enlisted on the ——, under the name of ——, which name I now declare to be incorrect. The name of ——, contained in the accompanying certificate of birth, I now declare to be my true name, and I make this solemn declaration conscientiously believing the same to be true, and by virtue of the

provisions of an Act made and passed in the sixth year of His late Majesty King William IVth.

[...]

The man should be warned that if the declaration so made be false or untrue in any material particular he is liable to be indicted for perjury.

2   For a clear account of the change of power in relation to the Uprising, see Lawrence James, *Raj: The Making and Unmaking of British India* (London, 1997), chapter 3, and especially pp. 293–4.

3   Stephen Bentley in 'Plain Tales from the Raj' oral archive, IOR Ems T6.

4   Ed Brown, quoted in Allen (ed.), *Plain Tales from the Raj*, p. 148.

5   Letter from William Guess to his sister, 8 August 1858, IOR Mss Eur C590.

6   Roberts, *Forty-One Years in India*, p. 519.

7   E. S. Humphries expands upon this point: 'No man was ever allowed to escape parade or a march because of over indulgence ... the day before ... he was just beaten, pushed and shoved along and made to keep up.' 'Plain Tales from the Raj' oral archive, IOR Ems T36, tape 2/10.

8   Ibid.

9   Ibid.

10 Stephen Bentley, quoted in Allen (ed.), *Plain Tales from the Raj*, p. 55.

11 Kipling, 'In the Matter of a Private', first collected in *Soldiers Three and Other Stories* (London, 1895).

12 Stephen Bentley, quoted in Allen (ed.), *Plain Tales from the Raj*, p. 185.

CHAPTER 5

1   I was elected the first female president of OUDS in 1968, four years after women had first been admitted as full members of the society, thanks to the lobbying of Maria Aitken and others. In the same year, Geraldine Jones became the first female president of the Oxford Union, following Ann Mallalieu, who had become

president of the Cambridge Union in 1967. The national press wanted to make a big issue of it, especially since I was elected in the fiftieth anniversary year of women's suffrage, but I was so self-involved that I regarded their interest as an intrusion and refused to give interviews.

2 During the Sepoy Rebellion, for instance, the elite Corps of Guides marched from their usual beat on the North-West Frontier down to the Relief of Delhi, a distance of 580 miles, averaging twenty-five miles a day. Brigadier Edward Greathed then covered sixty miles in thirty-six hours with a column of 2650 men when he went to the Relief of Agra.

3 Allen (ed.), *Plain Tales from the Raj*, pp. 171–2.

4 Patrick Tandy, private manuscript, 'Thim Days Are Gone'.

5 Stephen Bentley in 'Plain Tales from the Raj' oral archive, IOR Ems T6.

6 E. S. Humphries in 'Plain Tales from the Raj' oral archive, IOR Ems T36.

7 'Plain Tales from the Raj' oral archive.

8 Ibid.

9 Lawrence, 'English Women in Hindustan', p. 106.

CHAPTER 6

1 Pietro della Valle, quoted in Kaye, *Christianity in India*, p. 102f. The Italian nobleman and traveller mentioned these 'fair strangers from the west', which he encountered when he visited India in 1623, in his *Travels*.

2 Charles Lockyer, 'Account of the Trade in India', quoted in Carey (ed.), *The Good Old Days of Honorable John Company*, p. 200.

3 Later, as consciousness of colour grew in the Company's territories, some descendants of the Portuguese-Indians would become deeply offended at being categorised with the less well born Anglo-Indians. As one tries to understand the complexities of status in the Raj, these fine shades of colour and background multiply and overlap, just as they do in the Caribbean, for instance, where there are words to describe degrees of colour down to one-sixteenth.

4 The Princess Nasrat went on to have seven children with her husband Sutherland. Mary Fooks, the youngest daughter of that

marriage, lived well into the twentieth century and wrote about it
at the end of her life:

> My father was persuaded … to contract … a union with a niece of a
> turbulent Mahomedan chief there, a descendant of one of the Persian
> conquerors, to promote a friendship with the tribe. The only stipula-
> tion was that she was not to be forced to give up her religion. Her uncle
> swore that he would kill her but my father was warned never to let her
> be alone on his visits. My father offered to marry her by the rites of the
> Church, but she would not become a Christian … felt the union was
> binding in God's sight. My mother was a highly educated lady who read
> and wrote her own language and read the Koran and never let us touch
> it, keeping strictly to her own customs and a *purdahnashin*.

Sutherland took the family away to South Africa some years
before the Uprising, and told a friend there – who had asked why
he had left India at the height of his career – that he could sense
trouble looming, even though the Mutiny was still to be ten years
ahead. When Sutherland returned to active service he left his four
sons behind in South Africa, bringing his wife and three daughters back to India. Perhaps he had understood that by the
mid-nineteenth century the world was less tolerant of mixed-race
men, though, as ever, beautiful women of any background could
transcend the boundaries of race and class.

5   One woman who sailed on the fishing fleet, and subsequently
married, wrote to her cousin Maria in 1779, describing the experience: '… there were thirty of us on board … we were of all ages,
complexions and sizes, with little or nothing in common, but that
we were single, or wished to get married. Some were absolutely old
maids of the shrivelled and dry description, while others were
mere girls … ignorant of almost everything … This place has
many houses of entertainment of all descriptions and the gaiety …
after the arrival of a fleet from Europe is astonishing … the first
thing done is for the captains to give an entertainment, to which
they issue general invitations, and everybody … with the look and
attendance of a gentleman … is at liberty to make his appearance.
The speculative ladies dress … with all the splendour they can
muster … This is in truth their last, or nearly their last stake, and

all are determined to look and dance as divinely as possible. The gentlemen ... are of all ranks, but generally of pale and squalid complexions and suffering under the grievous infliction of liver complaints ... Not a few are old and infirm, leaning upon sticks and crutches ... these old decrepit gentlemen address themselves to the youngest and prettiest, and the youngest and prettiest, if properly instructed in their parts, betray no sort of coyness or reluctance.' From *MacIntosh's Travels*, quoted in Carey (ed.), *The Good Old Days of Honorable John Company*, pp. 93–4.

6 Julia Charlotte Maitland, in her *Letters from Madras*, thought that 'India is the paradise of middle-aged gentlemen. While they are young they are thought nothing of ... but at about forty, when they are "high in the service", rather yellow and somewhat grey, they begin to be taken notice of, and called "young men". These respectable persons do all the flirtation too in a solemn sort of way ...' Quoted in Edwardes, *Bound to Exile*, p. 38.

7 Paget, *Camp and Cantonment*, pp. 385–6.

8 Quoted in Carey (ed.), *The Good Old Days of Honorable John Company*, p. 93.

9 Lawrence, 'English Women in Hindustan', p. 122.

10 'From Camp to Quarters: or, Life in an Indian Cantonment after Field Service', part III, *Colburn's United Service Magazine and Naval and Military Journal*, part II, 1859, p. 385.

11 'We can at this moment recollect not less than half a dozen women, sober and well conducted, who, out of families of five, six, seven or nine, have reared respectively one, two or three children, or are now entirely childless.' Lawrence, 'English Women in Hindustan', p. 124f.

12 Paget, *Camp and Cantonment*, p. 386.

CHAPTER 7

1 Hull, *The European in India, or Anglo-Indian's Vade Mecum*, pp. 141–2.

2 Stephen Bentley in 'Plain Tales from the Raj' oral archive, IOR Ems T6.

3 George Annesley Mountnorris (Viscount Valentia), *Voyages and Travels to India, Ceylon, the Red Sea, Abyssinia and Egypt*, vol. I (London, 1811), pp. 197–8.

4   Stark, *Hostages to India*, p. 65.
5   This was a systematic disenfranchisement, and Anglo-Indians
    with a military background were left with two choices: to settle
    for a job in the band or with the horses, or to offer their military
    experience where it would be welcomed, which meant as merce-
    naries in the armies of the Maratha States, which were rebelling
    against the Company. The story of those who helped the Rajahs
    train their men, forming crack regiments such as the Bengal
    Lancers and leading their men against the very people whom
    they had been raised to think of as family, is a cracking yarn, full
    of twists of fate. When, for example, the new Maratha forces
    started to beset the Company's army, the Calcutta Council feared
    defeat at their hands and accused these 'Anglo-Indian' officers of
    'treachery to the motherland', but promised them amnesty if they
    would come back to the Company's side. Many of them did
    return, though one or two were executed by their Maratha over-
    lords when they attempted to leave. Those mixed-race officers
    who did return found themselves once more fighting for the
    'mother country' against the very regiments that they had
    founded. The amnesty was cancelled as soon as the crisis was
    past, leaving the Anglo-Indians once more disowned, caught
    between black and white and not quite belonging in either camp.
    But is a story for another book and has been told well by others,
    such as Geoffrey Moorehouse in *India Britannica* (New York,
    1983).
6   Lawrence, 'English Women in Hindustan', p. 122.
7   Satar, in 1848, Sambalpur in 1849, and in 1854 Jhansi and
    Nagpur swelled the territories of the Bengal Presidency when
    their ruling Rajahs died. Oudh was annexed in 1856, before the
    doctrine was repealed in 1858, following the Sepoy Uprising.
8   Lawrence, 'English Women in Hindustan', p. 124.
9   In 1868 – if he had lived so long – James would have earned four-
    teen annas, six pice a day. A private earned one anna, six pice,
    and a lieutenant-colonel thirty-five rupees, twelve annas and nine
    pice a day.
10 After the event, the Resident commented that the Contingent
    were very divided in their feelings towards their officers: four of
    the seven regiments, two of the four batteries and most of the 2nd

Cavalry (all but the small party left behind in Gwalior) killed none.

11   Since so much of the unrest was caused by a fear that the British wished to undermine the traditional faiths of India and impose Christianity, Coopland knew that he was a focus of the troops' hostility, writing to his sister that he found himself 'in the midst of a lot of savages (for most of them are nothing more)'. He was disturbed to find that his household servants were 'All very insolent … as if they were very forbearing in not at once murdering you.' G. W. Coopland, private letter, 1859.

12   Ibid.

13   The news came on 11 June that Delhi had been wrested from the mutineers three days earlier. In fact, the fight for Delhi was much later than this, and it was to take a long campaign of about eight weeks, with many losses, to gain control of the Moghul capital.

14   The Maharani of Jhansi became a heroine of the Uprising, fighting a rearguard action long after the rest of the country had been subdued, and has since been mythologised in Indian culture.

15   Kaye, *A History of the Sepoy War in India*, p. 317.

CHAPTER 8

1   Kaye, *A History of the Sepoy War in India*, p. 316.

2   For all his support of the fugitives in their escape from Gwalior, the Rana was subsequently granted a knighthood in the Order of the Star of India, and was also given a large land grant.

CHAPTER 9

1   The Taj Mahal, for instance, is thought to be a representation of Paradise. Its rectangular shape, with the tomb at one end and not in the centre, may be a veiled suggestion that with its builder, the Shah Jahan, interred there, he is in the place usually reserved for God.

2   Dushyant Singh is a member of the Bharatiya Janata Party, and represents the Jhalawar constituency of Rajasthan. His father, Shri Hemant Singh, was the last maharajah of Dholpur, while his mother, Vasundhara Raje, is the chief minister of Rajasthan and a member of the Sindhia royal family of Gwalior.

3   Heal & Sons, founded in 1810 by John Harris Heal, continue to

be one of Britain's leading furniture makers. Their catalogues provide an accurate description of High Victorian style as it was embraced by the middle classes. The 1854 catalogue of 'an officer's equipage for campaigning', for instance, provides interesting insights into Victorian military expeditions and usefully explains how a trunk, bedstead and other items could be loaded onto a horse. By 1858 they were producing catalogues with pictures of entire rooms, which should how households were organised and how various objects were arranged and displayed, and the 1881 catalogue talks of 'the reputation they have gained during the last 50 years for GOOD TASTE, SOUND WORK and MODERATE PRICES'.

4   Hope, *The House of Scindea*, p. 55. This building was described as 'a small Maida Hill-like villa on the right bank of the Chumbal, which the Raja of Dholpur kept for the use of English dak travellers'.

5   Rudyard Kipling, 'My Own True Ghost Story'.

6   Macpherson, the Resident at Gwalior, in his 'Report on the Mutiny to Government', 10 February 1858, described the Rani as 'an ardent, daring, licentious woman, under thirty, who rode in military attire, with sword and pistols, followed by forty horse from Kotah, and by a Brahminee concubine of her late husband'.

When the Rani of Jhansi was finally routed on 17 June 1858 she was drinking sherbet when surprised by some hussars. All but fifteen of her five hundred troops fled. The Rani's horse refused to jump a canal, and though shot in the side and cut by a sabre on the head she galloped off, but later fell and was burnt to death in a garden close by. Macpherson said that the Brahminee concubine never left her side and, although receiving a long sabre cut to her front, rose into the city where she was tended by a fakir and the Muslim head of police, and, 'dying in their hands, was reputed and buried as a Mahomedan convert'.

CHAPTER 10

1   Kaye, *A History of the Sepoy War in India*, p. 407.

2   In *Letters from Agra* (Edinburgh, 1898) Sir William Muir attests that only the 3rd East India Company Regiment, plus European artillery and two native corps were based there.

3 Raikes, *Notes on the Revolt in the North-western Provinces of India*, p. 66.
4 Coopland, *A Lady's Escape from Gwalior*, pp. 171–2.
5 Kaye, *A History of the Sepoy War in India*, p. 378.
6 Colvin brought a team of psychiatrists to Agra to look after his own ailing health, and perhaps a more poignant relic is the fact that the Agra Mental Hospital is still a centre of excellence for the treatment of mental illness.
7 Kaye, *A History of the Sepoy War in India*, p. 400.
8 Quoted in ibid., p. 402.
9 'From Camp to Quarters: or, Life in an Indian Cantonment after Field Service', op. cit., p. 385.
10 Carey (ed.), *The Good Old Days of Honorable John Company*, p. 401.

CHAPTER 11

1 See William Dalrymple, *White Mughals: Love and Betrayal in Eighteenth-Century India* (London, 2002) for more detail.
2 Sir James Outram, the liberator of Lucknow, was reputed to have bagged 191 tigers, 15 leopard, 25 bears and 12 buffalo during his leisure time in India.
3 The trident was Shiva's symbolic weapon, and it also echoes Poseidon and the sea which, in other myths, were agents of revenge.
4 In *Wide Sargasso Sea*, Jean Rhys calls her Antoinette, but she is the Bertha of Charlotte Brontë's novel.
5 Steel and Gardiner, *The Complete Indian Housekeeper and Cook*, p. 208.
6 Vere Birdwood, quoted in Allen (ed.), *Plain Tales from the Raj*, p. 182.

CHAPTER 12

1 Brydon's life was saved by a copy of *Blackwood's Magazine* that he had stuffed into his hat to protect him from the cold weather, and which in fact shielded him from an Afghan sword that sheared off part of his skull. He and his horse are mythologised in Elizabeth Butler's painting, *Remnants of an Army*, which is now in Tate Britain. His horse dropped dead, having carried him to Jellalabad,

but Brydon went on to be a regimental doctor at Lucknow, where he and his family survived the siege of the Residency in 1857.

2 The Corps of Guides, raised in 1844 by Lieutenant Harry Lumsden, were the first soldiers in the British or Indian army to wear khaki rather than the flamboyant colours then traditional in the military.

3 Qutb, the leading intellectual of the reformist Egyptian Muslim Brotherhood, urged his followers to withdraw from the moral and spiritual barbarism of modern society, and to fight it to the death. He was executed by President Nasser in 1966.

4 Letter from Syed Ahmad to a friend in Hyderabad, quoted in Allen, *God's Terrorists*, p. 78.

5 This is a pattern that seems to be continuing to this day: the leadership is educated, but most of its fighting force are from the peasantry.

6 Winston Churchill, quoted in Allen, *God's Terrorists*, p. 218.

CHAPTER 13

1 *General Report on the Administration of the Punjab for the Years 1849–50 and 1850–51*, p. 39.

2 Griffiths, *To Guard My People*, p. 403.

3 Quoted in 'Military Hygiene in India', *Calcutta Review*, vol. XXXIII, July–December 1859, p. 375.

4 Lawrence was, at this time, the Resident for Nepal. Later in his career he was to chair the first board of administration for the British Punjab.

5 Quoted in Craig, *Under the Old School Topee*, p. 49.

6 H. M. Lawrence Military Asylum, *Brief Account of Past Ten Years of the Institution* (Sanawar, 1858), p. 12.

7 'Plain Tales from the Raj' oral archive. Although always controversial, with debate and fury rumbling into the 1940s, when a survivor of the massacre assassinated Lt-General Sir Michael O'Dwyer, who had been Lieutenant Governor of the Punjab at the time of the massacre and supported Dyer, it transpired that not everyone disagreed with Dyer's actions: in a debate in the House of Lords his action was approved by 121 votes to 86.

Reginald Dyer, coincidentally, was from the hills near Murree and his father was the manufacturer of a celebrated beer drunk all over the subcontinent.

8 Eugene Pierce, quoted in Allen (ed.), *Plain Tales from the Raj*, p. 105.

CHAPTER 14

1 The Earl of Ronaldshay – later 2nd Marquess of Zetland – the Governor of Bengal and then Secretary of State for India, quoted by Sir Olaf Caroe in Allen (ed.), *Plain Tales from the Raj*, p. 197.

2 Winston Churchill, *The Story of the Malakand Field Force* (n.p., 1892), p. 5.

3 'Kidnapped' in Kipling, *Plain Tales from the Hills*.

4 The Kingdom of Swat existed from 1918 until it was absorbed into Pakistan in 1969.

5 Choksey, *Dentistry in Ancient India*, p. 11.

6 Quoted in *Journal of the Asiatic Society of Bombay*, 1926, p. 97.

7 *Harvard Dental Record*, 1929, p. 4.

CHAPTER 15

1 When I played hockey in the first eleven at my school, I remember my father joshing me for complaining that my hockey boots were too tight. He suggested that I simply take them off and play barefoot, as he had always done.

2 Cynthia Langdon-Davies, quoted in Craig, *Under the Old School Topee*, p. 133.

3 Mrs Allen in 'Plain Tales from the Raj' oral archive, EMST 1 (2/4)

4 Whiskey Weskin, the son of a fellow ISMD surgeon and a colleague of Bertie Quick throughout his career in India and Pakistan. Interview with the author.

5 Ibid.

CHAPTER 16

1 The passage, in a letter to Joan, reads: 'Isn't this life a funny thing, Freckles. 3 years ago I had only been in England a few months, new to the customs and people, in fact ... a greenhorn ... 2 years rolled their dreary length by during which the green youngster became more of a man in spite of many attempts to crush my search for something I badly wanted – human companionship to

cheer me up and lift me out of the slough of despondency of hum-drum hospital life & that awful gloom which only a stranger can feel in the extreme loneliness of a big city devoid of social rela-tionships, with no one to share the same interests & to have as a confidante; no one to look forward to; to consult in my petty troubles; to fill my empty time; to give my accumulated love to.'

2   The two friends were Eva Scutts and Joe Jagger, who were later to marry and become the parents of a Rolling Stone.

CHAPTER 17

1   Slightly misquoting Polonius in Shakespeare's *Hamlet*.

2   Sir Thomas Wyatt's translation of Petrarch's Rima, Sonnet 134, again slightly misquoted – he had clearly worked from memory. The correct version is:

> *I find no peace, and all my war is done;*
> *I fear and I hope, I burn and freeze like ice;*
> *[…]*
> *I desire to perish, and yet I ask for health;*
> *I love another, and thus I hate myself;*
> *[…]*
> *And my delight is causer of this strife.*

CHAPTER 18

1   The name Pakistan was an acronym first proposed by Choudhary Rahmat Ali in a pamphlet entitled 'Now or Never: Are we to live or perish forever?', published in January 1933. The name – origi-nally 'Pakstan' – was formed from the first letter of the constituent lands proposed for the new Muslim state: Punjab, Afghania (the North-West Territories), Kashmir and Sind. 'Stan' means 'coun-try' in both Urdu and Hindi, and also represented Baluchistan, the other province to be included. By the end of that year, the name had been changed to Pakistan to ease pronunciation, and in his subsequent book, *Pakistan: The Fatherland of the Pak Nation*, Ali included Iran in the acronym, thus Pakistan.

2   Annie Castledine (ed.), *Plays By Women: 10* (London, 1994), p. 19.

CHAPTER 19

1 The Netherlands, with its history of colonisation by the Holy
  Roman Empire, has a large and devout Roman Catholic population.
2 According to tradition, the present-day Parsis are descended from
  a group of Iranian Zoroastrians who emigrated to western India
  over a thousand years ago.

Bibliography

ON INDIA

Allen, Charles (ed.), *Plain Tales from the Raj: Images of British India in the Twentieth Century* (paperback edn, London, 2000)

——, *God's Terrorists: The Wahhabi Cult and the Hidden Roots of Modern Jihad* (London, 2006)

Carey, W. H. (ed.), *The Good Old Days of Honorable John Company: Being Curious Reminiscences Illustrating Manners and Customs of the British in India during the Rule of the East India Company from 1600 to 1858* (Calcutta, 1906)

Caroe, Sir Olaf, *The Pathans 550 BC–AD 1957* (London, 1958)

Fincastle, Viscount (A. E. Murray), and P. E. Elliott-Lockhart, *A Frontier Campaign: A Narrative on the Operations of the Malakand and Buner Field Forces, 1897–1898* (London, 1898)

Ghosh, Durba, *Sex and the Family in Colonial India: The Making of Empire* (Cambridge, 2006)

Griffiths, Sir Percival, *To Guard My People: The History of the Indian Police* (London, 1971)

Hawes, C. J., *Poor Relations: The Making of a Eurasian Community in British India 1773–1833* (Richmond, 1996)

Jasanoff, Maya, *Edge of Empire: Conquest and Collecting in the East 1750–1850* (New York, 2005)

Kaye, John William, *Christianity in India: An Historical Narrative* (London, 1859)

Keene, Henry George, *A Handbook for Visitors: Allahabad, Cawnpore and Lucknow* (2nd edn, Calcutta, 1896)

Peacock, E. B., *A Guide to Murree and its Neighbourhood* (Lahore, 1883)

Roberts, Frederick Sleigh, *Forty-One Years in India: From Subaltern to Commander-in-Chief* (London, 1897)

Spain, James W., *The Pathan Borderland* (The Hague, 1963)

Staines, James Richard, *Country Born: One Man's Life in India 1909–1947* (Croscombe, 1986)

Stark, Herbert Alick, *Hostages to India: Or, The Life Story of the Anglo-Indian Race* (Calcutta, 1936)

———, *The Call of the Blood: Anglo-Indians and the Sepoy Mutiny* (Rangoon, 1932)

ON THE SEPOY UPRISING

Bourchier, George, *Eight Months' Campaign Against the Bengal Sepoy Army During the Mutiny of 1857* (London, 1858)

Brown, Hilton, *The Sahibs: The Life and Ways of the British in India as Recorded by Themselves* (London, 1948)

Burton, Reginald George, *The Revolt in Central India 1857–59* (Simla, 1908)

Coopland, R. M., *A Lady's Escape from Gwalior, and Life in the Fort of Agra during the Mutinies of 1857* (London, 1859)

Hibbert, Christopher, *The Great Mutiny, India 1857* (Harmondsworth, 1980)

Hope, John, *The House of Scindea* (London, 1863)

Hull, E. C. P., *The European in India, or, Anglo-Indians' Vade-Mecum, To Which is Added a Medical Guide for Anglo-Indians by R. S. Mair* (London, 1871)

Jardine, William Ellis, Biographical notes on Residents at Gwalior 1782–1922, India Office Records, Eur Mss E237

Kaye, John William, *A History of the Sepoy War in India, 1857–58* (London, 1864)

Knowles, S., *How We Made Our Escape in the Mutiny of 1857* (n.p.)

Macpherson, Samuel Charters (ed. W. Macpherson), *Memorials of Service in India, from the Correspondence of S. C. Macpherson* (London, 1865)

Macpherson, Samuel Charters, 'Report on the Mutiny to Government', 10 February 1858

Nash, John Tulloch, *Volunteering in India: or, An Authentic Narrative of the Military Services of the Bengal Yeomanry Cavalry during the Indian Mutiny and Sepoy War* (London, 1893)

Ouvry, M. H., *A Lady's Diary before and during the Indian Mutiny 1854–8* (Lymington, 1892)

Raikes, Charles, *Notes on the Revolt in the North-western Provinces of India* (London, 1858)

Renford, Raymond K., *The Non-official British in India to 1920* (Delhi, 1987)

Rizvi, S. A. A., and M. L. Bhargava (eds), *Freedom Struggle in Uttar Pradesh: Source Material*, vol. 3 (3 vols, Lucknow, 1957–61)

Rose, A., *The Campaigns of 1857–8 in Central India* (n.p.)

Russell, Sir William Howard (ed. Michael Edwardes), *My Indian Mutiny Diary* (London, 1957)

Sawyers, Dr J., *Diary March 1858–August 1859, of Dr J. Sawyers, Assistant Surgeon*, India Office Records, Mss

Seton, Rosemary, *The Indian 'Mutiny' 1857–58: A Guide to Source Material in the India Office Library and Records* (London, 1986)

Sleeman, Major N. H., *On the Spirit of Military Discipline in Our Native Indian Army* (Calcutta, 1841)

Stocqueler, Joachim Hayward, *The Hand-book of India* (London, 1844)

Stokes, Eric, *The Peasant Armed: The Indian Revolt of 1857* (Cambridge, 1986)

Temple, Sir Richard Carnac, 'In the Century before the Mutiny', *Indian Antiquary*, vol. 52, 1923

————, *The Native Armies of India* (n.p.)

Times, The, The Armies of the Native States of India (London, 1884)

ON WOMEN AND FAMILY LIFE IN INDIA

The first port of call for anyone wishing to research families in India should be the India Office Records lodged in the British Library, and also the 'Plain Tales from the Raj' oral history of Imperial India compiled for the BBC, which is held at the School of Oriental and African Studies in London.

Atkinson, George Franklin, '*Curry and Rice,' on Forty Plates: or, The Ingredients of Social Life at 'Our Station' in India* (4th edn, London, 1911)

Bamfield, Veronica, *On the Strength: The Story of the British Army Wife* (London, 1974)

Barr, Pat, *The Memsahibs: The Women of Victorian India* (London, 1989)

Braddon, Sir Edward Nicholas, *Life in India* (Calcutta, 1872)

Craig, Hazel Innes, *Under the Old School Topee* (London, 1990)

Diver, Katherine Helen Maud, *The Englishwoman in India* (Edinburgh, 1909)

Duff, Rev. Dr, and Mr Skipwith, 'Married Life in India', *Calcutta Review*, vol. IV, 1845

Edwardes, Michael, *A Season in Hell* (London, 1973)

————, *Bound to Exile: The Victorians in India* (London, 1969)

————, *High Noon of Empire: India under Curzon* (London, 1965)

————, *The Necessary Hell: John and Henry Lawrence and the Indian Empire* (London, 1958)

Kincaid, Dennis, *British Social Life in India, 1608–1937* (2nd edn, London, 1973)

Lawrence, Lady, 'English Women in Hindustan', *Calcutta Review*, vol. IV, 1845

Maitland, Julia Charlotte, *Letters from Madras during the Years 1836–1839, by a Lady* (London, 1843)

Paget, Mrs L. G., *Camp and Cantonment: A Journal of Life in India in 1857–1859* (London, 1865)

Paxton, Nancy L., *Writing under the Raj: Gender, Race and Rape in the British Colonial Imagination 1830–1947* (New Brunswick, 1999)

Postans, Mrs, *Western India in 1838* (London, 1839)

Scott, H., Saunders and Ottley, letters to the Rt. Hon Sidney Herbert on the present condition of women in the army, 1854

Sharpe, Jenny, *Allegories of Empire: The Figure of Woman in the Colonial Text* (Minneapolis, 1993)

Shepard, Ethel, *A Marooned People: The Anglo-Indian Community* (London, 1930)

Steel, Flora Annie Webster, and Grace Gardiner, *The Complete Indian Housekeeper and Cook: Giving the Duties of Mistress and Servants, the General Management of the House and Practical Recipes for Cooking in All its Branches* (London, 1921)

Tytler, Harriet, *An Englishwoman in India: The Memoirs of Harriet Tytler 1828–1858* (Oxford, 1986)

ON DENTISTRY

Bengal Army Medical Regulations 1851

Bengal Council of Medicine Regulations 1877

Various departmental reports for hospitals and dispensaries in Calcutta, Punjab and the North-West Frontier, especially the Annual

Reports on Hospitals and Dispensaries, North-West Frontier Province, 1911–1915

Bishop, S. O., *Medical Hints for the Hills* (Darjeeling, 1888)

Bombay Army Surgeon, A, *Medical Hints for the Districts: Arranged for Government Officials, Their Families and Camp Followers* (Bombay, 1872)

Campbell, J. Menzies, *Dentistry Then and Now* (2nd edn, Glasgow, 1963)

Choksey, K. M., *Dentistry in Ancient India* (Bombay, 1953)

Cohen, R. A. (ed.), *The Advance of the Dental Profession: A Centenary History, 1880–1980* (London, 1979)

Dubois, Abbé Jean Antoine (trans. Henry K. Beauchamp), *Hindu Manners, Customs and Ceremonies* (n.p., 1816)

Hillam, Christine (ed.), *The Roots of Dentistry* (London, 1990)

Hogg, Francis R., *Practical Remarks Chiefly Concerning the Health and Ailments of European Families in India, With Special Reference to Maternal Management and Domestic Economy* (Benares, 1877)

Institute of Applied Manpower Research, *Development of Dental Education in India* (New Delhi, 1967)

Maganlal, R., *Dentistry in India* (n.p., 1936)

Modi, Jamshedi Jivanji, *Dentistry in Ancient India* (Allahabad, 1928)

Moore, Sir William, *A Manual of Family Medicine and Hygiene for India* (6th edn, London, 1893)

Glossary

agit-prop – agitational propaganda, usually meaning a form of theatre
   that had its heyday in Britain in the 1970s

arrack – spirits distilled from fermented fruits, grains, sugar cane or the
   sap or coconuts or other palm trees

ayah – native children's nurse or lady's maid

baille – four-wheeled ox cart, from Hindi 'bahalii'

bibi – native mistress or wife

badmash – a bad lot, a criminal

charpoy – a wooden bed with a stringed frame

chuprassy – attendant or messenger

Dewan – Prime Minister, or chief financial minister, of a state

ghat – steps leading down to a river, used especially by bathers

Ghazi – warrior of the faith. A Muslim fanatic devoted to the destruc-
   tion of infidels

havildar – sergeant in a native regiment

kitmutghar – butler

lashkar – the centre of military operations; a camp of native soliders or
   a body of Afridi soldiers

lingam – a symbol for the worship of Shiva, usually a short cylindrical
   pillar with a rounded top (from Sanskrit, meaning 'mark' or 'sign')

madrassah – school of Islamic studies

mofusil – the countryside outside the Presidency capitals of Bombay,
   Calcutta and Madras or, more generally, rural areas

munshi – secretary

nabob – deputy. Originally used to mean a governor, the term was
   adopted in the eighteenth century to describe the many men who

acquired a substantial fortune in India (from Urdu 'nawab', Arabic 'na'ib')

Presidency – one of the three main administrative areas of British Colonial India, Bengal, Madras and Bombay

punkah – a fan, correctly one suspended from the ceiling

purdah – the practice of seclusion

suttee – the ritual immolation of a wife on her husband's death; a woman who performs this act (from Sanskrit, literally 'faithful wife')

Talib – student

tulwah – an Indian sabre

Acknowledgements

This book would not have been written if Carmen Callil had not made some effort to persuade me that I could write, and if Lennie Goodings had not subsequently taken up the challenge to get me to do it, so my profound thanks to them both. My agent Jacqueline Korn has given me steadfast counsel, and my editor Joanna Goldsworthy and my copy-editor Zoë Gullen have brought their wisdom and attention to detail to bear on what, without them, would have been a chaotic text. I hope we will have the opportunity to work together again. Thanks, too, to Linda Silverman for marvellous detective work in unearthing photographs I had thought lost, and to Duncan Spilling for his work on the book jacket.

I knew little about India or my family's life there, and owe a debt to my Uncle Basil Quick, his wife Linda, and their friend Derrick 'Whiskey' Weskin, whose vivid recollections set me on the trail. Also to my aunt Esme Hughes and cousin Felicity Brandscheid for information about their part of the family. My cousins Basil Thyer and Guy Manns-Abbott set me on the path to my great-grandmother Margaret, and my cousin Eve Milner gave me photographs and stories of her side of the Quick clan. My brother Clive went to great trouble unearthing photographs of my parents and grandparents. I am deeply grateful to all of them.

John Walker and the Old Gallians who convene each year to

celebrate their attendance at the Ghora Gali Lawrence College and other hill station schools in India have given me insights that I could never have gained without them, particularly Lt-Col (retd) Stanley Tullet, Cecil Hopkins-Husson, Norma Probert, Bob Matthews, Maurine Fine, Robert and Cedric Pushong and Valerie Harrison. Sue Farrington at BACSA (the British Association for Cemeteries of South Asia) helped me find my great grandmother in Peshawar, and other friends in Rawalpindi were Juliet Siebold and Shahnaz and Brigadier Jaffar Khan, and Shahnaz Minallah who opened many doors. In Peshawar, Jaffir's former aide de campe Major (retd) Hamid Hassan and Bashir (Bash) Ahmad taught me the meaning of Pahktunwali, the Pathan code of courtesy. Niall Hobhouse introduced me to people and places in Central India that made my time there a glorious adventure, and Kavita Sanghi was especially generous in Indore and Mhow.

I have researched much of the material in this book in the India Office Records held at the British Library, a wonderful resource for anyone who has ever had a family connection to British India. I have consulted the books of Charles Allen, William Dalrymple, Geoffrey Moorehouse, Molly Kaye, Peter Hopkirk, and Eric Newby frequently and with great pleasure as I have been writing. David Gilmour kindly gave me his book on Curzon, and material about the army from his book on Kipling, and Mark Tandy gave me his father's unpublished memoir, all of which have made me know my subject better.

Finally I must thank my own William and Mary, and my friends Lucy Andre, Eva Kholokhouva, Consuelo Fernandez, Valerie Wade, Emily Bruni, Kate Hewitt, Kate Mortimer and Bob Dean, Charles Sturridge, Karl Johnson, Michael Maloney and Joe Mydell who have read or, even more indulgently, have allowed me to read them chunks of the manuscript on the way, and given me unstinting encouragement, and Cally for his generous help with the design.